The Schooled Heart

D1599397

The Schooled Heart

Moral Formation in American Higher Education

Released from
Samford University Library

edited by

Michael D. Beaty
Douglas V. Henry

BAYLOR UNIVERSITY PRESS

Samford University Library

LB
2324
.S356
2007

Studies in Religion and Higher Education 4

Editorial Advisory Board

Michael Beaty, Baylor University
Jean Bethke Elshtain, The University of Chicago
Stanley Hauerwas, Duke University
Stephen R. Haynes, Rhodes College

©2007 Baylor University Press
Waco, Texas 76798

All Rights Reserved. No part of this publication may be reproduced, stored in a
retrieval system, or transmitted, in any form or by any means, electronic,
mechanical, photocopying, recording or otherwise, without the prior permission in
writing of Baylor University Press.

Cover Design: Joan Osth
Cover Image: Used by permission of David Edmonson.

Library of Congress Cataloging-in-Publication Data

The schooled heart : moral formation in American higher education / edited by
Michael D. Beaty and Douglas V. Henry.
    p. cm. -- (Studies in religion and higher education ; 4)
  Includes bibliographical references and index.
  ISBN-13: 978-1-932792-94-2 (pbk. : alk. paper)
  1. Education, Higher--Moral and ethical aspects--United States. 2. Ethics--Study
and teaching (Higher)--United States. 3. Education, Higher--Aims and objectives--
United States. 4. Education--Religious aspects. I. Beaty, Michael D. II. Henry,
Douglas V.
  LB2324.S356 2007
  378'.014--dc22

                                                    2007004740

Printed in the United States of America on acid-free paper with a minimum of 30%
pcw content.

Contents

Part II

Christian Resources for Moral Formation in the Academy

Introduction

Retrieving the Tradition, Remembering the End

—Michael D. Beaty and Douglas V. Henry

The title of the volume you hold in your hands discloses our answer to a controversial question, a question that stands at the center of many debates about the nature and purpose of the modern American university. That question, quite simply, is this: should moral education figure centrally, or at all, among the purposes of the modern university? To that question, we offer in what follows an unequivocally affirmative response. The highest and best purpose to which the modern university can direct itself is nothing short of the moral formation of its students, or what in another time might have been called the schooling of the heart or the tutoring of the affections.

We regard this question as foundational within contemporary higher education, while acknowledging that others may not immediately see it so. The truth is that in contentious debates about large issues, the cacophony of claims and counterclaims most noticeably heard often drowns out attention to more basic questions responsible for dividing the ranks. Thus, disputes about one thing are often, at heart, disputes about another thing. For instance, recent and heated disagreement about the extent to which the classrooms of American universities are biased toward a politically liberal outlook—significant as that question may be—almost uniformly passes over the question of whether or not bias of some sort is avoidable or desirable.[1] Similarly, contentiousness in response to the National Collegiate Athletic Association's concern about its members' use of "hostile or abusive" nicknames, and more specifically its proscription of Native American mascots, invariably failed to rise above banal judgments about "political correctness." In both these and many other cases, assumed but unstated answers to the question of whether or not moral formation ranks among the university's defining tasks are operative, and most of the time, uncritically so. We contend that intelligent, discerning judgments about the "little" questions within American higher education are impossible in the absence of a clear understanding of the "big" questions about the proper nature, identity, and purpose of the university.

To be sure, we acknowledge those who continue in the vital tradition of scholars attentive to the place of moral education among the aims of the university, but predictably they fail to speak univocally about the issue. In response to the animating question of this volume, some leading American intellectuals, Stanley Fish and Richard Rorty, for example, answer forcefully, "No, the modern university's purpose is not to engage in moral education."[2] On the other hand, former Harvard president Derek Bok has argued that it is imperative for America's colleges and universities, especially its elite research universities and private liberal arts colleges, to recover the practice they once pursued with great vigor—the moral education of their students.[3] He argues that the nation's colleges and universities should serve the common and public good, not only by giving students the knowledge and information they need to compete in a highly information-driven, technological society and global market, but also by teaching them to think critically about the ideals of Western democracy and the moral demands of both global and local citizenship. Indeed, Bok calls upon the nation's elite universities to set the example by including in their curriculum the elements of a moral and civic education necessary to produce graduates prepared to fulfill their moral and social responsibilities. Bok's exhortations have been echoed by numerous other educators and social critics over the last decade or so.[4]

Yet while we are in sympathy with Bok's admonition that America's most prestigious universities must reclaim the task of moral education, we contend that a recommitment to this task on the part of America's institutions of higher learning is far more difficult than he admits.[5] This is because, in general, the nation's colleges and universities, and certainly most of their faculty, remain largely committed to the ideas and practices that displaced moral education during the last century. We are also convinced that Bok's recommendations for moral education, considered in themselves, ineffectually address the problems he identifies and thus would merely perpetuate them rather than offer a suitable solution.

From the outset, then, we confess that we aim to offer a significant contribution to the recovery of moral education as a defining aim and guiding commitment of American higher education. Put differently, within our general scope of inquiry there is no more crucial question than that of the purpose and identity of the modern university, and we profess that the university's core purpose is to be found in the morally discerning formation of human persons. We further acknowledge that our conception of the nature and practice of moral education differs in important ways from Bok's, though we admire many of his commitments and appreciate the attention brought to these questions by virtue of his professional and scholarly stature.

In order to make sense of the reasons why we share Bok's *cri de coeur* on behalf of the moral bankruptcy of American higher education, and also why we deem his exhortative solution to be lacking, we must tell a story. That story is one with which he, among many others, is familiar. It is the story of the old-time, nineteenth-century American college. Yet some of the most significant contours of the narrative, the ones largely explanatory of the challenges we face today, have been inadvertently—or in some cases perhaps by design—deprived of the attention they deserve. By retelling, and also by reinterpreting, that story in dialogue with Bok's own arguments for the recovery of moral formation in the university, we can clarify the crucial features of the ideal of moral education in the old-time American college, along with why that ideal was abandoned in the practice (if not the rhetoric) of modern American colleges and universities. It is likewise in light of that story that we then can make sense of a realistic and intellectually defensible alternative to Bok's, one that ought to be particularly appealing to religiously identified, especially Christian, colleges and universities.

A SHORT HISTORY OF MORAL EDUCATION IN AMERICAN HIGHER EDUCATION

As numerous scholars have pointed out, nineteenth-century American colleges and universities considered moral education to be an integral part, even the primary aim, of their mission.[6] The "old-time" college presumed that its central purpose was to educate the whole person, not primarily for a career, but rather so that he or she might become a well-formed person capable of both realizing a truly worthwhile life and exercising moral, social, and political duties correctly. The educational practices of the college or university were oriented toward developing the intellectual, moral, and religious capacities in such a way that they produced an educated class capable of exercising responsible leadership in church and the civic community. So, moral education included not only training in correct moral principles; it also entailed immersion in and formation by a tradition of inquiry whose primary aim was the cultivation of personal, social, and civic virtue. The task of moral education pervaded the entire life of the college, from curriculum, to chapel, to student behavior codes. Because the old-time college was typically a Christian institution, it presumed that human beings were creatures, dependent on God and one another, and that the diversity of legitimate intellectual or educational practices were ultimately unified within an intelligible whole.

As noted by Julie Reuben in her important book, *The Making of the Modern University*, this unity was nicely symbolized in the 1884 Harvard seal. At its center was the Latin word for truth, *veritas*, inscribed across three open books and encircled by the motto *Christo et Ecclesiae* (for Christ and Church). The seal symbolized the unity of all truth, a unity that brought religious truths in the holy scriptures, the moral truths in pagan literature, and the truths of science in the book of nature into harmony with one another.[7] Reflecting this commitment to unity, the American system of higher education aimed at organizing all knowledge—of the cosmos, human beings, and society—into an intelligible whole.

Reuben's book examines the institutional dimensions of a set of ideas essential to understanding the displacement of moral education in America. She underscores, as suggested above, that the old-time college assumed one of its primary tasks to be the moral education of its students. At the apex of this educational endeavor was the year-long senior course in moral philosophy. This class symbolized the belief that intellectual education was incomplete and would remain stunted without moral formation. It assumed that moral education included the inculcation of moral truths, but also that the larger task of moral formation required a substantive examination of social and civic roles and the concomitant duties which are necessary to sustain a healthy and well-ordered society.

By the 1930s, however, the intellectual landscape had changed significantly. Modern science had come to acquire the intellectual and cultural stature that theology and philosophy had shared in earlier eras. Because of significant strides in the intellectual and practical mastery of nature made in a variety of relatively new scientific subdisciplines, science was increasingly regarded as the only paradigm of reliable, publicly useful knowledge. In short, everything not subject to empirical methods of confirmation or disconfirmation as practiced by scientists was identified as unknowable. The philosophical version of this view is called positivism. It claims that morality is not about objective truths or facts; rather, morality is concerned with the realm of subjective values. Thus, there emerged what came to be known as the "fact/value" distinction, and thus the ideal of the unity of truth, with its implied harmony of morality, religion, and science, was split asunder. It was precisely this ideal that had constituted the underpinning of the morally formative activities of the nineteenth-century college or university. The development of positivism as a dominant perspective thus undermined the old-time college's self-identity.

AN EPISTEMOLOGICAL CRISIS: RELIGION AND MORALITY DISPLACED FROM THE UNIVERSITY

The story of the retreat of moral education from the modern American university largely parallels the retreat of religion from the university, a story told powerfully by Douglas Sloan.[8] Both developments were results of the insistence that knowledge is an entirely separate sphere of human activity from either morality or faith. A gloss on the parallel stories of the marginalization of morality and religion from higher education might go as follows. Faith and morality are essentially private matters. Their truths are impenetrable by, or inaccessible to, scientific knowledge. Christian churches rightly consider the truths of faith and morality to be necessary for human flourishing and proclaim them to the world. The function of modern colleges and universities, however, is to discover and transmit knowledge, those truths that are gained by experiment and publicly verifiable experience and that are the basis for technological and material success. Thus, neither faith (religion) nor morality is essentially connected with the primary function of a university education. While faith and morality may be made the subjects of personal concern, and while observable practices derived from them may be made the object of psychological or sociological inquiry, faith and morality themselves are not essential to the academic practices of the modern university and are best left on its margins—in extracurricular activities, for example. On this view, the notions of the unity of truth; the harmony of religion, science, and morality; and the centrality of moral education in the university appear anachronistic at best, and pernicious at worst.

Both Reuben and Sloan largely agree that academic leaders for the most part did not challenge the bifurcation of human life into the many dualisms so characteristic of modernity. Indeed, Sloan criticizes the leaders of the turn-of-the-twentieth-century Protestant theological renaissance for attempting to solve the problem of faith and knowledge by arguing for a new epistemological paradigm, a two-realm theory of truth that "assumes" and justifies a private/public dichotomy. Such a bifurcation of human thought, life, and belief marginalizes religious and moral truth claims from the primary business (that is, the primary academic

practices) of the university. It is easy to see how such a narrow conception of knowledge centered in positivistic science marginalizes both religion and morality and fractures the unity of truth, which provided both
the ideal of a harmony among academic practices and disciplines as well
as the conceptual foundation for the classic American college or university. Sloan, however, goes beyond Reuben's diagnosis of the fact/value distinction to argue that the two-realm theory of truth is an inadequate
response to the intellectual crisis that displaced religion and morality
from the principal academic centers of American culture.

The emerging intellectual consensus claiming science as the paradigm
of public knowledge produced what Alasdair MacIntyre has called an
"epistemological crisis" for the old-time college. Epistemological crises
occur when practices or beliefs that once had a clearly defined content and
a readily available justification cease to cohere or make sense. When a
community is in the throes of an epistemological crisis, evidence that once
pointed unambiguously toward a certain conclusion becomes open to
rival and often incompatible interpretations; a sense of self-deception,
error, irony, ambiguity, or skepticism often replaces what was once unri-
valed self-assurance and comfort in one's beliefs.[9] Moral education was
once the primary aim of the university. However, if morality is about subjective values rather than objective truths, then what place does moral
education have in the modern university if its primary task is to discover
and transmit knowledge (i.e., those truths that are gained by experiment
and publicly verifiable experience)? None, it seems. Logical and epistemological consistency is achieved by abandoning moral education as a substantive aim of the university. Thus, it is hardly surprising that by the
1930s, not even philosophy departments were interested in normative
ethics, the effort to discuss those ethical principles essential to right living.
Rather, in the English-speaking world, perhaps until the publication of
John Rawls's A Theory of Justice in the early 1970s, academic ethics occu-
pied itself with the logic of moral concepts, a quasi-scientific endeavor
consistent with the fact/value distinction.

THE ACADEMIC PROFESSION, THE MODERN UNIVERSITY, AND MORAL EDUCATION

The emergence of academic disciplines, and the notion of the academic
profession (and academic professional), is an integral part of the story of
moral education's marginalization in the university. This part of the story
is told in an especially powerful way by Christopher Jencks and David
Riesman in their classic book, The Academic Revolution.[10] They argue that
the major development in American higher education in the latter half of

the nineteenth and in the twentieth century was the ascendance of the modern university over older models of higher education. For the purposes of our sketch, an important aspect of the modern university is its link with the emergence of the academic profession comprised of various academic disciplines. Professionals are persons who have expertise over a specialized body of knowledge, acquired by formal education and apprenticeship. All professions claim autonomy, or the right to regulate themselves and their members. Autonomy includes determining the ends, methods, and standards of assessment for the profession, as well as other membership criteria. Professions are cosmopolitan rather than local, transcending their particular geographical places, institutions, and communities. As faculty become professionals, and experts over an increasingly narrow and sometimes esoteric body of knowledge and techniques, they become increasingly reticent to acknowledge or assume any authority to contribute to the moral formation of students.

Indeed, if Mark Schwehn and Bruce Wilshire are correct, the professionalization of academic life also created internal and external sources of alienation connected with the bifurcation of faculty allegiances.[11] Such alienation derives not merely from a conflict of professional understandings about teaching and institutional commitments to moral formation, but also from the dichotomy between professional commitments to research and institutional expectations for teaching, at least in our nation's major research universities. Schwehn reminds us that faculty members often complain of not being able to get "our work" done, with the implication that neither teaching, nor mentoring of students, nor committee service are "our work."[12] For some, at least, our professional work is research and publication, and so much the worse for teaching, to say nothing of moral education. This sort of disintegrated identity contrasts sharply with the ideal for faculty in the old-time college, where responsibilities began with teaching and included the moral formation of students, no matter what one's disciplinary specialty.

Thus, the story of the development of the modern university presents today's colleges and universities, and their faculty, with a double crisis. At the epistemological level, according to a certain understanding of knowledge, moral education is either neutral, objective learning about the moral points of view available or it is indoctrination. Thus, the notion that the college or university should be involved in moral education, when that means the moral formation of individuals with substantive commitments entailing that some ways of life are truly better than others, seems to be both morally and intellectually repugnant.[13] At the same time, the academic disciplines have developed in such a way that only a few faculty, at best, could be expected to consider moral education a part of their expertise. And those that do will all too often embrace some

version of the fact/value distinction that views morality in terms of subjective values, not the disciplined assessment of objective truth or false-
hood. But even this is not the end of the tale. It gets worse.

THE EMOTIVIST SELF, THE LIBERAL STATE, AND MORAL EDUCATION

Consider the motto of Baylor University, a university founded in 1845: *Pro
Ecclesia, Pro Texana*. No doubt for many non-Texans, placing the good of
Texas on apparently equal ground with the good of the Church is sheer
hubris. Yet this motto no doubt captures the self-understanding of most
old-time American colleges, an understanding broadly retained in the
public rhetoric of most of our nation's colleges and universities. In the
nineteenth century, both Christian and public universities existed to serve
church and civil society. These ends were often achieved by doing the
same kinds of things, and when they were not, the tasks or practices
appropriate to each end were understood as functioning in harmony with
one another. Indeed, they ideally were thought to be unified in a God who
issued both sets of obligations (to church and state) and who insured by
providential governance of all creation that serving these ends could be
done harmoniously and with integrity. On this view, moral and civic education presumed that moral truths about civic responsibilities were accessible by both reason and revelation. Thus, these aims were not only
thought to be realizable, but it was also supposed that right-thinking,
civic-minded people would agree on what constituted good moral and
civic education.[14]

It requires no imagination to see that the presumed agreement of right-
thinking people about moral and civic responsibility is *in absentia* today.
Indeed, the loss of consensus about the nature of moral and civic education is a major theme of our modern culture. Put differently, what is characteristic of modern democratic cultures in the West is the way in which
moral and civic education have acquired new social meanings in the latter half of the twentieth century. For example, Charles Taylor observes
that for most college students and many Americans, since morality is not
about facts but rather values, morality is choosing one's values and then
living consistently in light of one's fundamental choices.[15] Alasdair Mac-
Intyre agrees with Taylor's diagnosis, and he accordingly has dubbed our
culture an "emotivist culture," at the center of which is "the emotivist
self."[16] An "emotivist self" presumes that the source and center of the
moral life is choice, the free choice of individuals. Emotivism seems committed to the notion that the justification for morally praiseworthy character traits or the principles or rules which guide moral decision-making

is merely individual choice. The logical consequences of emotivism are that moral claims cannot be justified except by preference and the exertion of power, that moral disagreements are irresolvable, and that the notion of moral education is absurd, except as the acquisition of a certain kind of technical competence with respect to a variety of normative ethical theories and their application to practical cases, or else as the cultivation of taste among the like-minded.

A parallel view has developed about the nature of our civic or political life. According to John Rawls, for example, since people disagree about the best way to live, government should be neutral with respect to the comprehensive religious and moral views its citizens endorse.[17] Instead, government and the political arrangements it provides its citizens should be based upon a framework of procedures and legal rights that are neutral with respect to competing understandings of the good life for human beings. He calls his view political liberalism because (1) it endorses the two-hundred-year-old tradition of placing at the heart of the political arrangement such things as individual rights, equality before the law, and tolerance for dissenting points of view; and (2) it eschews the effort to defend the central commitments of liberalism with arguments that appeal to reason or human nature. It is procedural and pragmatic, not metaphysical, liberalism. At bottom, the claim that these arrangements are preferred by most self-interested agents is what Rawls offers as a "defense" of American (Western) democratic ideals. In the modern, liberal state, then, if Rawls is correct, not only does "justification" reduce to choice—the choice, ironically, that modern citizens of western industrialized democracies are bound to make—but any putative "education for citizenship" is unlikely to confront citizens with thick understandings of morality[18] and the good life, the kind of understandings religiously identified communions are likely to have. Consequently, in the education of their children Christians come to face a choice between conceptions of normative citizenship requiring ultimate allegiance to the liberal state[19] and conceptions of citizenship that do not.

BACK TO BOK

Bok admits that as the American culture became more pluralistic, and the university more professional and scientific, moral and civic education appeared increasingly to be mere indoctrination, out of place in a society that celebrates objectivity, tolerance, and the value of individual freedom. Thus, what counted as moral education in the nineteenth century was decried as "moralism"[20] in the twentieth century and was relegated to the province of pastors and demagogues. Morality had been

banished from the public to the private sphere, and the university culture was both complicit in and transformed by this exile. Bok's task, as
he sees it, is to provide a way to recover moral education in a democratic
culture significantly different from the culture enjoyed by the old-time,
nineteenth-century college.

Bok is hopeful that such a recovery can be achieved, in part because
of the interest in applied ethics that emerged in the late 1960s and continues today.[21] Bok concedes, however, that the practice of applied ethics
in the modern university does not much resemble the practice of moral
education in the university of the nineteenth century. Since the grand
narrative of modernity prizes the growth of individual freedom above all
else, rather than attempting to convey a set of moral or social duties or to
develop in students specific moral virtues, today's courses in applied
ethics aim to enable students to think for themselves about moral issues.[22]
This means, of course, that the task of university education insofar as it
has a moral or civic goal is to encourage the students to think more carefully about moral issues and to equip them to reason about issues more
effectively. But this approach runs the risk, says Bok, of producing students clever at arguing any side of an issue, but lacking any serious commitments of their own.[23] Indeed, this approach may encourage a socially
harmful form of ethical relativism—an inadequate approach, Bok insists.
As he puts it, though the ability to reason our way through the moral complexities of modern life is valuable, it may not be enough "to bring us to
behave morally."[24] Thus, according to Bok, when the modern university
debates the prospects of moral education, it is "caught between the evils
of indoctrination, on the one hand, and the hazards of ethical relativism
on the other."[25] Indeed, Bok believes that three critical questions face the
contemporary university: (1) How can a university combine education in
moral reasoning with the effort to teach by habit, example, and exhortation? (2) How can a university help students develop the desire and the
will to adhere to moral precepts in their personal and professional lives?
(3) How can a university create a serious program of moral education that
avoids both indoctrination and ethical relativism?[26]

These are serious and difficult questions and Bok charges that few colleges and universities are attempting to address them. Nonetheless, he
confidently advocates a contemporary program of moral education.[27] It
includes the following aims: (1) making students more perceptive in
detecting ethical problems when they arise, (2) acquainting students with
the best moral thought that has accumulated through the ages, and (3)
equipping students to reason about the ethical issues they will face in
their own personal and professional lives.[28] Most of this work will be
done, according to his proposal, in applied ethics courses.[29] In such

courses, students will be presented with moral problems that commonly arise in personal and professional life. Though many of these will appear to be dilemmas, he thinks that careful reasoning and argument will lead the students to see that in most cases reasonably clear solutions can be reached through appeal to "basic premises that almost all human beings share."[30]

Bok's proposal has at least three substantial difficulties. First, Bok himself claims that a successful institutional effort to avoid both indoctrination and ethical relativism will require the university to decide what moral standards, tendencies, and attitudes it wishes to teach by discussion, habit, example, and exhortation. Put slightly differently, to have an effective program of moral education, faculty must be recruited and retained who embody the preferred moral habits and who are committed to creating and nurturing the moral environment within which students can learn to lead ethically fulfilling lives. But this aim requires the modern university to embrace and espouse a coherent moral vision. Bok himself concedes that the modern university is beset by competing visions of its purpose and role.[31] In the current intellectual environment, any institutional effort by the nation's public and private research universities to decide which moral standards, tendencies, and attitudes are to be taught and praised in a preferred program of moral education will likely be seen as arbitrary and, hence, a poor fit with genuine education. Hiring faculty on the basis of such commitments will be viewed as unprofessional and a violation of academic freedom. Furthermore, being asked to cooperate with other faculty in the enterprise of moral education will likely be viewed as an obstacle to one's primary task and as a request to do something that one is untrained to do. So it is unlikely that any coherent moral vision will emerge that is sufficiently stable and enduring enough to support the kind of faculty hiring needed for Bok's program of moral education.

Second, Bok contends that most of the "hard cases," the standard fare in applied ethics courses, can be solved by appeal to "basic premises that almost all human beings share." However, many leading philosophers, both on the left and the right, argue that the deep moral problems that vex our culture are problematic just because they arise from the clash of fundamentally different moral points of view, each having basic premises which lead validly to different and incompatible solutions.[32] Unless we can adjudicate rationally between these rival and often alien moral points of view, Bok's contemporary program of moral education seems caught on the horns of his own dilemma. Appeals to honesty, promise-keeping, free expression, and benevolence are themselves principles subject to numerous interpretations and admit of the possibility of conflict.[33]

Third, Bok's commitment to applied ethics—envisioned as the neutral presentation of various ethical theories by virtue of which moral quandaries can be resolved—cannot be effective on its own terms, and thus cannot make much progress toward recovering the kind of moral education Bok rightly sees we need. For the combination of mutually incompatible ethical theories with hard cases often convinces students that no ethical theory is better than any other and that moral decisions are always fraught with ambiguity. Thus, centering moral education in hard cases is likely to produce the very ethical relativism and cynicism that Bok wishes to overcome. Further, applied ethics of this sort typically gives students the wrong idea of what ethics is all about and how morally admirable people are formed. Not least of all, this sort of approach tends to underwrite the "emotivist self" and a merely procedural democracy, both of which constitute shallow responses to our deepest moral concerns and difficulties.

For at least these reasons, it seems unlikely that Bok has proposed a contemporary program of moral education that could successfully address the problems of our modern culture, even if it were adopted widely by our nation's colleges and universities. We agree with Bok that moral education ought to be embraced by the university. At present, however, only institutions with a coherent vision of their task as a university, a vision in which moral education already has a place, are good candidates to assume this responsibility. The most likely candidates are the small liberal arts colleges, especially those that are religiously affiliated.[34] Our collection of essays is intended to provide a framework for moral education in such religiously affiliated colleges and universities, and especially those of Christian provenance. Lest our aims be misconstrued, let us be clear: we seek not to repristinate the old-time, nineteenth-century American college, as if that were possible, but rather to recapture for today its urgent commitment to substantive moral and intellectual formation.

HOW WE RETRIEVE THE TRADITION
AND REMEMBER THE END

This volume offers an alternative to standard models of moral education such as the one found in Bok's book, *Universities and the Future of America*. The alternative sketched in our essays challenges prevalent myths of moral neutrality, superficial dogmas of liberal citizenship, and prominent contemporary proposals for moral education. At the center of our proposed alternative is a genuinely liberal arts education, for such an education presumes that intellectual and moral formation is an integrated or unified endeavor. In addition, our alternative contends that all such truly complete liberal educational ventures presuppose some comprehensive viewpoint, and thus a metaphysical or theological stance of one sort or another. For Christians, the various academic practices that constitute a liberal arts education will naturally be grounded in a variety of interconnected theological truths that include humanity's creation in the image of God and the notion that all truth is ultimately unified in the triune God. Our effort in this collection of essays is to locate, within the current debate, our thesis that moral formation is an essential task in the university, and to explore the implications of this thesis for Christian colleges and universities by considering some of its significant theoretical and practical dimensions.

AMERICAN HIGHER EDUCATION'S UNSCHOOLED HEART

We frame our account at the outset with Warren A. Nord's "Liberal Education, Moral Education, and Religion" for several reasons. First, like Derek Bok, Nord acknowledges that moral education has little to no real place in the actual practice of many of America's leading colleges and universities. Second, like Bok, Nord offers a powerful critique of the current situation and a compelling case for a comprehensive program of moral education in America's public colleges and universities, a program that would require substantial reformation on their part. Foremost within his critique is the vulgarization of the liberal arts curriculum for various political and utilitarian ends—most especially, for professional and pre-professional education. The contemporary remnant of the classical liberal arts education goes by the vulgar name of general education, and it typically gives no real intellectual or moral direction to the undergraduate curriculum. Third, Nord's alternative program of moral formation does not rely primarily on courses in applied or professional ethics; rather, it relies on recovering a valid ideal of liberal arts education. Indeed, Nord's thesis is clear and refreshing: a genuine liberal (arts) education necessarily includes both moral education and a discussion of live religious perspectives on human nature, taking into account its moral dimensions and religious aspirations.

Fourth, Nord offers a positive and substantial program of his own. The aim of a liberal education is the moral and intellectual formation of students, and he sees these as inextricably linked. A genuine liberal education requires an integrated and well-ordered curriculum, all of which has moral import. Though moral formation is the work of the entire curriculum, he maintains that such a curriculum should include introductory and capstone courses of morally formative significance. Fifth, Nord

criticizes public education for a relentless secularism that typically rela-
tivizes moral views and excludes religious points of view from serious
consideration. Finally, Nord self-consciously addresses not only Bok's
plan for moral education in America's elite private colleges and research
universities, but also many of the essays in this volume. He discusses the
major themes any programmatic effort to retrieve the practice of moral
education as a significant aim in American higher education would have
to address. Not surprisingly, the rest of our essayists directly address
those themes, and often Nord's treatment of them.

One more word on why we use Nord's essay to frame the following
discussion. Nord's notion of a genuine liberal arts education relies on a
distinction that Bruce Kimball makes between (1) a "liberal arts" ideal—
an ideal Kimball and Nord identify with Cicero, classical and literary curricula, civic and social traditions, and self-conscious aiming at character
or moral formation—and (2) a "liberal-free" ideal—an ideal Kimball and
Nord identify with Socrates and unfettered philosophical and scientific
inquiry.[35] For Nord, a genuine liberal arts education combines the best
elements of both of these ideals, though he never spells out in any detail
what such a combination includes or excludes. We suggest that our collection of essays does spell out one philosophically sound way to combine these two ideals into a genuine liberal arts education, a way
especially congenial to Christian colleges and universities.

In his "Free Love and Christian Higher Education: Reflections on a
Passage from Plato's *Theaetetus*," Robert C. Roberts takes up several fundamental questions raised by Nord. What is a liberal arts education? Why
does it necessarily include moral formation? How does it differ from its
competitors? Is it a realistic programmatic initiative for the modern university? Roberts, too, worries that higher education in America is fundamentally distorted because our colleges and universities—under the
influence of cultural pressures—have strayed from their primary purposes. The education that many students and parents covet could be better described as training. They want those skills that will *equip* them to
make a living. Equipment can be employed and then discarded in favor
of other equipment more suitable for new tasks, Roberts points out.

Ideally, a liberal arts education forms persons rather than merely
equipping them for various jobs. That is, a genuine liberal arts education
contributes to the making of a complete and well-lived human life. But
such a life requires good character, and character accrues to a person in
such a way that it is not easily cast aside. Thus, Roberts contends that
the best kind of education possible is a genuine liberal arts education,
and that in such an education intellectual and moral formation are
inseparable.

We contend that Roberts sympathetically widens, deepens, and corrects Nord's account of liberal education. Roberts goes beyond Nord by arguing that any robust view of liberal education that includes both intellectual and moral formation of students will necessarily require an explicit theological or metaphysical framework, for such an effort depends on a particular understanding of not only human beings, but all of reality. For example, in contrast to contemporary metaphysical naturalists or materialists, both Plato and Aristotle insisted that education is a formation in love, and necessarily, a formation in character. It is a formation in free love, the love that is most appropriate to one's true human nature, in contrast to enslaving and corrupting loves. Christian liberal education is an education that promotes love of the good, which includes love of God and neighbor, as well as the proper ordering of our love of all other created objects. Insofar as love and the habituation of one's desires and affections are essential to the pursuit of truth and the acquisition of the intellectual virtues, we may properly speak of the morally and intellectually well-formed person as having a "schooled heart," a notion inspired by Roberts's own work on the virtues and moral psychology.

Roberts corrects Nord's account of the "liberal arts" ideal by showing that it is not insufficiently critical, as Nord thinks, and thus does not require the corrective of a "liberal-free" ideal. There are no doubt defective understandings of it and flawed efforts to practice it. But neither defective understandings nor flawed practices are intrinsic to the proper conception of the liberal arts ideal. In addition, Roberts argues that Nord's account of a liberal-free ideal of moral formation is internally incoherent, despite the strengths and attractiveness of his defense of moral formation in American higher education. First, the successful practice of a liberal-free version of moral formation depends on the moral virtues, so it is self-deceptive to think that it can be carried out independent of a moral point of view. Nord wants students, as does Bok, to be able to assess a variety of moral outlooks. But the development of such capacities requires a moral stance. The notion of a morally neutral capacity for the assessment of a moral outlook is incoherent. A genuinely liberal education requires moral formation in one's own moral tradition, even as one develops the ability to understand sympathetically and assess competing points of view.

Finally, like Nord, Roberts commends Bok for urging the modern university to reclaim its commitment to moral formation. And he suggests that the kinds of practices Bok commends may be the best that can be done in the secular, modern university. Nonetheless, they may be deficient, suggests Roberts, for the tasks Bok wants done. Since the secular university has evolved into a vehicle that is fundamentally ill-adapted to the education of a complete human being, a very different kind of vehicle, with a different design, is needed. We agree with his assessment.

In "Returning Moral Philosophy to American Higher Education," Nicholas K. Meriwether defends a pedagogy of ethics that can be read as an elaboration of the two fundamental objections Roberts raises against Nord. It is also an attempt both to spell out and defend an alternative to Bok's commitment to moral neutrality as a principled pedagogical stance, which is, perhaps, the standard approach in the academy. Meriwether compares and contrasts two basic approaches to moral formation in the university. The "pedagogy of mediation" requires that those who teach ethics adopt a neutral and mediating role, often the primary pedagogical practice in applied ethics courses. Instructors never indicate their own views but merely present the different alternatives, mediate between those thinkers who espouse them, and attempt to lead students into a deeper understanding of the competing theories and the factors that make particular issues controversial. Finally, and most importantly, they prod students to develop the higher intellectual skills necessary for understanding complex issues and encourage them to identify more clearly what they believe, while submitting the implications of their beliefs to critique.

Meriwether submits this pedagogical stance, and the assumptions that privilege it, to a sustained critique. In its place, he articulates and defends an alternative he calls the "pedagogy of profession" and responds to objections to it. The core of his view, which follows from Roberts's critique of Nord and Bok, is that moral education requires, at a minimum, a pedagogy in which the classroom instructor "presents, argues for, defends, and applies a normative ethical theory" to both the ordinary and extraordinary facets or situations of human life.[36] Moreover, he recommends that such a course be a capstone course, one that must be taken by every student to meet their general education or liberal arts education requirements.

Were such courses adopted and taught in accord with the "pedagogy of profession," twenty-first-century American colleges and universities would be retrieving the best aspects of nineteenth-century moral education as practiced in the old-time Christian college, as well as a set of practices with a much older history, as MacIntyre makes clear.[37] Like Bok, but unlike Nord and Roberts, Meriwether seems inclined to invest the moral formation of students in a particular course taught in a particular way at one particular juncture of students' experience rather than to see moral formation as the cumulative work of a well-ordered set of courses, a significant portion of which is identified as liberal arts education.

Stanley Hauerwas writes prophetically, provocatively, and powerfully. Some, both critics and friends, would say he writes outrageously. Readers of his *"Pro Ecclesia, Pro Texana:* Schooling the Heart in the Heart of Texas" will not be disappointed. In this essay, he insists that Christians are living in dark times: we live in a country out of control, find ourselves in churches nearly indistinguishable from Rotary Clubs, and work in or attend universities unable to tell the truth about the darkness of the situation. He insists that Christian colleges and universities are no less implicated in this conspiracy of silence than their secular sisters. Most bluntly, he accuses the Church of making a Faustian bargain with the nation-state, allowing its most basic convictions to be privatized. Thus, like Roberts, he contends that most Christian universities have failed to provide a genuine alternative to modern, secular, American higher education.

At the heart of his essay are the following five theses: first, the contemporary American church is far too accommodating to the culture. He claims that the modern university and the modern nation-state "are mutually supportive projects." The modern state's central task has always been to replace the church as the object of ultimate loyalty. It has seduced even Christians into giving this secular liege *de facto* unconditional allegiance because of its ability to deliver some measure of earthly happiness to most of its citizens, and promissory notes to the remainder. Second, for Christians the principal locus or community within which moral formation takes place and is intelligible is the church. Third, while Christian universities are not the church, they ought to be servants of the church. So compromised are American universities in their allegiance to the modern state that even Christian colleges and universities have largely accepted the modern university's understanding of academic ethics and proper pedagogy. Fourth, if Christian universities are true to their first calling they must reject accommodationist strategies and any model of education that preserves and promotes the morally stunting and distorting views of the larger culture. Fifth, at the very least, Christian universities should help our students discern when to say yes and when to say no to the culture.

Hauerwas provides a provocative and insightful diagnostic narrative of our present dilemmas, though he has all too little to say about what moral formation might look like in Christian universities. His essay is suggestive, but teasingly so, and the essays that follow do much to address what moral formation might look like if its rootedness in the Christian gospel were taken seriously. The Christian gospel offers a narrative of formation and transformation, a story that is about the redemption of the whole person, that is particular and concrete, that is unabashedly agonistic, that is, paradoxically, about both peace and justice. Indeed, Hauerwas reminds the reader that if a university or college is Christian, then its efforts at moral formation must aim at telling the whole truth, including the uncomfortable truths, about human beings. The moral formation that takes place in such a university must ultimately be grounded in and bear witness to the God made incarnate in Jesus Christ, a Jew, the Savior whose life, death, and resurrection is the fundamental witness of the church. Thus, a Christian process of moral formation must be grounded in the church's story of God's creative, redemptive, and reconciling work in the world.

CHRISTIAN RESOURCES FOR MORAL FORMATION IN THE ACADEMY

In view of the trajectory of the first half of the book, what follows next begins to elaborate on the concrete, morally and intellectually interconnected virtues that properly characterize schooled hearts within the Christian university. That is, it attempts to sketch out some of the tradition-embedded contours of morally formative education, given the cumulative case laid out by Nord, Roberts, Meriwether, and Hauerwas. While a comprehensive account of the biblical and traditional sources that define the relevant virtues of morally well-formed students falls outside the scope of this project, we nonetheless offer a clear-eyed representation of the kind of account needed.

Thus it is that David Lyle Jeffrey's essay begins where Hauerwas's leaves off, and what Hauerwas leaves speculative and unstated, Jeffrey identifies and states. Jeffrey makes good on Hauerwas's commitment to Christian particularity by addressing four virtues: wisdom, community, freedom, and truth. However, Jeffrey does not valorize any virtue *simpliciter*, but only as it is expressed in the tradition-bound terms of biblical teaching as interpreted by the church. In taking this approach he shows how Christian universities must avoid the deracinated celebration of the virtues typical of universities wedded to the thin, morally reformative approach endorsed by Bok and the insufficiently confessional model proposed by Nord. Following Jeffrey's turn to concrete Christian particularity, Paul J. Wadell and Darin H. Davis drive in their chapter to the core of contemporary student culture and demonstrate how apt and timely a response morally formative Christian higher education is, with its particular virtues, to the morally misshapen and despairing lives typical of students today. Rounding out the essays in this section are contributions from Shawn D. Floyd, Stephen K. Moroney, Matthew P. Phelps, and Scott T. Waalkes that take one specific Christian virtue, humility, and demonstrate how unavoidably confessional it is, how inextricably bound up with moral and intellectual life it is, and how fruitfully exemplified within the practical context of classroom pedagogy it might be.

To be more precise, Jeffrey's essay, "Wisdom, Community, Freedom, Truth: Moral Education and the 'Schooled Heart,'" has at least three important resonances with Roberts's. First, if virtue cannot be taught, then education must necessarily be a technical or instrumental education. Jeffrey insists that Christian colleges and universities must resist the seductive and corrosive influences that encourage a flattening of education to mere instrumental ends. To avoid such a catastrophe, Christian colleges and universities must order their loves properly. Second, Jeffrey follows Roberts's admonition that moral education be both an articulation and application of particular moral virtues. Jeffrey bids us focus on *sophia* (wisdom), especially as it is articulated in the biblical tradition. Third, because a biblical understanding of wisdom takes one to matters of the heart, and involves both knowledge and the affections, Jeffrey also sees the value of speaking of moral formation in terms of the schooling of the heart. Yet, he contends, any adequate account of a schooled heart requires a proper understanding of the kind of community within which real freedom is found, a freedom grounded in transcendent truth.

Jeffrey makes explicit, in ways none of the other essays do, a biblical framework for thinking about the task of moral education, and in so doing, he exhibits intellectual suppleness and verve in bringing it into contact with the intellectual riches of the larger Christian tradition. His essay illuminates the intersections between biblical and nonbiblical insight, understanding, discernment, and wisdom in a way that exemplifies precisely what he speaks about. It demonstrates how it is that the intellectually and morally well-formed Christian will move from the Scriptures into the world and back again in increasingly wider and deeper swaths.

Like Roberts, Jeffrey challenges the dichotomy posed by Nord. Nord, taking his lead from Bruce Kimball, equates the liberal arts ideal with a stifling conformity to tradition and his liberal-free alternative with a freeing of the individual from tradition. Jeffrey reminds the reader that the understanding of freedom enjoined by Seneca, the biblical writers, and Augustine is much more subtle than Nord's characterization allows for. It is opposed to both individual license and heavy-handed dogmatism. Ironically, but not surprisingly, appeals to autonomy often degenerate into one or the other of these vices. As Jeffrey so powerfully argues, genuine freedom is neither freedom from all authority, nor the tyranny of dogmatic inflexibility in thought. The kind of freedom of thought that is essential to intellectual and moral formation depends on the authority of truth, an authority often recognized in the voice of a teacher or the expressions of a community. Free obedience then ensues; generous liberality on behalf of the good of others is one of its finest expressions.

In "Tracking the Toxins of *Acedia:* Reenvisioning Moral Education," Paul J. Wadell and Darin H. Davis provide a diagnosis of what they take to be an insidious cultural vice, *acedia* (which encompasses notions of indifference, callousness, and lethargy), and then they suggest a way to reenvision moral education in response to *acedia's* detrimental role in the culture. For if *acedia* is the ill that they contend it is, and if our young are especially vulnerable to it, then helping initiate students into a quest for goodness is the most important work that educators can do. More particularly, they argue that three virtues integral to the moral life—hope, courage, and perseverance—are especially important as qualities that enable their possessors to resist or overcome cultural *acedia*. They make specific recommendations regarding how moral formation in the university might cultivate hope, courage, and perseverance, despite the pervasiveness of *acedia*.

In investigating *acedia*, Wadell and Davis take very seriously two points Roberts makes in his essay. First, they hold that Christian moral philosophers ought to articulate and trace the implications of particular Christian virtues and, by implication, correlative vices. Second, their essay may be read as an application of Roberts's suggestion that because different metaphysical frameworks will understand virtues and vices differently, one must begin with a specifically Christian account of a virtue or a vice in relation to the cultural context against which it is best understood. They thus argue that *acedia* is not merely sloth or lethargy, but, on a Christian understanding, it is an expansive indifference toward moral and spiritual excellence, and its expansiveness makes it especially harmful to our personal and social well-being.

Their explication of *acedia* presumes the kind of teleological eudaimonism Meriwether praises. Davis and Wadell make clear that if our lives as Christians are a quest or journey toward the good—understood as a radically different kind of happiness that necessarily includes friendship with God through Christ—then such a quest requires the enabling virtues of hope, courage, and perseverance (among others, to be sure). And they make clear why *acedia* is a vice impeding the attainment of our true good, how *acedia* is defective with respect to our true good, and why the virtues are necessary to combat this kind of defect.

Another important contribution of their essay to this volume comes in its insightful discussion of a Christian understanding of vocation and how this is a pedagogical resource for moral formation in the Christian university. They argue that at the center of moral formation must be a theologically grounded understanding of vocation; namely, vocation is a call to respond to the good, a goodness made known through God's incarnation in Jesus the Christ. Their account is enriched by reference to literary texts and contemporary television, and one sees how easily these tools might be used in pedagogically useful ways in either philosophy or literature classes to prod students to attend to the debilitating aspects of modern culture. As Iris Murdoch insightfully insists, following Plato, attention to the good is a significant portion of moral formation. Yet, as these authors point out, our culture too easily distorts our attention in the form of reality TV and similar fads and fashions. A useful feature of the essay is its practical suggestions for how courses that reflect these concerns could be constructed, and how familiar courses might be reformed or reconstructed if these ideas were taken seriously.

Shawn D. Floyd's essay, "Could Humility Be a Deliberative Virtue?" acknowledges that in one version of moral education in a pluralistic democracy, moral education involves presenting students with competing moral theories and, via dialectical discussions, helping students decide for themselves what their moral beliefs will be. On this view, it is inappropriate for the teacher to advocate any theory over another because it requires one to commit oneself to a substantive account of the good as true, and thereby to abdicate the morally neutral position allegedly proper to the role of the teacher. Violation of moral neutrality results in indoctrination rather than a genuine education, on this view. As noted above, Meriwether denies that the doctrine of moral neutrality is essential to the pedagogy of moral formation, and Floyd clearly joins him in his opposition to the necessity of moral neutrality.

Indeed, while Floyd acknowledges the view that moral education requires moral neutrality, he points out that many liberal theorists who discuss moral formation in a democratic culture themselves reject the doctrine of moral neutrality. Indeed they embrace the view that all moral education requires substantive commitments and insist that liberal ideals rightly provide the basis of moral education for students living in a democratic, pluralist society. Like Warren Nord, many call this "liberal education." Its aim is to produce good citizens of a democratic culture, namely "deliberative citizens" who exemplify civility, tolerance, and respect for freedom.

Floyd asks if theologically grounded virtues might contribute to a good civic education as understood by proponents of liberal education, and he argues that some can, including humility. He argues that humility is necessary (though perhaps not sufficient) to foster and sustain the practices regarded as central to democratic education. More specifically, he argues that humility should itself be considered a deliberative virtue. Floyd's strategy is straightforward and effective. First, he identifies two important objections against the very possibility that humility (understood theologically) might be necessary to foster democratic practices. Then, he presents a positive case for humility as essential for the practices of civility, mutual respect, and reasoned deliberation about political goods and procedures. He argues that such practices can only be sustained by those who are shaped by more fundamental dispositions, that humility is one of the necessary fundamental dispositions, and that Aquinas' account of humility can help us understand why this is the case.

In the final essay of the book, Stephen K. Moroney, Matthew P. Phelps, and Scott T. Waalkes give vital expression to how a theologically cogent understanding of humility might contribute to a morally formative classroom pedagogy. Because "Cultivating Humility: Teaching Practices Rooted in Christian Anthropology" focuses on how humility might be developed in students, it is a natural follow up to Floyd's chapter. The authors note their indebtedness to MacIntyre's account of virtue and its relation to practices and tradition. Moreover, their work is clearly indebted to recent work in virtue epistemology on the intellectual virtues. The authors insist that humility is not only a moral virtue; it is also an intellectual virtue. They then survey some of the recent literature that argues for humility, but that does little to address the issue of how this virtue is cultivated in students.

They draw from the accounts of Mark Schwehn and Parker Palmer, both of whom insist that humility is a virtue that enables students to be receptive to and engage in a variety of learning practices. Following Roberts, in the first part of their essay, they develop a Christian account of humility grounded in a Christian anthropological account of human beings. Humility is the proper response to the fact that (1) others are made in God's own image and may have something valuable to teach us, (2) we are limited creatures whose knowledge is tightly circumscribed by our finitude, and (3) we are fallen creatures whose thinking is distorted by our sin—both personal and corporate.

The authors note that most other discussions of humility as an intellectual virtue offer little pedagogical advice. So, a key question is: How might a Christian understanding of human beings and humility contribute to the development of sound, effective pedagogical strategies for the cultivation of humility? An especially important feature of this essay is that the authors are from different academic disciplines—theology, psychology, and international studies. To suggest a variety of pedagogical strategies that cultivate humility, each individual contributor illustrates teaching strategies that are rooted in one of the three aspects of their Christian anthropology, that draw upon discipline-specific resources, and that offer rich resources for cultivating humility in students. Their contribution is to provide educational themes in their diverse disciplines that help confront students with the necessity of theologically grounded humility. Then they identify a host of humility-promoting practices that fit well into their three different intellectual disciplines, and that also are clearly transferable to other disciplines. Their helpful illustrations may prompt teachers to imagine analogous practices in their own disciplines.

CONCLUSION

The contributors to this volume agree that American higher education ought to reclaim one of its historically prominent and primary purposes—the moral formation of students. They agree that the principal vehicle of such an effort is a genuinely liberal arts education. Necessarily, commitment to this ideal requires a reformation of many current practices in American universities, from smorgasbord approaches to general education to thin or impoverished courses in applied ethics. Our authors agree that a genuinely liberal arts education integrates intellectual and moral formation—for these notions are unified in any true account of what is genuinely good for human beings.

Taken together these essays provide a theoretical and practical sketch of an alternative to the common contemporary approaches to moral education in American higher education. Though there are important disagreements among our authors, in the main, they agree that Christian approaches to moral formation will be tradition-based and tradition-constituted, confessional or professional, and agonistic. Rather than emphasizing rules/principles or consequences, the model sketched makes understanding and emulating good persons of primary importance, and regards the virtues as the principle terms of moral discourse, while allowing that rights and duties are derivative, indispensable elements of moral life in community. The model presumes that proponents will at times have deep disagreements not only with those who embrace a very different account of reality, and thus a very different metaphysical or theological point of view, but also with one another. Yet, these disagreements are constitutive components of a healthy moral tradition. Additionally, the model sketched does not presume that moral education in Christian universities is ultimately "for democracy," that is, that its end purpose is to make good democratic citizens. It does presume that the right sort of moral and intellectual formation will equip men and women with the kind of character that enables them to participate in well-formed political processes, be they democratic or otherwise. It further suggests that formation as Christian persons involves the development of those virtues characteristic of Christians, and that such formation may be useful for participation in democratic processes, to include the practice of dissent. Our authors, then, reject the notion that religion is merely useful to prop up civil society.

Our hope is that our sustained reflection on the place of moral formation in American higher education will contribute to a recovery of the coherent purpose once generally acknowledged in American colleges and universities, but long since displaced after the turn of the twentieth century. In this way we aspire to offer a compelling answer to a nearly universally acknowledged deficiency in American higher education, as poignantly described by Bok. Yet we acknowledge that not all of our readers will find our solution wholly satisfactory. Some will resist its particularity, and especially its Christian particularity, even while acknowledging that it is precisely the theologically grounded, tradition-constituted character of the moral education we propose that enables it to succeed where Bok's approach cannot. Others will hesitate over the conception of freedom developed herein, for it ultimately abjures hyper-individualistic license, emotivist latitudinarianism, and the supposition that human beings lack an essential nature and thus are free to become whatever they want to be. They will demur from the freedom acquired by students as a result of the morally formative education we have in mind—hard-won and taking more the nature of a learned skill than a preexisting status— because it is tethered to a concrete conception of what is good for human beings. Still others, however sympathetic they may be to the need for tradition-constituted education in virtues such as freedom and humility, or to the desirability of regarding freedom as a right necessarily circumscribed by the good, will be reluctant to embrace the explicitly confessional or professional pedagogical methods to which we point, holding instead to the instructional advantages of withholding from students their own considered judgments and leading them indirectly to ultimately well-warranted conclusions.

To these predictable worries, we have three responses. First, our principal concern is to develop a coherent understanding of what a morally well-shaped university education might involve within the context of the Christian tradition within which we find ourselves, and not for the sake of universal humankind. Indeed, the only way we see to offer an account of the role of moral formation within higher education that would appeal to anyone and everyone would be to dilute it to the point of ineffectuality, just in the way that Bok does. We do not see any way of addressing the morally bereft character of American higher education to which Bok points, then, without embracing a thick account of human nature and the moral life. In this sense, we acknowledge the inescapably limited scope of our account.

Second, we hope that even those who are dubious about the theologically concrete commitments we embrace, and thus about the morally formative education which we advocate, will discern analogous ways of addressing the problem that we face in common, if we would recover for

American higher education the noble and morally enabling purposes it once served. We acknowledge, for instance, that other concrete, metaphysically supple, tradition-sustained approaches to the moral life are possible, and that indeed our own account is substantially indebted to such classical alternatives, both Greek and Roman. Thus, we would rather see those who dissent from the particular moves that we make choose to develop their own rich, thick alternative accounts of the moral life, key virtues, and ultimate ends that education should serve instead of settling for the rootless and shiftless "vision" of the moral life typical within the American academy today. That is to say, we believe that there are methodological lessons to be learned from the account that we offer about moral formation in higher education, even if the first principles from which we operate are unpersuasive to others.

Finally, we invite correction of our errors, such as they may be. After all, to invite such correction is part of the legacy of Christian moral formation that is ours, just as it is part of the legacy of the liberal arts tradition that is ours as well. In this book, no one expresses better or more concisely the principled theological grounds for welcoming the exposure of one's mistakes than Stephen Moroney, Matthew Phelps, and Scott Waalkes: others are also created in the image of God and worthy of charitable acknowledgment; we are limited, finite, and ever incomplete, not least of all in the scope of our understanding; and we are broken, fallen creatures all too easily satisfied with less than that to which we should aspire. In this spirit, then, we encourage others, especially those who disagree with us, to help us advance the significant conversation at stake in this book and others like it, for the matters here at hand are far from trifling and surely deserve no less than our best efforts and patient attention.[38]

Part I

American Higher Education's Unschooled Heart

Chapter 1

Liberal Education, Moral Education, and Religion

—Warren A. Nord

Liberal education comes in various shapes and sizes. I will discuss two historically influential conceptions of liberal education, both of which have clear implications for how we think of moral education. Though their emphases are different, they are, in fact, complementary, and I will argue that an adequate account of moral education requires that we draw on both. I will also argue that serious study of religion is essential to both liberal education and moral education. (What will give this thesis particular punch is that I make this claim regarding public as well as private higher education.) First, however, a few comments about why moral education is such a problem in higher education.

WHY MORAL EDUCATION IS A PROBLEM

There are several reasons.

First, there is the stubborn prejudice that we either learn morality at mother's knee—or we do not learn it at all. Certainly, it is believed, it is too late in college to learn to be moral.

Second, it has become increasingly common to think of higher education primarily in economic terms. Surveys of incoming freshmen show that they value higher education chiefly for the jobs that their degrees will buy them (and the money they will make in those jobs). They are not the only ones. More and more, parents, legislators, and policymakers think of education in economic terms (whether the goal be jobs for my kids, educated workers for my business, or American competitiveness for success in the international marketplace). Not surprisingly, higher education has become more narrowly practical in response to the utilitarian values, pressures, and policies of the larger culture. This is not simply a recent phenomenon; almost from the beginning, American public schools and universities had a practical bent. But it is becoming more pronounced. Not surprisingly, both secondary and higher education have become increasingly uncoupled from more traditional emphases on virtue and the search for moral truth.

Third, it is widely believed that in a pluralistic liberal democracy, public universities must remain morally neutral; individuals should be free to make their own moral (and religious) judgments. Again, there has been a steady development in this direction over the last two centuries, but many would say that the trend accelerated during the liberal and antiauthoritarian 1960s. Moral education is often seen as synonymous with *moralistic* education, that is to say, indoctrination. Within most colleges and universities, the availability of electives and the absence of a core curriculum grant students the right to shape, within broad limits, their own educations; the result is cultural fragmentation and skepticism about a common morality.

Fourth, in accepting the fact-value dichotomy of the scientific method, many scholars have come to believe that the *real* world is one of pure factuality, while value-judgments are subjective. Talk of what is good and evil, morally right and wrong, is conceptually impossible within the framework of modern science and much social science. Modern science has also marginalized God and theology, and discredited ways in which religion makes sense of morality. To the extent that students come to an understanding of nature that is derived from the value-free sciences, and of human nature derived from the value-free social sciences, morality will almost inevitably seem irrational—a matter of blind faith, arbitrary personal decisions, or mere social conventions—and hardly a fit matter for *education*, as opposed to socialization or training.

Fifth, while the humanities have also been shaped by modern scientific naturalism, *postmodernism* has flourished in the humanities over the last several decades. In this context I take postmodernism to be the view that we are epistemologically constrained by the particularities of our cultures and subcultures, so that we inevitably interpret the world in terms of our own time and language, our own class, race, and gender. There is no way of stepping outside our cultural skins, outside the social locations that shape our ways of making sense of the world, to discover what is *objectively true*; indeed, *it makes no sense* to talk of objective truth. A part of what makes this view *post*modern is that it rejects the claim that science (the approach to knowledge characteristic of modernity) has any special standing in providing us with knowledge of the world; rather, science simply provides *one narrative among many* for interpreting the world, no more objective or reasonable than any other. The problem with postmodernism is that it makes moral judgments *relative* to (or *internal* to) a tradition, a culture, a language-game, a narrative, or a worldview— in which case moral education becomes a matter of politics or power, not education (properly understood).

Sixth, as research became a major responsibility of faculty (a development that had taken place by the end of the nineteenth century in universities) specialization inevitably followed in its wake. Aided and abetted by the influence of modern science, scholars defined their research and their teaching more and more narrowly, rejecting the older commitment to the "unity of truth" (the idea that knowledge and virtue were one). The idea of a core curriculum that all students should study gave way to electives, distribution requirements, and a dizzying array of courses offered by professors whose hearts were in their specialties. Not surprisingly, the traditional nineteenth-century capstone course in moral philosophy (taught by the president of the college, typically a minister) had disappeared by the end of the century as ethics becomes one specialty among many. It was no longer reasonable to leave morality "to the benign amateurs who were not intimidated by cosmic questions or their own ignorance."[1]

All of these reasons for marginalizing or discrediting moral education in colleges and universities are controversial. All of them are, I believe, misguided.

TWO CONCEPTIONS OF LIBERAL EDUCATION

In his very helpful book, *Orators and Philosophers: A History of the Idea of Liberal Education*, Bruce Kimball charts the history of two quite different, sometimes competing ideals of liberal education.[2] The first—which he calls the *artes liberales* (liberal arts) ideal—is grounded in the classical canon. It assumes that moral truths and the ideals of civic virtue are to be found in classical literature, and it is largely a literary education. It forms character, and is meant to be the ideal education for public leaders (historically, mostly men of leisure), and as such, it has typically been elitist. A liberal arts education binds students to the past, to tradition. While

Kimball traces the liberal arts conception back to the Greek rhetorician Isocrates, Cicero is its patron saint. It was the educational ideal of late Greece and Rome, the early Middle Ages (during which it took on Christian hues), the Renaissance, and early America. In so far as a traditional religious ideal has been to nurture children and students in the faith, as it is embodied in the Bible (a classic to be sure), the liberal arts conception lends itself to religious ends.

The second conception of liberal education—which Kimball calls the *liberal-free* ideal—takes as its patron saint the philosopher Socrates, and is moved by the continuing search for truth. It values free, critical inquiry and tolerance; it is skeptical. It inclines toward egalitarianism and individualism rather than elitism and tradition. It pays scant attention to the classics but is concerned with philosophical inquiry and scientific experiment. It assumes no truth from the past, but is critical, constantly looking for new truths; it underwrites the idea of progress. It *liberates* students, rather than binding them to tradition. The liberal-free ideal was foreshadowed in Greek philosophy and in the philosophy of the high Middle Ages, but it came into its own only with the scientific revolution, the Enlightenment, and nineteenth-century research universities. Arguably, it had become the dominant conception of liberal education in American universities by the end of the nineteenth century (though the liberal arts ideal lived on in smaller, more traditional "liberal arts colleges" and in the occasional rhetoric of university presidents).

A famous exchange, from the end of the nineteenth century, captures the difference nicely. In 1880 T. H. Huxley, the greatest promoter of Darwin and modern science, argued that education should be founded on "an unhesitating faith that the free employment of reason, in accordance with scientific method, is the sole method of reaching truth."[3] Matthew Arnold responded by claiming that education is rather a matter of teaching "the best which has been thought and uttered in the world"; it speaks to "our need for conduct, our need for beauty."[4] Huxley argued for the liberal-free ideal, Arnold for the liberal arts.

I have already noted that much of what passes for education nowadays does not fall under either umbrella.

THE LIBERAL ARTS IDEAL AND MORAL EDUCATION

A *liberal arts* education, on Kimball's account, is a moral education; its purpose is to form character, to nurture virtue, to shape the identities of students by initiating them into a community, a tradition, a narrative that interprets and orients their lives.

It is sometimes said that our most fundamental values are *caught* more than they are *taught*, and there is something to this. Character is, to a considerable extent, formed early in our lives. We are not argued into it; the virtues are not in any real sense chosen. Rather, children learn to be honest, to work hard, and to be compassionate by observing their parents, by internalizing the moral values of their communities, and by being initiated into civic and religious traditions. Alasdair MacIntyre has argued that "I can only answer the question 'What am I to do?' if I can answer the prior question 'Of what story or stories do I find myself a part?' We enter human society, that is, with one or more imputed characters—roles into which we have been drafted—and we have to learn what they are in order to be able to understand how others respond to us and how our responses to them are to be construed. . . . Deprive children of stories and you leave them unscripted, anxious stutterers in their actions as in their words."[5]

We live (granted, less now than in the past) in what Robert Bellah and his colleagues have called "communities of memory" that give shape and substance to our identities.[6] We are not individuals, pure and simple (*social atoms*, as is sometimes held in the social sciences), but members of communities (national, ethnic, religious, and linguistic) shaped by institutions and traditions, by webs of influence and obligation that tie us not just to other people in our own time, but to the past—and the future. To be oblivious to the traditions and roles we inherit is a little like having amnesia: if we do not know where we have been, we do not know where we are going; indeed, we do not know who we are.

Over the last several decades there has been a resurgence of interest in "virtue ethics" and a reassertion of the centrality of character to morality among philosophers and theologians. At the same time "character education" has become fairly common in our nation's schools. As the father of a teenager I am inclined to think this is all to the good. Our relentless cultural emphasis on individualism and autonomy has often blinded us to the importance of moral socialization and character. If all goes well, children are socialized or trained by their parents, their religious communities, and their schools to be honest, hard-working, and compassionate people who, when confronted with moral problems, will act honestly and compassionately. It is often noted that the etymology of the word *character* suggests that character is "engraved" on our being. Indeed, whatever our commitment to critical thinking, we must rely, in the beginning at least, on the virtues we acquired as children and the traditions within which we find ourselves. We must have a starting place. Children must be socialized before they reach the age of reason, but even beyond that elusive age it is fitting and important that students continue to be nurtured in moral and civic practices and traditions.

Like schools, universities must have a moral ethos. Derek Bok has argued that a "comprehensive program of moral education" in universities would include "discussing rules of conduct with students and administering them fairly, building strong programs of community service, demonstrating high ethical standards in dealing with moral issues facing the university, and . . . being more alert to the countless signals that institutions send to students and trying to make these messages support rather than undermine basic norms."[7] Through honor codes and student government the university creates a moral community and nurtures the development of moral and civic virtues such as integrity, civic responsibility, community, hard work, and excellence. Faculty and administrators must use moral language to define the goals and practices of their institutions. Bok notes that in doing so, universities are not (indeed, they cannot be) morally neutral; in using moral language the university commits itself to moral standards of right and wrong—a stance incompatible with moral relativism. Happily this is not (for all our pluralism) particularly controversial; indeed, Bok suggests, such moral values "are all so fundamental and so universal that they have proved essential to virtually every civilized society."[8]

James Davison Hunter has complained that the "quest for inclusiveness" in moral education "can be pursued only by emptying lived morality of its particularity—those 'thick' normative meanings whose seriousness and authority are embedded within the social organization of distinct communities and the collective rituals and narratives that give them continuity over time."[9] There is much to this, particularly in regard to character education programs in public schools with their virtue-of-the-week pedagogies. Much character education is thin, unimaginative, and dreary. Still, I'm inclined to think that the institutional context for Bok's academic virtues is not hopelessly thin. There is a rich academic tradition into which students can be initiated, one that overlaps with various civic, moral, and religious traditions. Moreover, it is no small thing for universities to go on record about matters of right and wrong.

Of course, the purpose of a liberal arts education is to ground our virtues and values in thick moral, civic, and religious traditions by way of the curriculum, in what is taught about history and literature, nature and human nature. Some colleges and universities still do take it as their task to locate students in the American constitutional tradition, or within the history of Western civilization, in order to give students civic and moral identities.

Stanley Hauerwas has claimed that students come to college unprepared to engage "in reasoned discourse to know better the good and true. They lack the virtues necessary for sustaining the life of the mind, as there exists no community capable of directing them to the good in the first place."[10] Hence, it is the task of the university "to *train* those with the wisdom to help us all know better what is best about us. Such training comes by the discipline of confronting texts and figures of the past and present in the hope of continuing discussion of our forebearers."[11] For Hauerwas, to say that a college or university is Christian "is to say that certain matters cannot be left out of the conversation if we are to know better what it means to be Christian. Thus, it might [rightly] be expected that the curriculum of a college that claims Christian identity would look different from those that do not. But even more important, it means that what is taught as history, or psychology, or sociology at such schools, and how they are taught, might be different."[12] Not just *might* be different, *must* be different. A Christian college or university would teach students how Christians (Catholics, or Protestants, or Evangelicals) make sense of the world and how they should live their lives. It would nurture Christian virtue—and, in the process, *transform* students' values, goals, and desires.[13]

I agree that it is tremendously important to locate students in traditions. My concern here is about the fact that this can be done in relatively open or closed ways. At the rightward end of a spectrum of possibilities, some very conservative religious colleges marginalize criticism of their tradition by failing to give their students the intellectual resources to think critically about it; faculty may even be required to sign statements of allegiance to that tradition.

At the leftward end, liberal religious colleges or universities might simply insist that the school's own religious tradition be included within the curriculum along with other secular and religious traditions (which are taken seriously, and are taught by scholars sympathetic to them). Between these two ends of the spectrum lie a variety of possibilities.

The potential virtue of a liberal arts education is that it locates students in thick moral, civic, and religious traditions that give them ground on which to stand in confronting the materialism, pluralism, and often mindless individualism of popular culture and the relativism of so much of our intellectual life. The great danger of a liberal arts education—as one moves rightward along the range of possibilities—is narrowness and dogmatism. It is not just that the religious tradition in question may turn out to be fundamentally mistaken (most everyone agrees that historically this has often happened, sometimes with morally devastating consequences). It is also the case that if students are not given the resources and encouragement to think critically about the traditions into which they are initiated then education degenerates into training or indoctrination.

TRAINING AND EDUCATION

Ordinarily we think of training as primarily a matter of drill, discipline, and habit rather than critical reflection. We *train* children to read and write and do math. We toilet train children, rather than educate them in toiletry. We educate students, by contrast, when we provide them with a measure of critical distance on their subjects (and their lives). Most of us would say, for example, that it is not the task of educational institutions to train or socialize students to be good Democrats or Republicans; rather, a good education will enable them to think in informed and critical ways about both political parties. Indeed, most of us believe that the truth about politics and public policy is most likely to be discovered as a result of open and informed discussion of the alternatives. As students mature and proceed through the grades, the extent to which they are trained and socialized (a necessity for children) should diminish, while their education, properly conceived, should take root and grow.

Of course, much of what passes for education might better be termed *training*. This is the case in secular as well as in religious institutions. In professional schools we talk of training doctors and lawyers and MBAs. This is not just a matter of drill and habit—training can be intellectually quite sophisticated. Rather it is a matter of initiating students into a particular way of practicing medicine or law or business, rather than educating them to think critically about alternative ways of practicing their profession. (How many business schools take seriously Marxist or communitarian or religious ways of thinking about human nature, values, decision-making, and economic institutions?) Similarly, students who study science are, much more often than not, *trained* to think scientifically rather than *educated about* science. They are taught through textbooks that convey the truth authoritatively and never raise questions about the adequacy of scientific method for making sense of the world. (The philosopher and historian of science Thomas Kuhn once claimed that science is taught more dogmatically than any subject in the curriculum other than theology.[14] One might respond that theologians, at least, must always study some science in the course of their education; scientists are never required to study theology.)

No doubt I have drawn this distinction between education and training too starkly; some nuance is needed. My point is that much education (including traditional liberal arts education) can fall short of being truly educational if it fails to enable and require students to think critically about the fundamental beliefs and values that define the commitments of their discipline, school, or tradition.

Similarly, much of what is called character education might more aptly be called character socialization or training: it does not rise to the level of being truly educational; it does not raise critical questions about the moral and civic traditions into which it socializes students. This is not necessarily to denigrate character education. As I have said, students must be trained or socialized before they can be educated; they must have a starting point for moral deliberation. Indeed, in today's culture, we need a little more socialization before we initiate them into the rough and tumble of a *liberal-free* education.

But that transition is essential, for, as the philosopher E. M. Adams has written, "the measure of one's provincialism and cultural slavery is the extent to which one is blindly in the grips of one's culture without critical understanding and mastery of it. The measure of one's education," by contrast, "is the extent to which one has a critical understanding and mastery of human culture."[15]

ETHICS COURSES

Derek Bok gives a passing (one paragraph) nod in the direction of literature, history, and the social sciences' capacity to enlighten students morally, but when it comes to critical moral thinking he puts his money on courses in applied and professional ethics. The typical course in applied ethics, he suggests, "does not seek to convey a set of moral truths but tries to encourage students to think carefully about complex moral issues. . . . The principal aim of the course is not to impart 'right answers' but to make students more perceptive in detecting ethical problems when they arise, better acquainted with the best moral thought that has accumulated through the ages, and more equipped to reason about the ethical issues they will face in their own personal and professional lives."[16] Bok notes the spread of courses in applied and professional ethics over the last couple of decades.

There are, of course, many kinds of ethics courses, taught in quite different ways. But they are not usually required courses. There is no small irony in the fact that for all the importance commonly attributed to morality, ethics courses are nonexistent in K-12 schooling and are typically electives in higher education (though courses in professional or applied ethics have often become required in professional schools). Indeed it can only be astonishing, on reflection, that we require students to learn about the most abstract, complicated, and obscure scientific theories but leave them completely ignorant of all moral ones. How many students have any understanding of utilitarianism, Kantian moral theory, social contract theory, or liberation theology? How many have even heard of John Rawls or Reinhold Niebuhr? Arguably, the *de facto* position of the educational establishment is that students need not be particularly educated about morality.

We also marginalize critical thinking about morality by compartmentalizing ethics in philosophy departments (in accord with the conventional academic division of labor). Ethics has become a specialty with little, if any, direct relevance to other disciplines. This in itself is not the problem—no doubt ethics should continue to be a philosophical specialty—but the other disciplines have, in turn, largely been demoralized. (I will take economics as an example of this below.) Of course the fact that ethics has become a *philosophical* specialty means, in most universities, that *theological* voices are typically left out of the discussion. (Why include Reinhold Niebuhr along with John Rawls?) While courses in the history of ethics may include religious thinkers prior to Kierkegaard, recent and contemporary religious voices are almost always left out.

One might also fret about the *abstractness* of philosophical ethics. As in most any discipline, abstraction simplifies the messiness of reality. This has real advantages (particularly in terms of clarity and logical rigor)—but it also has disadvantages. Most important, it decontextualizes ethics from historical and cultural settings (other, usually, than the context of the history of *philosophy*—which is not unimportant). Yet, moral judgments and theories are inevitably entangled in complex webs of scientific, social, and spiritual facts, assumptions, and beliefs. They are tested, in part, by their implications for human suffering and flourishing—and require some sense of how, historically, moral ideas and ideals have played out in the past. Moreover, appreciating the moral demands on us requires a *sensitivity* to people's suffering and to the human condition. This is not to say that a narrowly philosophical ethics is not essential to our critical thinking about morality; it is to say that moral education must be embedded in a historically and culturally textured liberal education.

Perhaps the greatest concern of those who approach ethics courses from the vantage point of the liberal arts ideal is the danger of moral relativism. Hauerwas suggests that such courses simply "underwrite the presumption the students have prior to taking such courses. Students assume that ethics names that part of life in which you have to make up your own mind . . . [and] that when it comes to what we care about, it is finally up to us to decide what we 'value.'"[17] Bok is aware of this:

> At this point, universities confront a serious dilemma. They can try to impart a preferred moral code by every reasonable means at their disposal. . . . [But] if they do, they risk imposing their views on students in a manner that conflicts with principles of intellectual freedom basic to the modern university. To avoid this danger they may elect simply to teach students to think more carefully about moral

dilemmas without attempting to dictate answers. This is the method followed in most contemporary courses in applied ethics. Useful as it is, however, it runs the risk of making students clever casuists, adept at arguing any side of a difficult moral or social problem but lacking strong convictions of their own that they try to put into practice. In short, efforts to create a serious program of moral education seem to be caught between the evils of indoctrination, on the one hand, and the hazards of ethical relativism, on the other.[18]

Bok concludes that this dilemma awaits resolution.

But there is no dilemma here. First, *if* moral judgments and theory can be reasonable (granted, a controversial claim nowadays), then moral views are not "imposed" on students any more than scientific views are "imposed" on students. Rather, teaching ethics is a matter of reasoned argument; it is education, not indoctrination. Second, while the university may wisely resist taking a position on controversial matters of philosophical or religious morality (unlike in those matters of broad moral agreement where, Bok holds, the university *should* make its stance clear), *individual faculty* members are surely free to take positions. This is the implication of Kimball's *liberal-free* ideal; it is also inherent in the ideal of academic freedom. A liberal education is properly understood in terms of the reasoned search for truth. It is essential, here, to distinguish a political from an educational conception of liberal education. Arguably, in a pluralistic, liberal society, public universities should retain broad neutrality in *curricular* matters about which there is deep intellectual and cultural disagreement. This is a constraint on institutions, however, not on individual faculty members who retain academic freedom.[19] There may be pedagogical reasons why, in particular situations, neutrality is a wise strategy, but why, in principle, should a professor of ethics be required to keep her views to herself in matters of morality?

The American Association of University Professors' founding document, its 1915 *Declaration of Principles*, singled out scholars who work in philosophy and religion—the domains of "ultimate realities and values"—as particularly in need of the protections of academic freedom. The *Declaration* notes that in interpreting "the general meaning and ends of human existence and its relation to the universe, we are still far from a comprehension of final truths, and from a universal agreement among all sincere and earnest men." (No doubt some believe they comprehend final truths, but there is clearly still no universal agreement about those truths today.) Here, as elsewhere, the *Declaration* continues, "the first condition of progress is complete and unlimited freedom to pursue inquiry and publish its results." Moreover, "it is scarcely open to question that freedom of utterance is as important to the teacher as it is to the investigator." Indeed, the confidence of one's students "will be impaired if there is suspicion on the part of the student that the teacher is not expressing himself fully or frankly, or that college and university teachers in general are a repressed and intimidated class."[20]

The *Declaration* is clear that academic freedom does not provide a license for indoctrination. In dealing with "controversial matters," the university professor,

> while he is under no obligation to hide his own opinion under a mountain of equivocal verbiage, should, if he is fit for his position, be a person of a fair and judicial mind; he should, in dealing with such subjects, set forth justly, without suppression or innuendo, the divergent opinions of other investigators; he should cause his students to become familiar with the best published expressions of the great historic types of doctrine upon the questions at issue; and he should, above all, remember that his business is not to provide his students with ready-made conclusions, but to train them to think for themselves, and to provide them access to those materials which they need if they are to think intelligently."[21]

Moreover, according to the AAUP's 1986 "Observations on Ideology," where "ways of finding out and assessing the truth are precisely what is under debate, good teaching requires exposing students to all major alternatives. A department ought to try to insure that different currently debated and important approaches to its subject are presented to its students fairly and objectively, so that students are able to make informed choices among them."[22] Academic freedom cannot trump liberal education. But it does institutionalize the right of professors to teach the truth as they understand it, especially in the realm of "ultimate realities and values."[23]

REASON AND RESPONSIBILITY

Conservatives, vividly aware of humanity's sinfulness, believing in the Fall more than in moral progress, convinced that Truth is to be had within their traditions, wary of the Enlightenment, modernity, and the danger of too great a freedom, generally believe that education must always guide and sometimes constrain students. The problem with this attitude is that much of the world's evil is the result of business as usual; much evil may even be, as Hannah Arendt famously suggested, *banal*. It is not enough to be a person of character; there are, after all, people of formidable character and considerable virtue who do the wrong thing for lack of critical judgment. We cannot rely uncritically on our communities and tradition. All too many of us learned sexism and racism from our communities, including, of course, our religious communities. Indeed, over the last several centuries, religious establishments have often sided with the forces of reaction and have had to be dragged, by the forces of Enlightenment, into accepting democracy, civil rights, the rights of women, academic freedom, and more generally, social movements of equality and social justice. (And, clearly, not all yet do.)

Not all moral progress stems from the Enlightenment, and the Enlightenment clearly has a shadow side. Still, we must attain a measure of critical distance on our character, our communities, and our culture—all of which require reformation from time to time. The possibility of progress in human affairs requires that we think critically about the fundamental ideas and ideals of our cultures and traditions. The powerful advantage of a liberal-free education is that it is self-correcting. There cannot be (or at least there should not be) any orthodoxy. The different disciplines (and the different traditions they encompass and address), in conversation with each other, provide a system of checks and balances; academic freedom enables (and, in the long run, ensures) genuine self-criticism.

In an apt phrase, Mark Schwehn has written that, at their best, universities practice "education in and for thoughtfulness."[24] The Enlightenment emphases on "reason, tolerance, and freedom of inquiry that are preserved and defended at the best universities have served as a powerful corrective to the sometimes violent effects of religious fanaticisms."[25]

But Schwehn adds, the "Weberian ethos" [that is, the calculating, disenchanted understanding of reason] "still prevails, and that ethos does obscure the highest and best calling of the university itself: the spirited search for the truth of matters."[26] Hauerwas has argued that just as Socrates corrupted the youth of Athens, "the contemporary university's degraded form of the Socratic method does so in a more direct and almost inevitable manner. In the name of exposing students to critical questions through a chaotic curriculum filled with equally chaotic courses, we only reinforce the disdain for reasoned discourse." Students require the virtue that is nurtured within a guiding community or tradition. But such virtue, he claims, is seen in our culture "as an impediment to freedom."[27]

There is a good deal of truth in these charges. It is crucial (as Hauerwas insists) that students come to see that moral judgments are not simply matters of personal choice or social convention. And, in fact, it is hard to justify convictions about moral truth (or reasonableness) against the background understanding of the world that so much of higher education conveys—the assumptions, for example, that we can understand reality—nature, psychology, history, and economics—apart from moral and religious categories, that the study of ethics can be compartmentalized, that rationality must conform to scientific method, or that we are caught up in a thorough-going postmodernist relativism. And there is something close to a *secular orthodoxy* in much higher education. Moreover, the curriculum of most universities is chaotic. It does not guide students in a search for truth—much less *moral* truth. It leaves them largely on their own, partly, no doubt, because such guidance would be an "impediment to their freedom." True, as Derek Bok argues, an enlightened university does not totally abandon students. While the ethics courses Bok advocates strike Hauerwas as exemplars of chaos based upon a thin view of philosophy called "critical thinking," Bok also shows, as we have seen, how universities (at their best) nurture various kinds of civic, moral, and intellectual virtues. Moreover, many courses in history and literature (and other subjects) will require students to study various civic, moral, and (occasionally) religious traditions—though it is no doubt also true that most professors do not see their task as one of moral education, and do not structure their courses to explore in self-conscious ways the moral or existential dimension of their subjects. All things considered, public universities fall well short of the ideal.

But the ideal is critically important. The ideal, however, is not simply freedom. The ideal is *the free, but disciplined search for moral truth*—for ever since the Enlightenment, it has been widely and rightly held that truth is best discovered if culture is free (and if there is academic freedom in universities). The ideal is the open, informed, and thoughtful willingness to think critically about one's own deepest beliefs and values. At its heart, a liberal education, *properly understood*, is a moral education: it initiates students into an ongoing conversation about the truth that matters most within a community of scholars who disagree among themselves, where an institutional orthodoxy cannot dull the need to be critical of one's own commitments.

The fact that a (good) liberal education is necessarily a moral education should not be surprising, for morality requires that we pursue a liberal education. Why, after all, should we care about seeking the truth? I cannot argue for it here, so I will just say that to be a person is to have responsibilities—*person* is a moral category, and perhaps the most fundamental responsibility we have is *to be reasonable, to live examined lives.*[28] One cannot be a morally responsible person if one practices business as usual, either by way of accepting uncritically one's culture or even one's countercultural tradition.[29]

THE LIBERAL-FREE IDEAL AND MORAL EDUCATION

Now back to Kimball—this time to his conception of liberal-free education (or, from now on, simply "liberal education," in contrast to his "liberal arts" education). Rather than describe what typically passes for a liberal education, I am going to take the general idea that Kimball gives us and propose what I take to be a *sound* liberal education, drawing out the implications for moral education and religion.

The governing ideal, once again, is that students should be initiated into an open and critical search for truth. I suppose I should say right away that a liberal education cannot leave students on *their own* to search for truth. At the end of the nineteenth century Andrew Dickson White declared that at Cornell, "[f]our years of good study in one direction are held equal to four years of good study in another"[30] and at Harvard (and some other colleges) students were, for a while, free to pursue an entirely elective curriculum. Happily, such ideas quite quickly and rightly fell by the wayside—at least in their most excessive forms. Universities must provide guidance, *a curricular structure* within which students pursue a liberal education.

My proposal is that we think of this curricular structure as having four dimensions, each of which must be related to the others by way of a structured conversation.

First, if the ideal is to initiate students into a search for truth we must ask: *the truth about what?* The obvious answer would seem to be: *the truth about things that matter most.* (I suppose that no truth is trivial, but surely some truths are more important—much more important—than other truths.) No doubt we do not typically think this way about the curriculum. We acknowledge that undergraduates must be able to write well (clearly this is important), but after that the curricular structure dissolves, more often than not, into a set of distribution requirements dictated primarily by tradition and academic politics. Over the last century we came to define that structure largely in terms of methodological approaches—the natural sciences, social sciences, humanities, and arts. Of course, from the vantage point of our respective disciplines, judgments about what matters most would be suspect. Indeed, the whole idea of "what matters most" will strike some as absurd. On either naturalistic or post-modernist grounds, such judgments become either subjective or matters of politics and ideology.

When the philosopher David Hume was in his "philosophical closet" (as he put it) he came to any number of strange (we might say absurd) conclusions, few of which he could accept when he stepped outside his closet. My own view is that when we step outside our disciplinary closets it is clear enough that what matters most are our existential concerns about good and evil, suffering and flourishing, justice and injustice, love and beauty, God and the ways in which we find meaning in life—concerns that are inescapable simply because we are human. Given our deepest needs and concerns, *how should we live our lives? This is the moral question.* Needless to say, this question can be answered in many ways.

Still, the most important criterion (though not the only one) for assessing the content of both curricula and courses is their relevance to the moral concerns of life.

This, then, is the first dimension of a liberal education: it must have *depth—existential or moral depth*. It must address who we are and how we should live our lives. What, after all, could be more important? This is the domain of morality—and, traditionally, of religion.

Second, a liberal education is a *broad* education. It is not narrow, or specialized, or merely vocational. It introduces students to the major ways in which humankind has made sense of the world, their lives, and their ultimate concerns. This is not simply because it is good to be aware of the diversity to be found in the world. The idea is that if students are to think critically—if they are not simply to be trained—they must understand the alternatives. What do they know of England, who only England know? Indeed, one might wonder, what do they know of science, who only science know?

If students are to think critically about the moral dimension of their lives it is essential that they learn about moral traditions and theories that help them to distinguish among the possibilities open to them. Few people believe, as did Rousseau, that if we could shuck the corrupting layers of civilization our natural goodness and innate reason would be sufficient to the task at hand. We are the heirs, happily, of a good deal of richly textured moral reflection, embodied and given shape in various theories and traditions, institutions and ideologies, philosophies and theologies, art and literature.

Morality is not intellectually or culturally free-floating. It is rooted in historical, cultural, and intellectual contexts that make sense of it. It is entangled with our convictions about human nature, the law, personal relationships, feelings of guilt and love, traditions, religious experiences (maybe), assumptions about what the mind can know, and our convictions about the meaning of life. A *broad* education will give students insight into people and cultures in all of their richness, and it will introduce them to the major traditions and theories for making sense of our lives morally.

To which alternatives do we introduce students? There is clearly not time in the day or pages in the textbooks for serious considerations of all alternatives. If our quest is for the truth, then we can safely discard intellectually dead alternatives, though there may well be reasons for studying them in the context of history. If we do not have time to consider all the *live* alternatives then a good liberal education will introduce students to *the major* live alternatives—that is, to those that are most influential (for good and evil). Some of those alternatives are religious

Third, we take other cultures and intellectual traditions seriously only if we enable students to understand them as their members or advocates understand them—not as *we understand* them given our preconceptions and values. It is hard to improve on John Stuart Mill who wrote that students must hear arguments "from persons who actually believe them . . . in their most plausible and persuasive form. . . . Ninety-nine in a hundred of what are called educated men . . . have never thrown themselves into the mental position of those who think differently from them . . . and consequently they do not, in any proper sense of the word, know the doctrine which they themselves profane."[31]

Of course people in other cultures and traditions just are, to some considerable extent, what they take themselves to be (rather than what we take them to be). They believe what they do, and they act as they do, for reasons that make sense to them; they live within structures of meaning that give coherence and direction to their lives. If we miss this essential fact, if we miss their world, then we miss *them*. Most important, we must be able to see and experience the world as others do if we are to acquire the perspective that enables us to think critically about our own assumptions and values. A liberal education must provide students the resources to make sense of the world from *within* alternative cultural, intellectual, civic, moral, and religious traditions, taking them on their own terms as their practitioners do.

No doubt it is not easy to get inside another culture or tradition. To the extent possible we should use primary sources, allowing people to speak for themselves. In particular we should use literature and art that nurture what Martha Nussbaum calls the "narrative imagination."[32] (Much moral shortcoming, after all, results from a failure of *imagination*.) The goal here is those *thick* accounts of how people live and die, suffer and flourish, that gets us beyond abstractions. This undermines our natural parochialism and any uncritical egotism or ethnocentrism. It makes it difficult to *dehumanize* people, a precursor to much of the great evil that has been done in human history. The English novelist Ian McEwan wrote of the 9/11 hijackers that if they

> had been able to imagine themselves into the thoughts and feelings of the passengers, they would have been unable to proceed. It is hard to be cruel once you permit yourself to enter the mind of your victim. Imagining what it is like to be someone other than yourself is at the core of our humanity. It is the essence of compassion, and it is the beginning of morality. The hijackers used fanatical certainty, misplaced religious faith, and dehumanising hatred to purge themselves of the human instinct for empathy.[33]

Here the humanities do most of the heavy lifting. In the humanities, unlike the sciences and social sciences, students are often required to read primary sources as much as the work of contemporary scholars.

Fourth, as I suggested in my comments on a "liberal arts" education, we are not simply external observers of history, self-contained, morally unencumbered individuals or *social atoms*; we are caught up in history, we are *historical beings*, enmeshed in traditions, in webs of influence and obligation that tie us not just to other people in our own time, but to the past—and the future. In giving students a past, by situating them in communities of memory, we give them moral identities. The study of history reveals the shallowness of living entirely in the present, a pervasive sin of our current culture. No doubt the more *liberal* the education, the more it will make clear to students that they are characters in an anthology of stories, not just one master narrative. Moreover, it will make clear that history is a contested domain, open to various (liberal and conservative, secular and religious) interpretations. Still, we cannot escape history if we are to think critically. All thinking takes places within traditions (even creative thinking)—though we can, with education, think ourselves into other traditions in order to acquire critical perspective on our own.

Clearly, we cannot understand the present without understanding the past—we cannot understand race relations in America without understanding the history of slavery, Jim Crow, and the civil rights movement—and lacking that understanding we forego the evidence we need in deciding how to live (and vote and legislate now). History is, in part, a record of the moral experiments of humankind. It is commonplace to quote Santayana to the effect that those who forget history are condemned to relive it. The point, of course, is that our lives might well be changed by the lessons of history—and Santayana's use of the word *condemn* points to the gravity of the lessons. I do not mean anything so particular as drawing conclusions from our experience in Vietnam that might apply to Iraq—though that may be possible too. It is rather a matter of acquiring some deep appreciation for the possibilities and limitations of human character and social institutions, the nature of suffering and the varieties of ways in which people flourish, the grounds of hope and sources of evil. In fact, in some sense moral judgments and theories can be tested historically; we can acquire some sense of how well policies, practices, and theories affect human suffering and flourishing, and whether they ennoble or demean us.

There is another reason why the study of history is so crucial. Though not all historians write or teach about history in *narratives*, most do. Much literature takes the form of narratives (be they epic poems, novels, or short stories). Western religions (more than their Eastern counterparts) have conceived of reality as having the structure of a narrative—

one authored, ultimately, by God. In fact, most scholars within the humanities work within the idea that we best understand reality—at least human reality—as a narrative or set of overlapping narratives. Why is this important? Because narratives locate the intelligibility of human beliefs and action in a rich meshing of reasons, purposes, intentions, and cultural meanings rather than in some matrix of causal laws. In historical narratives we encounter *thick* descriptions and *rich* explanations of people and cultures, not just social atoms bouncing off each other in ways that can be captured in quantifiable laws.

Fifth and finally, it is not enough simply to introduce students to various cultures, traditions, moral theories, or historical periods in turn, like items on an academic cafeteria-line. A good liberal education will initiate students into an on-going *conversation* about how to make sense of the world and how to live our lives, about what is true, good, and evil. (This is the particularly Socratic nature of our inheritance: we seek truth through conversation.) Through such conversations the four dimensions of a liberal education—its existential depth, its breadth, its commitment to understanding from the inside, and historical narratives—are connected.

As things stand now, at most universities students are free to choose among a dizzying array of (often narrowly focused, highly specialized) courses that are unlikely to cohere in any meaningful way and cumulatively may leave them largely culturally illiterate and ungrounded. Texts rarely acknowledge that their subject matter may be interpreted in fundamentally different ways. And in spite of a widespread acknowledgment (in principle) of the value of interdisciplinary studies, undergraduates are too rarely required to participate in interdisciplinary discussion. As the literary critic Gerald Graff has put it, college curricula are typically *separatist* "with each subject and course being an island with little regular connection to other subjects and courses."[34] As we actually practice it, education is essentially a sequence of monologues, something closer to *serial socialization* than to a conversation; it is more a matter of training students than educating them. (I am reminded of the good soul who, when asked for an opinion of Dr. Johnson's new dictionary, replied: it is "most instructive, though I did seem to notice a trifling want of connection."[35]) Graff's proposal, one that I endorse, is to "teach the conflicts"— indeed, to use this as an organizing and connecting principle for a liberal education.[36]

How, then, do we teach the conflicts, the tensions, the controversies? Ideally it would be through a carefully integrated core curriculum. Academic politics make such a curriculum virtually impossible, however, though interdisciplinary courses certainly are possible. One of them should be something like the old nineteenth-century capstone course in

moral philosophy (though who would teach it is something of a problem). The other alternative is *introductory* courses and texts that map the
controversies.

Virtually all courses deal (even if only implicitly) with questions of
moral or existential concern, and the way in which those questions are
answered will, almost inevitably, be controversial in our culture. Take
economics, for example. Introductory economics textbooks typically
teach students neo-classical economic theory: economics is a "value-free"
science and the economic world can be defined in terms of the competition of self-interested individuals with unlimited wants for scarce
resources; values are subjective, personal preferences; and decisions
should be made according to cost-benefit analyses that maximize whatever it is that we value and that leave no room in the equation for duties,
the Sacred, or those dimensions of life that are not quantifiable. Economics is one thing; morality and religion are, quite clearly, something else.

This is controversial. Of course, no religious tradition has ever held
any such view, and it is not irrelevant that a number of studies by economists have shown that students who study neo-classical economic theory end up more self-interested than when they began.[37] Students do not
typically learn about the *subject* of economics, which is replete with moral
and spiritual issues and problems (materialism, self-interest, the dehu-
manization of work, the dignity of people, the sacredness of the environment, and the nature of justice, for example) and is open to various
interpretations (conservative and liberal, secular and religious).[38] Instead
they learn to think about the economic domain of life as it is interpreted
by mainstream economists; they learn a social science discipline. And this
is almost always done *uncritically*. Economics textbooks devote few
pages, if any, to justifying their methodological assumptions, their interpretive framework for making sense of the subject at hand; that is, students are given little critical perspective on the assumptions that shape
economics as a discipline.[39]

I am not so quixotic as to recommend that economics courses balance
neo-classical theory and social science with moral philosophy or theology
at every turn, but I do think that economics texts should include at least
one substantive introductory chapter in which social scientific ways of
understanding economics are contrasted with various philosophical and
religious ways of making sense of the economic domain of life. Indeed,
every introductory text and course should provide students with historical and philosophical perspective on the subject at hand, mapping con-
nections, tensions, and conflicts with other disciplines and domains of
the culture—including religion.[40]

Or take science. The interpretation of nature that modern science provides is widely acknowledged to undercut rather than support traditional

ways of thinking about morality and religion. Consequently, science texts and courses should devote some time and space to mapping the relationship of science, morality, and religion—and the controversies that attend them. Is there a purpose or meaning built into nature? Are we morally grounded in nature? Has science become scientism and overstepped its legitimate bounds? In fact, scientists, philosophers, and theologians are in the midst of an extraordinarily lively cultural conversation about design, purpose, and meaning as they relate to biological evolution, cosmological evolution, the environment, the origins of life, genetic engineering, biological accounts of morality, spirituality and healing, and the relationship of brain and mind. Yet, we keep students almost entirely ignorant of these fascinating and important conversations. Science texts typically dumbdown this conversation, if they refer to it at all, as if it were nothing more than a replay of the Scopes trial, with anti-intellectual fundamentalists warring against all the rest of us reasonable folk. But there are at least seventeen, not just two, ways of relating science and religion; the conversation is rich and exciting and important.[41]

It is essential to keep in mind that the purpose of *introductory* science and economics courses is not to train scientists and economists. It is to contribute to the liberal education of students, not least with regard to the moral dimension of life. Courses cannot be disciplinary monologues; they must establish relationships with other disciplines and domains of our culture in a way that allows students to think critically about them. No doubt upper-level and graduate courses may serve the purpose of training economists or scientists and need not be constrained by the requirements of a liberal education—though even here a somewhat greater liberality of mind would be helpful.

The point is that if a liberal education is to move us toward the truth, we cannot settle for serial socialization in the various disciplines. Students must be initiated into cross-disciplinary conversations. The curriculum must be structured to facilitate such conversations. Electives and distribution requirements are not sufficient.

There is a set of moral virtues internal to the practice of liberal education. In probing the existential depths of life and experience, a liberal education nurtures sobriety and moral seriousness. In opening ourselves to alternative ways of thinking and living, we practice humility (a virtue totally absent from the textbooks and courses that orient most students within a subject). In our efforts to think and feel ourselves into the hearts and minds of others we take them seriously as persons, according them at least a measure of respect—and compassion often follows in the wake of our ability to empathize with others. In studying history we are caught up in communities of memory that nurture a sense of gratitude to those who suffered so that we might flourish and that ground our responsibility to those who come after us. In engaging other people and cultures and traditions in conversation we nurture civility and, insofar as we can sustain such conversations, we nurture community, for we recognize that we are engaged together in the quest for a better world. The moral virtues and the intellectual virtues are, in fact, entwined; it is impossible to disentangle them.[42]

RELIGION

Traditionally, religions have addressed the deepest existential questions about human existence, and theological alternatives to secular ways of making sense of life continue to possess a good deal of vitality. Religious voices must be included in the curricular conversation; that conversation is *illiberal* to the extent that it dismisses or marginalizes religion. It is true that many (not quite a majority) of our public universities have departments of religious studies, but courses in religion are always electives (indeed, this is the case at many private universities) and, as I will suggest, religious studies courses do not always take religion as seriously as they should. Indeed, public higher education is so systematically and unrelentingly secular that it verges on indoctrination. It uncritically nurtures in students a secular mentality.[43]

There are two major reasons why religion is not taken seriously in higher education. First, while it is widely acknowledged that it is proper, maybe even important, to study religion as a historical or sociological phenomena, it is also widely believed (primarily because of naturalistic and postmodern intellectual commitments) that religious ways of making sense of the world are no longer intellectually respectable, even if religion is a live alternative for many people. Of course, there is no consensus about whether religion is intellectually respectable. From the vantage point of a research university in America it may well appear from the absence of religious voices that there is some such consensus. But that seeming consensus is achieved primarily by exiling the dissenters to divinity schools, seminaries, and religiously affiliated liberal arts colleges. Or perhaps I should say the vocal dissenters are exiled, for some keep their dissent quiet. Surveys have shown that a majority of scholars take religion seriously in their personal lives, but most manage to compartmentalize those religious convictions from their scholarly work.[44]

Quite apart from this "silent majority" there continues to be a lively religious counterculture that is, I suggest, intellectually respectable in the following sense. It is shaped, in part, by scholars and intellectuals, many with advanced degrees from our most prestigious research universities, who understand and in many ways work within the dominant culture, but who also draw on theological traditions to rethink and reform the conventional wisdom of our time and place. Though some religion is mindless and disdains intellectual respectability, most is not and does not. Most religious scholarship has not gone the way of astrology or lapsed into purely private and irrational faith. Theologians and religious scholars continue to grapple in informed and sophisticated ways with secular modernity and postmodernity. No doubt many scholars in the dominant culture find their efforts worthless, perhaps even dangerous; indeed, I suspect that many assume that all religious thought is simply a variation on fundamentalist anti-intellectualism. But such naiveté does not justify excluding religious voices from the curricular conversation; to do so, as I have suggested, is *illiberal*.

If religious ways of making sense of the world (and of living our lives) are to be taken seriously, universities should have departments of religious studies, and if students are to be liberally educated they should be required to take a least one course in religious studies that takes religion seriously as a live alternative for making sense of the world (though I should much prefer a more integrated core curriculum).

Of course, much hinges on how the field of religious studies is defined. While much coursework in religious studies allows students to hear religious voices—to encounter primary source texts drawn from various religious traditions—religious ways of thinking and living are often not allowed *to contend with* the secular alternatives. Typically students encounter religions only in historical contexts, rather than as live options in their intellectually, morally, philosophically, or spiritually most compelling forms, for understanding the world here and now. Many faculty in departments of religious studies are wary of the idea that students should study religion as part of a larger search for moral (and perhaps even spiritual) truth, for this cuts against the grain of the secular methodological commitments of the field (and raises fears that departments of religious studies will be confused with divinity schools).[45] As a result, students often do not learn how to think religiously in courses in religious studies so much as they learn to think in secular ways about religion.[46] I have argued elsewhere that theology—a *critical* rather than *dogmatic* theology—must be a subfield of religious studies even in public universities.[47]

The second reason that religion is not taken seriously as part of a search for moral or spiritual truth in public universities is misunderstanding of the First Amendment and academic freedom. It is uncontroversial that teachers in public schools and universities have the Supreme Court's permission to teach about religion. They cannot proselytize, but they can teach about it. This is uncontroversial; no Supreme Court justice has ever dissented from this claim. Arguably, however, a stronger claim can be made—that public schools and universities are required by the Establishment Clause of the First Amendment to teach about religion.

Ever since *Everson v. Board of Education* (1947), the Supreme Court has interpreted the Establishment Clause ("Congress shall make no law respecting an establishment of religion") to require governmental *neutrality* in matters of religion. More particularly, it has required two kinds of neutrality: neutrality among religions, and neutrality *between religion and nonreligion*. The question for my purposes is this: what does it mean to be neutral between religion and nonreligion? Justice Black was clear in *Everson* that neutrality is a two-edged sword: "State power is no more to be used so as to handicap religions, than it is to favor them"[48] and ever since *Everson* the Court has held that government may not inhibit or denigrate religion any more than it can promote or practice it. In *Abington Township v. Schempp* (1963), Justice Clark wrote that public schools (and presumably universities) could not establish a "religion of secularism," preferring "those who believe in no religion over those who do believe."[49]

But, of course, this is just what has happened. Schools and universities *do prefer* the views of those who do not believe over those who do. No doubt many of the particular claims made by scientists and secular scholars can be reconciled with much religion. It is at the level of philosophical presuppositions that they are more often in tension, for they assume conflicting conceptions of causality and meaning, evidence and rationality, and when the adequacy of secular categories for making full sense of the subject at hand is uncritically conveyed, it is impossible to sustain a pretense of neutrality. In fact, the only way of being neutral when all ground is contested ground is being *fair* to the alternatives. That is, given the Court's longstanding reading of the Establishment Clause, public schools and universities must require some study of religion.

Consider a multicultural analogy. Until the last several decades textbooks and curricula routinely ignored women's history and minority literature. We are now (almost) all sensitive to the fact that this was not a benign neglect, but a form of discrimination or oppression, and it would now be utterly naive to hold that the old texts and curricula were neutral in matters of race or gender. Of course, as multiculturalists are well aware, the problem was not just that minority and women's history and literature were ignored; it was that conflicting, distinctively male and white ways of thinking and acting, and patterns of culture, were taught to children uncritically.

Similarly, it is anything but neutral to ignore religion, much less teach uncritically secular and scientific ways of thinking and living that conflict (at the philosophical level) with religious alternatives.

But if the state must be neutral with regard to religion, what about individual teachers? Clearly teachers in public primary and secondary schools must remain neutral, for they are "agents of the state," hired to teach an official curriculum. Teachers in universities, however, have academic freedom and this alters the situation.

I noted above that the AAUP's 1915 *Declaration of Principles* singled out scholars who work in philosophy and religion—the domains of "ultimate realities and values"—as particularly in need of the protections of academic freedom. I suspect that the authors of the *Declaration* were more concerned, in 1915, with protecting scientists and critics of religion from religion than they were with protecting advocates of religion, but the principle of academic freedom surely cuts both ways. Academic freedom must protect the right of scholars to pursue *all* kinds of truth. This is not to deny, of course, that there may be good pedagogical reasons for remaining neutral in many situations. Moreover, religious claims or conclusions cannot be introduced into a class gratuitously, or as a matter of dogma; they must be germane to the course and justifiable by reputable scholarly methods.[50] (Needless to say, when religious claims are germane and when the methods are reputable will be matters of considerable controversy.) The Supreme Court has indicated that academic freedom can be grounded in the First Amendment, though it has done little to spell out a substantive doctrine of academic freedom.[51]

Moreover, it has never ruled in a case involving the academic freedom of a teacher to take sides *in a matter of religion* where the Establishment Clause might also come into play. Still, the principles seem clear. Because scholars have academic freedom they cannot be taken to speak for the state, to be agents of the state, and hence are not bound by the Establishment Clause, which is binding only on government and its agents. No doubt a department of religious studies cannot be a seminary in miniature; it cannot have as its purpose to promote any religious claims or religion generally. The university, as a state institution, must remain neutral among religions and between religion and nonreligion. At the same time it can, and must, allow individual scholars to take sides on religiously contested questions.[52] After all, what would academic freedom be worth if we had to carve out an exception for the most important concern that scholars can address?

CONCLUSION

First, one lesson of history is that much (but not all) moral progress comes about because of free institutions, educational institutions not least. For all of its shortcomings in practice, the liberal-free ideal of education—of initiating students into an open, if structured, search for truth, especially moral truth—is a powerful corrective to orthodoxies and dogmatisms.

Second, I have to acknowledge how far short of a *good* liberal education most universities fall. Too often, scientific naturalism and postmodernism have discredited morality and the idea of moral education. Most higher education is chaotic; it leaves students too much on their own.

Third, because religious traditions continue to possess a good deal of cultural and intellectual vitality, religious voices must be included in the curricular conversation. Moreover, religion cannot be just an object of study; it must be a live option for students to take seriously in deciding how to live their lives. This is not typically the case, and most higher education is illiberal as a result.[53]

Fourth, a good moral education must combine the liberal arts and the liberal-free ideals. In schools, both private and public, a rudimentary liberal arts education properly shapes the character of students, particularly younger students, giving them moral direction in life by locating them in traditional communities (particularly in the community of the school itself, but also in the American constitutional tradition, and in Western civilization). This is a *conservative* education. A liberal-free education gives more mature students the resources to think critically about virtues, culture, and traditions that often go unquestioned within (at least the more conservative) varieties of a liberal arts education, opening up the possibility of reforming them.

Fifth and finally, there is considerable virtue in having a mix of (predominantly) liberal arts and (predominantly) liberal-free colleges and universities. While there are considerable dangers in a conservative liberal arts education, there is also considerable danger in the morally thin and chaotic education that most colleges and universities provide in the name of liberal (or liberal-free) education. Some mix of the two ideals appears wise, especially in our current state of disarray.

Chapter 2

Free Love and Christian Higher Education

Reflections on a Passage from Plato's
Theaetetus

—Robert C. Roberts

Plato's *Theaetetus* begins with Socrates inquiring of Theodorus the geometer whether he knows of any young men "devoting themselves to geometry or to any other sort of liberal study" (143d).[1] Theodorus commends Theaetetus, a youth who combines "a rare quickness of intelligence with exceptional gentleness and . . . an incomparably virile spirit . . ." (144a). Boys this intelligent are usually impetuous and unsteady, Theodorus observes, but Theaetetus's "approach to learning and inquiry, with the perfect quietness of its smooth and sure progress, is like the noiseless flow of a stream of oil" (144b).

Theodorus has remarked about the physical resemblance between Socrates and Theaetetus. Socrates points out that Theodorus is hardly reliable for that sort of judgment, since he is not a painter, but being a practitioner of liberal studies he might well be credited should he "praise the mind of either of us for its virtue and intelligence" (145b). In fact, the real similarity between Socrates and Theaetetus is spiritual, and throughout the dialogue Socrates, the intellectual midwife who, by his questions, teases the minds of his interlocutors into the possession of truth, treats the young man as a worthy recipient of his efforts at education.

Theodorus, Theaetetus's more conventional tutor, hovers in the background during much of the dialogue, and Socrates begins the discussion of knowledge by commenting that though knowledge is what people like Theodorus are nominally trying to purvey, he himself "cannot make out to [his] own satisfaction what knowledge is" (146a). In an earlier dialogue Socrates would have gone on to claim that if education aims at purveying knowledge we can hardly expect to be successful educators if we do not know what knowledge is—and we certainly do not know what knowledge is if we cannot specify its necessary and sufficient conditions in a formal definition. He does not say that here, but he does spend about 75 percent of the dialogue trying, unsuccessfully, to draw such a definition out of Theaetetus.

The passage I want to examine is not part of that 75 percent. It is a digression from the dialogue's main business of defining knowledge, but not from the larger business to which this project would supposedly contribute: the business of educating young people whose talents and inchoate virtues make them promising candidates for the best kind of education. After several failed attempts at a definition, Socrates comments, "one theory after another is coming upon us, Theodorus, and the last is more important than the one before," to which Theodorus replies: "Well, Socrates, we have time at our disposal" (172c). Theodorus's reference to the leisure of inquiry that the little discussion group is currently enjoying prompts Socrates' digression.

TWO TYPES OF EDUCATED CHARACTER: FREE AND UNFREE

No doubt the issues raised by the appearance of a philosopher in a court of law are in the back of Socrates' mind throughout the dialogue, since he takes his leave at the end by saying that he "must go to the portico of the King-Archon to meet the indictment which Meletus has drawn up against me" (210d). He asserts that it is natural for people who have spent much time in philosophical study to "look ridiculous when they appear as speakers in a court of law"; however, this is because it is only the philosophers who have been trained as free people, while those "who have knocked about from their youth up in law courts and such places seem, on comparison, to have been trained as slaves" (172c–d). As it turns out, the freedom that Socrates' education has afforded him does not save him from death at the hands of the slave-minded lawyers. That the slave-minded live and the free-minded die is perhaps not a historical anomaly.

Socrates' digression consists of contrasting, colorful descriptions of two types of character—the one of the free individual, produced by a genuine and liberal education; the other of the unfree individual, produced by a technical or haphazard "education." At the center of this digressory account stands a contrasting depiction of the hearts of the educated person and his unfree counterpart.

In the education that produces the slavish character, knowledge is subordinated to concrete accomplishment. Socrates' example is the orator in the law courts whose discourse is always devoted to achieving some end such as convincing a jury, or gaining an acquittal or a conviction. The lawyer's topics are preset by the exigencies of situations in court, and he is under a time limit to say what he has to say. Through a legal education in this sort of context, the young person

> acquires a tense and bitter shrewdness; he knows how to flatter his master and earn his good graces, but his mind is narrow and crooked. An apprenticeship in slavery has dwarfed and twisted his growth and robbed him of his free spirit, driving him into devious ways, threatening him with fears and dangers which the tenderness of youth could not face with truth and honesty; so, turning from the first to lies and the requital of wrong with wrong, warped and stunted, he passes from youth to manhood with no soundness in him and turns out, in the end, a man of formidable intellect—as he imagines. (173a–b)

Given Socrates' experience with lawyers, maybe he can be forgiven this perhaps overly dismal sketch. Surely just and honest lawyering is possible, but Socrates' point would be that it requires an education that goes beyond technical training in legal argument. The truly honest lawyer will have somehow learned to love truth and justice, to take pleasure in an argument not just because it wins the case, but because it is sound and compelling, because the conclusion is true and if accepted would secure a just state of affairs. And such an education would, surely, include mentoring by honest older lawyers and practice in a context that is less cutthroat than the one Socrates describes. But the contrast that Socrates is drawing with the free intellectual agent is not primarily directed at lawyers. I think his point is that any education that takes the intellectual goods of truth, knowledge, insight, and understanding as nothing more than means to other human ends corrupts the soul. It may be a training in something or other—legal practice, business practice, political manipulation, manufacturing, entertainment, or what not—but it will not be a *human education*.

Who, then, are the beneficiaries of a true human education? What do they look like, according to Plato's Socrates? It will not surprise us that they are philosophers. They have been trained in the kind of free pursuit of knowledge exemplified in the *Theaetetus* itself. Unhindered by the external constraint that the lawyer studied under, the philosopher has been brought up passing freely from one argument to the next, "and he does not care how long or short the discussion may be, if only it attains the truth" (172d). Socrates is not talking about the dilettantes and hangers-on, or the professors who teach courses in "philosophy" just to make a buck. He is talking only about top-notch specimens, about whom he says,

> From their youth up they have never known the way to market place or law court or Council Chamber or any other place of public assembly; they never hear a decree read out or look at the text of a law. To take any interest in the rivalries of political cliques, in meetings, dinners, and merrymakings with flute girls, never occurs to them even in dreams. The philosopher is no more aware whether any fellow citizen is well- or ill-born or has inherited some defect from his ancestors on either side, than he is of how many pints of water there are in the sea. He is not even aware that he knows nothing of all this, for if he holds aloof, it is not for reputation's sake, but because it is really only his body that sojourns in his city, while his thought, disdaining all such things as worthless, takes wings, as Pindar says, 'beyond the sky, beneath the earth,' searching the heavens and measuring the plains, everywhere seeking the true nature of everything as a whole, never sinking to what lies close at hand. . . . [He] hardly knows whether [his neighbor] is a man at all; he spends all his pains on the question, what man is, and what powers and properties distinguish such a nature from any other. . . . [He tries to induce others] to drop the question, 'What injustice have I done to you or you to me?' and to think about justice and injustice in themselves, what each is, and how they differ from one another and from anything else. . . . (173d–e, 174b, 175c)

Plato draws a picture of people possessed and obsessed—in love with the most important kind of knowledge Plato can think of. They have their sights on something so good that all else pales by comparison—or even disappears from view. These passionate knowers are not the disinterested spectators, indifferently open to all reality, of modern popular epistemological mythology. And what they love is worth seeking and having for its own sake, quite independently of whether it's "useful" for other purposes. The education that develops this epistemic purity of heart is one in which inquiry is practiced simply for the sake of the highest kind of knowledge. It is the perfect antithesis of the merely technical training of Plato's lawyers.

In contrasting the product of a purely technical education with that of a liberal or philosophical education, Socrates is not talking about a policy that might be adopted or a skill that someone might deploy for awhile and then exchange for the opposite policy or skill as suits his fancy. The person emerging from such an education is not just equipped; he is formed. What accrues to him, for better or worse, is a character. Socrates makes this clear by representing each of the orientations in terms of its peculiar sense of humor. He cites

> the story of the Thracian maidservant who exercised her wit at the expense of Thales, when he was looking up to study the stars and tumbled down a well. She scoffed at him for being so eager to know what was happening in the sky that he could not see what lay at his feet. Anyone who gives his life to philosophy is open to such mockery. (174a)

To the maidservant, whose merely technical education has ingrained in her soul as patently obvious that it is far more important to be aware of one's surroundings than to know the nature of the universe, Thales's folly (and no doubt the irony of the fact that some people think he is a wise man) comes across with the perfect spontaneous immediacy of factual perception. The sense of humor that Thales's mishap triggers into laughter is an unstudied valuational response disposition based on her conception of the epistemic goods. It is as though her perceptions automatically follow the principle, *only knowledge that makes you a living is worth having.* So Thales strikes her as an utter incongruity, from the human point of view.

The philosopher, too, has a sense of humor, but with different canons. Socrates comments:

> When a despot or king is eulogized, [the philosopher] fancies he is hearing some keeper of swine or sheep or cows being congratulated on the quantity of milk he has squeezed out of his flock; only he reflects that the animal that princes tend and milk is more given than sheep or cows to nurse a sullen grievance, and that a herdsman of this sort, penned up in his castle, is doomed by sheer press of work to be as rude and uncultivated as the shepherd in his mountain fold. He hears of the marvelous wealth of some landlord who owns ten thousand acres or more, but that seems a small matter to one accustomed to think of the earth as a whole. When they harp on birth—some gentleman who can point to seven generations of wealthy ancestors—he thinks that such commendation must come from men of purblind vision, too uneducated to keep their eyes fixed on the whole or to reflect that any man has had countless myriads of ancestors and among them any number of rich men and beggars, kings and slaves. . . . When the philosopher drags the [lawyer who has laughed at him] upward to a height at which he may consent to . . . stop quoting poetry about the happiness of kings or of men with gold in store and think about the meaning of kingship and the whole question of human happiness and misery, what their

> nature is, and how humanity can gain the one and escape the
> other—in all this field, when that small, shrewd, legal mind has to
> render an account, then the situation is reversed. Now it is he who
> is dizzy from hanging at such an unaccustomed height and looking
> down from mid-air. Lost and dismayed and stammering, he will be
> laughed at, not by maidservants or the uneducated—they will not
> see what is happening—but by everyone whose breeding has been
> the antithesis of a slave's. (174d–175a, 175c–d)

The philosopher's sense of the incongruous, like the maidservant's, is an aspect of deeply ingrained valuation and orientation. It is a trait of his character, traceable to his deepest and most fundamental concerns and attachments and pervasive patterns of thought. Though it is based in much deliberate reflection, it is a disposition of spontaneous perception, of "seeing" with something like the immediacy of sense perception. And what he sees when he looks out on the human world is a great deal of foolishness.

The last thing I want to note about Plato's vision for a genuinely human education is his refusal to distinguish sharply, as we might tend to do, between a love of the epistemic goods and a love of what we (but not Plato) would call the moral good. A human education is one that forms in a person a free love of the good, simply. The development of the intellect and the development of the heart cannot be separated. This judgment of the shared identity of moral and intellectual education is based in Plato's metaphysics, in which only the good is finally real and thus the proper object of knowledge. What modern people regard as the realm of the knowable—the physical world of particulars, the world accessible to our organs of sense perception—is not the proper object of knowledge because it is not good. Since evil haunts "this region of our mortal nature,"

> we should make all speed to take flight from this world to the other,
> and that means becoming like the divine so far as we can, and that
> again is to become just with the help of wisdom. . . . In the divine
> there is no shadow of injustice, only the perfection of justice, and
> nothing is more like the divine than any one of us who becomes as
> just as possible. It is here that a man shows his true spirit and power
> or lack of spirit and nothingness. For to know this is wisdom and
> excellence of the genuine sort; not to know it is to be manifestly
> blind and base. All other forms of seeming power and intelligence in
> the rulers of society are as mean and vulgar as the mechanic's skill
> in handicraft. (176b–c)

The implication here seems to be at odds with the whole history of epistemology starting with Aristotle, though the Christian tradition, all the way back to the Bible, has its reservations about the trend.[2] Beginning with Aristotle, the intellectual virtues are distinguished from the virtues of character and assigned to their own special faculties of the soul. In our own day it is widely thought that being "morally" good is quite irrelevant to the achievement of extraordinary intellectual accomplishments such as creative scholarship and the highest levels of scientific discovery. The intellect, with its powers of insight and understanding and proof, are one thing, and the heart, which may or may not be conformed to the good, is another. If this post-Platonic tradition is right, then higher education, aiming as it does chiefly at the formation of intellectual skills, can certainly not afford to make moral education more than a pious sideline or, more consistently, should just ignore it altogether. Under the influence of Aristotle's division, the Christian university, which assumes the importance of moral character and assumes some responsibility for fostering it, will nevertheless not think of moral formation as *part* of intellectual formation, but will see these as two separate tasks.

FREE LOVE IN THE CONTEXT OF CHRISTIAN EDUCATION

What can Christian educators learn from this digression in the *Theaetetus*? If Plato is right, it will be essential to the task of an education that aims to form students for the intellectual life to form them also in such virtues as justice, generosity, humility, courage, perseverance, and love of God and neighbor. I think we will want to affirm Plato's formal points while reevaluating them in terms of specifically Christian metaphysical/axiological content. A genuine human education must be more than training in how to accomplish ends. It is a formation in love, and this is a formation of character, indicated by a distinctive sense of humor and other affective dispositions. A merely technical education is not a human education, for it does not fulfill us, does not put us in relation with good, does not give us the most important kind of knowledge, does not give us virtue. In fact, it probably corrupts us, as Plato suggests, by giving us a false impression of being educated, of being a person "of formidable intellect—as [one] imagines."

A genuine education aims at the formation of not just any love, but of a free love. What makes a love free? I think the basic formal idea is that of a love that is appropriate to the human soul. We see all kinds of enslaving loves, the most obvious of which are substance addictions. Here one is attracted to something that is so deeply and immediately at odds with one's social and physical nature that to continue to take it is to destroy oneself incontestably and rather quickly. Another example is Anna Karenina's love for Vronsky. Plato thinks there are many other cases as well, cases that are somewhat less obvious and more controversial, such as a love of money or social standing. For him the one thing that is completely healthy and liberating for a human being to love is the eternal world, utterly stable Beauty, Justice, the purely Good, the Divine. To love this is to be free because it is to enjoy a realization of one's true nature; it is to enter into relationship with, and reflect the nature of, one's perfectly suitable other. Since that divine world is the best thing there is, the only really good and really real thing, to know it is the aim of proper intellectual aspiration. But to know that world is to be good. This knowledge is a state of character. So intellectual and "moral" virtue are the same.

If education is formation in love and proper love is love for what is worthy, then a first principle of Christian education will be to promote the loving of God with all our heart, soul, mind, and strength. God is the first and most worthy object of our love, and the knowledge of him is the first and most worthy kind of knowledge, for to know him is to love him (and to love him is to know him). And to know him in this way is eternal life: "And this is life eternal: that they might know Thee, the only true God, and Jesus Christ whom Thou hast sent."[3] So here the intellectual and the moral virtues coincide, and the business of Christian higher education must be to promote them together, to teach the love of the good as the basis for the knowledge of the good.

But Christians' conception of the relationship between God and the physical and social world differs vastly from the one Plato expresses here. God is not the only good thing; the world of the divine is not the only thing worth knowing and loving, not the only possible object of free love. "If anyone says, 'I love God,' and hates his brother, he is a liar." "He who says 'I know him' but disobeys his commandments is a liar." The Christian believes that God's glory (his lovableness) is manifested in the sensible world, and the social world is not to be fled but to be understood, admired, lamented, and improved. Our Lord Jesus, who most perfectly revealed the nature and will of the eternal, was not above "meetings and dinners" in the way that the Platonic paragon is. (I do not remember any biblical sanction for merrymaking with flute girls, but there is plenty of sanction for merrymaking and girls, and flutes can be used to glorify God.)

Plato suggests that the intellectually virtuous person is indiscriminately uninterested in particulars, whether this be the congenital defect in the neighbors' family tree or an injustice between you and me that needs resolving. The paradigmatic Platonic individual distinguishes among items that ordinary people would call knowledge and ascribes worthiness to some of them and little or none to others. He posits a clear hierarchy of intellectual "goods," with conceptual knowledge attained by dialectic at the top, but at the top of the top especially important Forms (not all Forms are created equal). So the discrimination of instances of knowledge is not foreign to Plato; and one could make the case that the hierarchy is determined by the kind of considerations that we would call moral. Justice is near the top, the Good is at the top. Sometimes Beauty is at the top, but this is not just prettiness; it has moral depth. The different cases of knowledge vary in degree of importance, and the degree of importance is determined in part by the "epistemic" value of explanatory power, and in part by their "moral" value.

The educated Christian, like the Platonic paragon, loves intellectual goods for their own sake, but also like the Platonist sorts them in part by reference to moral standards. For the Christian, moral virtues like justice and agape enable discrimination concerning which intellectual goods ought to be pursued—or, better, which truths are intellectual goods. Particular truths that have the character of gossip are not to be contemplated or savored, while particular truths about a neighbor's unusual generosity and perseverance in the good are to be dwelt upon and enjoyed. A Christian education inculcates an instinct against the one and for the other. A Christian may properly decide not to pursue the truth about how to build a hydrogen bomb, though that truth is challenging and within her reach; and her reasons will be what we call "moral."

Christians are interested in the Form of justice (that is, in understanding the *concept* of justice), but they are also interested in particular justices and injustices, and the interest in the concept derives in large part from the interest in the particulars. The educated Christian does not try to induce others to drop the question, "What injustice have I done to you or you to me?" so as to think more purely, more righteously, of what justice and injustice are in themselves. Rather, he is interested in Justice, in large part, so that he can make sure that he and his neighbor are living on just terms down here in the sensible world of particulars. The Christian considers it a pretty significant intellectual failing if somebody is so interested in what justice is that he fails to notice an injustice he is systematically doing to his neighbor, or so interested in what man is that he does not notice that his neighbor is a man.

The educated Christian's sense of humor will both resemble and differ from that of Socrates. Socrates finds the eulogy of a despot or king funny because he is aware of something much greater than kings and despots. Eulogizing them strikes the philosopher as eulogizing a swineherd would strike the uneducated. The educated Christian's reason for laughing at the eulogy is similar, but does not ultimately depend on the belief that everything in this world here below is of no value. Rather the basis on which kings and despots pretend to importance is no real basis of superiority. The Christian will also laugh with the maidservant at Thales's absent-mindedness, but without devaluing Thales's concern for intellectual goods in the way she does—in case she is, as we have speculated, the product of a purely utilitarian education. Thales is funny, not because he overvalues astronomy, but because he is so one-sided in his intellectual interests that his humanity seems to be in question.

So Plato's picture of the moral/intellectual character of the philosopher is in some ways very different and even morally and intellectually shocking to the Christian. Much of the difference between these characters, and thus the difference between their educations, is determined by their different underlying pictures of reality, their different theologies or metaphysics. Can we generalize that human education—that is, one that aims to form the virtues and makes no sharp distinction between the intellectual and the moral virtues—always turns on a theology or a metaphysics? I think that is a safe generalization.

In the current university scene, Plato's metaphysics is not much of a competitor to Christian education, but the metaphysics of scientific naturalism is. Scientific naturalism construes nature (which it takes to be everything there is) as nonteleologically mechanistic. The working of this mechanism exhausts the realm of truth. Thus naturalism attempts to separate the good and the true and to relegate conceptions of the good to individual or communal choice, noncognitive feelings, or projection. If truth applies in morality, it does so very differently than in science. Naturalism sanctions and prescribes a merely technical education, and thus a nonhuman education, a training in skills but not an education in virtues. Yet if Plato's analysis of the how-to legal education can be applied to this case, an education under naturalist auspices does nevertheless tend to form character. At its worst it creates despair about personal teleology. Personal goals are just whatever they happen to be—fame, reputation, tenure, money, power, whatever suits one's fancy—and "education" provides the techniques by which to secure whatever one happens to want, which in some cases may even be scientific truth, if *that* happens to strike one's fancy. So one conclusion we can draw from our discussion of the *Theaetetus* is that education of persons is indexed to metaphysics (in a way that merely technical training need not be). Secular universities, which may pose as offering a merely instrumental, "value-free" education, are in fact training people in a certain kind of metaphysics, and thus in a certain moral/spiritual character. Not that they always succeed, of course, any more than Christian colleges and universities always succeed in forming Christian character.

A COMPETING VISION OF "FREE" LOVE

Warren Nord, in his challenging paper in this volume, distinguishes two kinds of liberal education (and implicitly two corresponding conceptions of freedom), neither of which corresponds to the one I have outlined in response to Plato's *Theaetetus*. A *liberal arts* education is grounded in a classical canon of texts, often including canonical religious texts, and it aims to inculcate the moral and political virtues implied by those texts; but it falls short as an intellectual education because, being a nurturing in *one* moral outlook, it does not train the student in a thoroughly critical assessment of *all* worldviews and moral systems. A *liberal-free* education introduces students to a representative sample of the moral systems and encourages a free (in the sense of not being grounded in any single system) critical conversation about them. In other words, one trains the intellect without grounding it in any particular morality. Nord is particularly concerned to outline a liberal education that can be pursued at public universities, one that neither favors nor actively disfavors any religion or other contestable moral system, and for this purpose he endorses the liberal-free model of liberal education. Like Plato, he roundly rejects a merely technical education as not serving human freedom in any significant sense.

In a public university, perhaps a liberal-free education is as close as one can come to a liberal education. Perhaps a genuinely liberal education, of the kind that we find in the *Theaetetus* and that I have commended as possible in the Christian university, is incompatible with the nature of a public university, as an entity that systematically seeks to be morally neutral. I have compared Plato's conception with that possible in a Christian university, a university that is not constrained to be neutral with respect to moral systems. Let me now raise some doubts about the viability of a liberal-free education.

A liberal-free education seems to be an unstable reversion to the old separation of the intellectual from the moral life. The public university supposedly trains its students to be radically critical of all moral viewpoints, and the "freedom" and excellence of human life that is thus engendered by this "liberal education" consists in this intellectual power to make critical assessments. But the rational assessment of moral viewpoints is (as Nord seems to acknowledge) itself a moral enterprise. For example, it requires an empathic, imaginative entering into the viewpoints of the moral practices that are under assessment; it requires a humble willingness to set aside one's own prejudices during the examination; it requires a certain implicit respect for other human viewpoints. But such empathy, humility, and respect are themselves virtues, aspects of a moral orientation. Nord comments:

> There is a set of moral virtues internal to the practice of liberal education. In probing the existential depths of life and experience a liberal education nurtures sobriety and moral seriousness. In opening ourselves to alternative ways of thinking and living, we practice humility. . . . In our efforts to think and feel ourselves into the hearts and minds of others we take them seriously as persons, according

them at least a measure of respect—and compassion often follows in the wake of our ability to empathize with others.[4]

Where did these virtues come from? It would be highly implausible to suppose that such capacities in the students were engendered entirely by the techniques of rational assessment that are central to a liberal-free education in a public university. More plausibly, these capacities derive from the students' own moral systems, which are then enhanced and deepened by the exercise of empathic critical assessment of alien moral viewpoints. Only a person who has achieved a certain maturity within a particular moral viewpoint will be able to probe the existential depths of life as it is lived in some other moral tradition. Only a person who is already morally serious about truth will ever come to practice the kind of humility that allows one to admit that another's moral outlook may include some good that is lacking in one's own. But in that case, the liberal-free education is not quite what it was advertised to be. It is covertly parasitic on one or more of the particular moral frameworks toward which it is supposed to be taking a neutral stance. The notion of a morally neutral capacity for the assessment of moral outlooks appears to be incoherent.

The liberal-free educational enterprise seems to limp along exploiting rather unsystematically the bits of moral capital that the students and faculty have brought into the university from their churches, synagogues, mosques, or their Stoic or humanistic liberal democratic homes. We might wonder whether a more robust, deeper, and objective version of the critical intellectual freedom at which the liberal-free education aims might be achieved by frankly admitting that rational assessment of moral systems depends on the assessor's having a moral system of his own. Then liberal education might consist in training students deeply in one moral tradition (their own), acquainting them with the best of thought in that tradition in the context of pursuing its practices (its prayers, its worship, its expedients of reconciling those who are alienated and succoring those in need, etc.), for moral thought divorced from its practices is abstract and unreal. Among the intellectual practices of a moral tradition like Christianity is that of assessing other moral viewpoints and thinking critically about features of one's own. As Nord points out, this cannot be done well without virtues like empathy, love, respect, humility, and honesty. Since all of these virtues are native to Christian soil, they naturally support and are supported by a Christian liberal arts education. So it looks to me as though the goal of a liberal-free education is much more likely to be achieved by a sectarian education of the right sort than by a public education straining unnaturally (and a bit self-deceptively) for moral and intellectual neutrality.

Another assumption that may lie behind Nord's optimism about liberal-free education in the public university is that virtues really can be prized loose from moral traditions. The virtues of humility or forgivingness may have originated in the Jewish or Christian traditions, but it is possible to separate the virtues from the theologies, the metaphysics, the distinctive conceptions of human nature of these originating traditions. I have suggested the contrary in following Plato's distinction between two radical senses of humor, and in distinguishing Platonic justice from Christian justice. In each case, while the two virtues are both called "sense of humor" or "justice," they actually are very different character traits because of the difference in the implicit metaphysical background. No doubt countless variants and syncretisms of virtues are possible, and many of these variants will bear family resemblances that may explain why a single virtue-name covers the different variants. Thus Stoic courage, Aristotelian courage, and Christian courage are all called courage, but they involve different emotional patterns, connect differently to other virtues, and differ in their supporting metaphysics. Stoic courage is a matter of recognizing that the things the uncourageous person fears do not really threaten anything genuinely good, and so courage is the rational elimination of fear. Aristotelian courage, by contrast, involves proper fear of real threats but occupies a mean between fearing too little and fearing too much, and is balanced by a corresponding mean of confidence; in Aristotle's world, but not the Stoic's, contingencies can bring real harm.

Christian courage, like the Aristotelian and unlike the Stoic variant, is compatible with real fear, but unlike both, the confidence derives from a personal relation to a loving God who transcends all such passing harms as may cause the fear. Thus Christian courage depends intimately on such other virtues as faith and hope. These three courages may, in certain circumstances, eventuate in identical behavior—say, the competent performance of some difficult action under threat of harm. Thus, superficially they may seem to be the same trait; but they are actually quite different. A similar story can be told about any virtue. So the hope that an advocate of liberal-free education might harbor for a set of *virtues* that are noncontroversial, tradition-independent, and morally neutral is based on an illusion created by common vocabulary.

Nord criticizes the liberal arts style of liberal education for failing to train students to be radically critical. They are trained in the virtues of their own tradition, true, but they lack something in intellectual maturity because they have not been trained to turn their critical powers on *all and any* moral viewpoints. No doubt this is true of some liberal arts education, but it is not implied by the idea of liberal arts education as such, nor is it true of the best liberal arts education. Of course not every moral tradition is equally equipped with moral and critical resources; traditions come in varying depths of development. But a moral tradition, such as Christianity, that has been sufficiently richly developed over many centuries by gigantic minds such as Paul, Augustine, Thomas Aquinas, John Calvin, Søren Kierkegaard, and countless lesser lights, will have within it enormous critical resources that can be directed both at alien moralities and at itself. And it will have virtues of the types that Nord mentions—humility, respect, honesty, empathy, courage—that enable its best intellectual practitioners to tap the critical resources of its most articulate opponents.

PRACTICING FREE LOVE IN THE CHRISTIAN UNIVERSITY

Derek Bok, in his book *Universities and the Future of America*, struggles with the question of how to implement moral education in the curriculum of a secular university. He documents a precipitate decline in general American morality during the last half of the twentieth century, and asks what universities might do to stem and reverse the trend. The divorce rate tripled between 1960 and 1990; children are spending less time with their parents and more with the TV; teenage drug and alcohol abuse, pregnancy, suicide, and crime are up 100–200 percent in the same time period. Parents are less involved in their children's schools. White-collar crime has risen dramatically. The percentage of citizens who distrust corporate America doubled between 1970 and 1990. Employees do not trust management. Government scandals have sapped people's confidence in the probity and effectiveness of government officials. People want the services that government provides but do not want to be taxed to pay for them.

Until well into the nineteenth century, higher education in America had the express, even overriding, aim of forming leaders of moral character—in Thomas Jefferson's words, "an aristocracy of talent and virtue." The expedients were Bible study, moral philosophy, a great deal of hortatory discourse throughout the curriculum and extracurriculum, codes of conduct enforced by sanctions, the watchful eye of every faculty member, careful selection of faculty members for the soundness of their character and theological views, and a senior capstone course in moral philosophy which often consisted in the university president dictating from lectures which were to be copied down as faithfully as possible into students' notes and recited back on the following day.

After the Civil War this style of university education went into decline and was gradually replaced by the modern research university. The earlier methods of moral instruction and control came to seem too paternalistic and faculty were increasingly hired for their academic expertise rather than for the morality of their life and views. Although the public rhetoric of the universities continued to include the claim to form character, the truth was that the college experience, at least in the large secular universities, no longer did so. Indeed, the tendency may now to be to reverse whatever gains in character a student may have achieved prior to college.

Clearly, secular universities are no longer the kind of institutions that might help to resist or reverse American moral decline. And yet the college years seem a golden opportunity for influencing the character of America, if only the right kind of institution could be devised. Bok's main task is to suggest ways that the secular university might become such an institution. Bok's proposed program for moral education has several aspects. Courses in applied ethics at both the college and professional school levels will sharpen the student's powers of moral reasoning and help the student get in touch with the moral commitments and sensitivities that he brings with him to school. The school will have rules governing the ethical conduct of students, but these will always be backed up with plausible reasons, which will be clearly laid out for the students to see, and rules will be enforced consistently and fairly. Students will be encouraged to put their morality into practice during their college years in strong programs of community service. The university will model high ethical standards in the investment of its endowment and in holding its faculty to high standards of professionalism.

Bok's proposals are praiseworthy. Anything that can be done to restore a bit of moral tone to the secular universities must be to the good—perhaps even to the good of larger America. But to someone whose model is the Christian liberal arts college or university, the proposals bring to mind the old tires and miscellaneous scrap metal that U.S. soldiers in Iraq recently wired to the sides of their military trucks and jeeps in lieu of genuine, integrally built armored vehicles. The make-shift, patched-on armor may stop a bullet here and there, but the overall construction of the vehicle is not well adapted to the purpose. If the moral formation of a university's students is to be integrated with their intellectual formation in anything like the Platonic or Christian vision of the fully mature human being, the overall design and construction of the university must have that aim expressly in its sights. Since the secular university has evolved into a vehicle that is fundamentally ill-adapted to the education of a complete human being, a very different kind of vehicle, with a different design, is needed.

The earlier American college (which was virtually always a Christian college) is not a perfect model. As Bok points out, some of its methods of moral instruction and control were better adapted to an unsophisticated constituency than they would be to people who read widely and think carefully. In particular, such colleges were legalistic and paternalistic, focused on behavior and memorization of precepts, in ways that fell far short of the best classical and Christian moral thought and practice. But other features of such colleges are well worth retention, emulation, and development. Central to the education of each student must be a coherent moral-metaphysical framework, a comprehensive world-and-life view from the vantage point of which alien views of the world can be evaluated, in which the student can be trained to think autonomously and deeply about science, history, literature, and the practical worlds of work, family, and public affairs. Moral philosophy will be central, including the applied ethics courses that Bok advocates. But the moral philosophy central to the curriculum should not, in my opinion, be the usual metaethics and rehearsal and evaluation of all the normative theories of the modern period. Instead it should concentrate on exploring the way moral concepts actually work, with special attention to the concepts of virtue and vice, with the aim of heightening moral self-awareness in terms of the grand moral traditions of classical and Christian thought. Finally, the moral coherence of the university, both intellectual and communal, cannot be achieved and retained without another of the features of the earlier American college—the careful selection of faculty members for the coherence of their own moral character and beliefs with the envisioned university community. This must be done as far as possible without compromising the academic excellence of the school, but neither are Christian orthodoxy and orthopraxy to be slighted in the interest of such excellence.

Character education at the college level may seem problematic in that by the time students get to college their character is already well under way of being formed. Our task does seem to be primarily one of continuation and deepening; mostly we build on the formative contributions of earlier schooling, chiefly at home but also at school. So we must look for students who, like Theaetetus, are already on their way to knowing the good and loving knowledge for the right reasons, students in whom some seeds of goodness have begun to sprout.

But this task of building, continuing, and deepening is still a very significant one. Given our sinful, forgetful, and ever-unfinished nature, none of us ever outgrows our need for Christian education. How do we deepen character that is already there, refining the love of the good which is also a love of knowing it, a desire to penetrate and explore it ever more profoundly? Like Theaetetus's dialogue with Socrates, much of the most powerful teaching that goes on in the university involves the close interaction of an older person, more mature in his loving understanding of what is real, with a younger one. In this interaction the junior Christian works as an apprentice inquirer under the guidance of the older Christian. But apprenticeship is not quite the same thing as "going to school" under somebody. It is more in the nature of a partnership, albeit here one partner has a more leading and guiding role than the other. In the common endeavor of Christian education that I envision, both parties grow in understanding and in appreciating what they understand, though the "learning curve" of the younger partner is usually steeper. The growth is of at least two kinds: the student becomes more proficient in the skills of inquiry, but through the work-in-association she also absorbs attitude and affective tone from the older person. From her senior associate she learns a style of living, a way of being with particular reference to inquiry. This partnering character of Socrates' teaching, sometimes facilitated and undercut by his rascally irony, was one of its most powerful features, and one from which the Christian educator can learn. It cuts the distance between teacher and pupil, trimming the teacher down to a more real-life size, and expresses a kind of humility (though in Socrates' case the humility was attenuated a bit by the irony). Humility is a major Christian virtue. As the Apostle Paul notes in Philippians 2, our Lord intentionally cut himself down to our size to become our teacher. The Christian university teacher will, I think, use irony less often than Socrates did. The humility in which the Christian teacher expresses his or her love for God and for what God has made, and his passion for understanding both, will be another of the virtues that the student is put in a position to absorb through her apprenticeship with her teachers in the Christian university.

Chapter 3

Returning Moral Philosophy to American Higher Education

—Nicholas K. Meriwether

> For who would dare to call himself a philosopher if he had
> handed down no rules of duty?
>
> —Cicero, *De officiis*

INTRODUCTION

Imagine yourself as an undergraduate attending a college that takes with
utmost seriousness the moral formation of its students. In addition to
earnest appeals to civic virtue in convocations and the occasional lecture,
and encouragement to community service in dorms and college clubs,
the curriculum culminates in a rigorous, year-long capstone course in
moral philosophy. In the fall of your final year, you file into class with
your fellow seniors and, peering anxiously into the well of the lecture
hall, you see none other than the college president himself reviewing an
overstuffed binder for the first day's lecture.

For the next hour, and in the weeks and months to follow, the president lays out in a rigorous, systematic way a foundation for personal

morality and public duty, much in the manner of a biology or chemistry course. In effect, his lectures in moral philosophy seek to develop through deductive logic and empirical observation a harmonious synthesis of our various moral duties, viz., to family, to society, and to God, and also to demonstrate how the performance of these duties contributes to one's personal happiness. Although explicit references to other thinkers, or even the major theorists of Western civilization, are relatively few and far between, he has borrowed liberally from the thought of others. The textbook for the course is written by the president himself, and in his lectures he makes little effort to offer views opposing his own; when they are treated, it is always in order to show the superiority of his own view to theirs. For the course is not a survey in Western moral theory, nor is it designed merely to encourage moral reflection. The point of the course is to provide the student with a moral philosophy that will guide him through life's challenges. Accordingly, the president is not loathe to apply moral norms in delineating what he believes to be appropriate student behavior, and like most others, you cannot help but occasionally experience the unwelcome sting of remorse at your own failings. He is also quite clear in his stance regarding issues of public controversy, much to the delight of those who agree and the chagrin of those who differ. Naturally, some students resent the loss of time they might otherwise have spent on courses within their chosen field, but since the college prides itself on its commitment to the moral formation of its students, and because the course is required, the vast majority do not consider it burdensome. Besides, a good many of the students respect and appreciate the foundation that the president provides, and it is not unusual for discussions of his views to turn into lively debates at the refectory and in the dorm rooms.

Regardless of whether the students agree or disagree, by graduation they all readily concede that they have been provided with a vigorous, substantive theory of morality that demands either adoption or repudiation (however qualified) and that will reverberate in their lives for years to come.

What I describe above would have been a standard feature in the nineteenth-century liberal arts college; it is virtually unheard of today. Required courses in moral philosophy, which had been part of university education for centuries in the West, effectively died out by the early twentieth century. Should we view the demise of the requirement in moral philosophy as a welcome liberation from the hidebound pedantry and autonomy-destroying indoctrination of traditional education? Or should we view it as contributing to the desultory, goalless nihilism of higher education critiqued by the late Neil Postman:

Modern secular education is failing . . . because it has no moral, social, or intellectual center. There is no set of ideas or attitudes that permeates all parts of the curriculum. The curriculum is not, in fact, a "course of study" at all but a meaningless hodgepodge of subjects. It does not even put forward a clear vision of what constitutes an educated person, unless it is a person who possesses "skills." In other words, a technocrat's ideal—a person with no commitment and no point of view but with plenty of marketable skills.[1]

My objective in what follows is to provide a compelling case for a requirement in moral philosophy as a capstone course in the secular or religiously affiliated university or college curriculum within the context of a pedagogy of ethics instruction that complements and justifies such a requirement. Central to that case is, of course, the theme of this volume, viz., the pressing need for university-level education to contribute to the moral formation of students, and just as importantly, the need to critique the reigning assumptions and tendencies within the academy that undermine or dilute any such effort, such as relativism, nihilism, and positivism. I shall argue that this can only be achieved if combined with the rejection of the dominant progressive approach to ethics instruction that emphasizes the instructor's neutrality, unguided discussion of ethical dilemmas, and autonomous choice, an approach I call a pedagogy of *mediation*.

Ethics education requires at a minimum a pedagogy of *profession*; that is, one that presents, argues for, defends, and applies a normative ethical theory. To this end, I shall critique the dominant contemporary approach to moral education that purports to teach ethics in a neutral or mediatorial manner, and address some standard objections to using the ethics classroom to profess a normative ethical theory.

As Michael Beaty and Douglas Henry make clear at the outset of this volume, the history of moral formation in American higher education is one of retreat, eventual abandonment, and—by the late 1960s—a partial-yet-confused recovery from that abandonment. I call it *partial* because a university expresses its priorities and commitments primarily through what it requires in order to obtain a degree. When an area of inquiry is not a required part of the curriculum, as is the case with ethics in the vast majority of secular and religious institutions, it cannot be considered central to the mission of that institution, regardless of how much character formation "talk" is included in catalogs and brochures. According to one rather comprehensive study, institutions in which students report the greatest gains in character formation "go well beyond simply offering opportunities for their students to reflect, refine, and test their values, ethics and attitudes. . . . [These] institutions . . . present a range of character-testing activities and *require* their students to take part in more than a few."[2]

Yet if one is going to require character-formative activities, we must also require a systematic exposition of the foundations of public and private moral responsibility, unless we assume, against all experience—not to mention the wisdom of the ages—that students enter college with complete conceptual clarity on the nature of the human good. And so I also call that recovery *confused*, because if ethics is taught merely as case studies-oriented "applied ethics" within the framework of progressive theories of moral education (and it generally is), it is as likely to disorient the students' moral beliefs as strengthen them. The requirement in moral philosophy that I propose will be informed in significant ways by the moral philosophy course of the nineteenth century described above, but will also differ in important respects. The profession of moral philosophy cannot occur in a cultural-historical vacuum; it must be sensitive to the age and ethos it inhabits, and we are alas far removed from a time in which moral formation was an accepted and welcomed component of higher education.

THE PROFESSION OF A NORMATIVE ETHICAL THEORY: A BRIEF SKETCH

According to Bernard Rosen, "a normative ethical theory provides us with a general means of arriving at moral judgments that apply to specific situations, events, persons, actions, and things."[3] Thus, an instructor who provides guidance for controversial issues such as the moral permissibility of homosexual marriage, abortion, euthanasia, capital punishment, war, affirmative action, gun control, and so forth, by expounding a theory of morality, that is, an account of the nature of right and wrong, good and evil, is professing and applying a normative ethical theory.[4] Examples of normative ethical theories include natural law theory, Christian ethics, virtue theory, utilitarianism, Kantian or Rawlsian deontology, or some combination of these, as for example a natural law theory grounded in theism supplemented by an account of Christian virtues such as is found in Thomas Aquinas. To profess a theory is to do in effect what I describe above: to recommend it to students as the instructor's considered view of the matter, to make inferences from it as to the correct view of moral controversies, and to combine the presentation of the theory with a critique of theories and arguments that oppose the instructor's positions as implausible, unreasonable, or otherwise inadequate. Like the nineteenth-century moral philosophy course, this approach would draw from research within other disciplines to support its positions, including human biology, psychology, political science, anthropology, or sociology, with one key qualification that I will describe below. Where appropriate, the instructor would also take issue with assumptions within these fields that he believes undermine moral realism, such as moral relativism, latent or explicit positivism, or unreflective reliance on the fact-value distinction. In so doing, the goal of an ethics course would be, like the moral philosophy requirement of the nineteenth century, to serve as a kind of capstone course, unifying the disciplines for the purpose of establishing and defending a comprehensive, coherent, and integrated view of public, private, and professional morality.

An important clarification at the outset: mediatorial or progressive vs. professing or traditional approaches have more in common than is often recognized, and the differences, though profound and significant, can also be exaggerated. The mediatorial approach does not dispense with shaping and molding students; neither does the professing approach forfeit critical thinking. Indeed, the language of virtue acquisition is by no means absent from contemporary mediatorial methodology, though it is typically recast as the impartation of skills or habits that encourage the correct sort of approach to ethical reflection.[5] And despite the fact that the mediatorial approach lays much heavier emphasis upon dialogue, the professing approach may allow a prominent place for "conversation," "dialogue," and "engagement" without, however, collapsing into a consensus theory of truth.[6] Robust dialectic is critical to good pedagogy, although it is often more difficult to realize in practice than is commonly admitted, for the simple but obvious reason that *many* students are intimidated even by affable and nonthreatening instructors.

Still, it's fairly safe to say that, for all parties to this dispute, erstwhile quintessential moral education pedagogy—the Francis Wayland model of reading lecture notes aloud while students scribble away (as described in the opening sketch)—is no longer applicable to today's university classroom. Allowing for a spectrum of degrees to which either model (profession or mediation) is embraced, perhaps the essential distinction between a mediatorial and a professing approach can be expressed as follows: a moral pedagogy is one of profession in which the instructor is explicit regarding his own commitments and openly defends his position from criticism in the explicit hope that students will adopt his view. The instructor makes clear at some point where his sympathies lie, and treats alternatives as rivals to be defeated, even if he allows and encourages robust criticism and approaches his own views fallibilistically. In the mediatorial model, the instructor's commitments are intentionally suppressed, and an attempt is made by the instructor to appear neutral. Students are encouraged to choose which moral theory they wish to embrace without the instructor indicating which view he endorses.

FROM PROFESSION TO MEDIATION

An examination of the successes and failures of nineteenth-century moral philosophy will help clarify what is needed to complete its recovery and render it coherent and genuinely beneficial today. Thus, in laying out the central features of my proposal, I focus on elements of the story that are not emphasized above in Beaty and Henry's "Retrieving the Tradition, Remembering the End." The old moral philosophy's strengths include its pedagogical approach, which emphasizes the profession of a substantive moral theory; the status of the course in moral philosophy as a required capstone course; and, perhaps most controversially, the placement of moral theory within the context of teleological eudaimonism. Its chief weakness, on the other hand, consists in the manner in which instructors in moral philosophy sought to ground moral belief.

Despite seismic epistemological shifts over the period leading up to the new methods of scholarship of the late nineteenth century, the consensus among American institutions of higher education of the seventeenth through the mid-nineteenth centuries was that all truth was unified in God, and that knowledge of all the arts and sciences had spiritual and moral implications that should be conveyed to students throughout the curriculum. The nineteenth-century course in moral philosophy, typically taught by none other than the college president, represented the apex of the collegiate curriculum, integrating scholarly learning with the well-lived life. It was not a survey course, nor was it terribly concerned to answer or engage alternative theories. Rather, "The senior year course in moral and mental philosophy" writes Julie Reuben, "was the capstone of the college education. It drew together the knowledge learned in the previous three years and placed it in a Christian framework." [7] Accordingly, the course was anything but a mere examination of the logic of ethical concepts and their meaning and use. It was not *interpretive* in that sense, but emphatically *evaluative* and *exhortative*, and unabashedly strove to arrive at definitive moral conclusions. [8] The idea was to provide "a handy system of ethics that would comprehend most of the student's concerns and answer, as neatly as possible, a number of theoretical questions." [9]

However, the epistemological shifts following the scientific revolution did impact moral education in significant ways; in particular by convincing moral philosophers of the nineteenth century that moral philosophy itself must be approached *scientifically*. Thus, despite the emphasis in Christian colleges on organizing knowledge within a unified Christian worldview, moral philosophers attempted to make the specifics of moral philosophy independent of revealed religion, a move reflecting also the proliferation of denominations during this period.

Nevertheless, the instructors believed that their putatively scientific methodology was compatible with, if not directly supportive of, Christian faith. The study of morality could be conducted in ways analogous to the study of other areas of human inquiry; indeed, moral philosophy was better understood as moral *science*.[10] In this way, the moral truths discovered in and through their theological traditions could be transmitted to a society that was slowly abandoning that tradition as an unquestioned source of knowledge. According to Meyer, as the "authority of the Church and of Scripture was being replaced by that of the private conscience," the American Victorian ethic expressed in the moral philosophy textbooks "wanted to restore a lost sense of legitimate authority, to reawaken moral passions once kindled by faith, to revitalize a diminishing capacity for ontological wonder without resorting to special revelation, sectarian dogma, or arbitrary personal assertion." Moral philosophy was seen "both as a secular supplement to and as an ethical justification of religious faith."[11] Thus, in keeping with what they considered the spirit of the age, the moral philosophers sought to appropriate the methods and terminology of the natural sciences. A representative analogy appearing in many textbooks of the period is that moral science "describes man's relation to the moral order . . . just as astronomy describes earth's relation to the solar system."[12]

Clearly, then, the pervasive adoption of quantitative modes of knowledge to the exclusion of qualitative modes, a development that the moral philosophers sought to accommodate, was having its effect long before the end of the nineteenth century. The quantitative mode emphasizes explanation on the basis of physical cause and effect, analysis, quantification, measurement, and mechanistic (and deterministic) external relationships.[13] It is the astounding success of this approach in the natural sciences that made the latter the paradigm for all areas of human inquiry. The qualitative mode encompasses the faculties of human knowledge and perception that are the domain of religious belief, value, meaning, purpose, and thus the "ends" of human moral action, i.e., justice and goodness. Thus, qualitative modes of perception constitute an independent mode of human knowing, and are irreducible to the quantitative mode.[14] But the quantitative mode's success in natural science made it appear to be the only legitimate approach to knowledge, and thus applicable to all human inquiry, including morality. The qualitative mode appeared sectarian, subjective, and private by comparison, and thus unable to provide a social ethic or to serve as a proper object of inquiry.

This is not to suggest that if the instructors had only had a methodology that privileged qualitative modes of knowledge, moral philosophy would have weathered the tremendous changes in higher education of the late nineteenth and early twentieth centuries. The "disciplinary regime" that centered on the disciplining of the faculties of the mind through "hard work in abstract subjects" such as classical languages and mathematics had effectively succumbed to intense pressures for curricular reform in most schools by the 1890s. The requirement in moral philosophy does not appear to have been a direct target of these changes, but simply went down with the core curriculum ship.[15] Thus, the pressures of professionalization and specialization were arguably just as significant. Yet as long as a quantitative scientific methodology seemed to harmonize with the qualitative claims of moral philosophy, as it appeared to do in the version of natural theology embraced by the nineteenth century moral philosophers, the inherent tensions between the two were repressed, and human values could plausibly be inferred from the facts of nature. Eventually, however, the triumph of the quantitative became complete when the social sciences—which until the 1890s were viewed more-or-less as adjuncts to moral philosophy—separated themselves and embraced positivism, wherein only that which could be observed exclusively through the quantitative methodology of the natural sciences could be a proper object of knowledge. As a result, that which was nonquantifiable and nontestable—moral philosophy, along with theology and metaphysics—was relegated to the noncognitive sphere of the subjective and private. From that point, the sphere of fact and the sphere of value were irretrievably separated. Since moral belief was not a proper object of knowledge, a requirement in moral philosophy as a distinct area of inquiry simply no longer made sense.[16]

Yet qualitative concerns are irrepressible. Those within the quantitative paradigm never fully abandoned qualitative concerns; rather, they subsumed them as mere reflections or corollaries of the quantitative mode. For example, progressive scientific humanism, as described by George Marsden, is in effect a qualitative ideal of human progress rooted in quantitative scientific advance.[17] Scholars within this intellectual tradition, which effectively replaced the comparatively more religiously orthodox moral philosophy of the nineteenth century, believed that the application of the quantitative methods of science to human problems would result in qualitative advances in human welfare, and believed that ethical and religious ideals would advance alongside science, with, of course, the latter and its methods in the lead. Thus, to the degree that a quantitative approach produces what are assumed to be the right qualitative results, the need for students to be exposed to substantive moral philosophy as a distinct intellectual experience was lessened, since as science continues to advance, the proper application of scientific assumptions and methodologies to human concerns (through the social sciences), will make such exposure unnecessary. And despite the fact that by the late 1960s, the awareness of the need for treating ethics as a dis-

tinct area of inquiry had reemerged, the teaching methodologies continued to take their cue from the quantitative mode informing the methodology of the natural sciences: an emphasis upon method, not content;
open, nondirected, free inquiry rather than impartation and exhortation;
and a positivistic prejudice against the existence of moral absolutes, and
toward defining moral norms as the products of the right kind of process.

A momentous casualty of these developments was the ability of nineteenth-century moral philosophy to place moral action within a context
of teleological eudaimonism.[18] I call a moral theory *teleologically eudaimonistic* when it provides an account of human moral action such that
when a person does what is right in and of itself (and in the typical for-
mulation, out of utter, complete selflessness, which is the mark of true
virtue), he achieves his purpose in the universe, does what is beneficial
for society, and achieves personal happiness.[19] This is possible only
because such theories view the universe as inherently purposive and
meaningful, that is, as *teleological*, a perspective that requires the epistemic integrity of qualitative modes of knowledge. One finds versions of
teleological eudaimonism in many of the world's religions, as well as in
the moral philosophies of Plato and Aristotle. But in the Western moral
tradition, the harmony of the individual good, the common good, and
the moral law is possible only because the universe is designed and
directed by a merciful and benevolent God, who infuses man, society,
and nature alike with his divinely ordained purposes, and sees to it that
obedience and disobedience receive their due reward and punishment, if
not in this life, then in the life to come.[20]

Christian teleological eudaimonism thus harmonizes Bishop Butler's
three classes of duties, commonly referred to in nineteenth-century moral
philosophy textbooks: particular duties to oneself and one's family and
friends, duties to the common good, and duties to that which is right in
and of itself. It is not that these never conflict, but the conflict is, in the
grand scheme of things, only temporary. Thus, the sanction for doing
what is right in and of itself—say, refusing to torture the child of a terror-
ist to force him to divulge a plan to detonate a dirty bomb—is the idea
that in the grand scheme of things, God in his providential wisdom will
make all right. It is indeed the loss of this teleological justification for
moral action that makes the sanctioning of sacrificial moral action so very
difficult, if not impossible, in secular approaches to ethics. If, however,
one rejects the positivistic notion that only quantitative methods can provide warrant for moral belief, and recognizes that moral, religious, and
metaphysical beliefs may count as knowledge without demonstration
from quantitative sources of knowledge, one has ample warrant for a teleologically eudaimonistic moral theory.

Not least of all, the story of the demise of moral philosophy, and the replacement of a pedagogy of profession with a pedagogy of mediation, cannot be told without due attention to the impact of Darwin's theory of evolution. By the end of the nineteenth century, the Protestant synthesis of theism, morality, and natural theology grounded in a quasi-scientific methodology, and thus in a metaphysical-axiological unity, was gradually being replaced by new methods of scholarship emphasizing free inquiry and scholarly consensus.[21] The driving force behind the development of the new approaches was the need to accommodate better Darwin's theory of evolution. The specific content of moral theory, naturally, could not help being affected by these new approaches. By 1879 John Bascom, a former student of Mark Hopkins, President of Williams College, and author of two books on moral philosophy, had already articulated the view that would serve as an *idée fixe* of progressive theories of moral education well into the twentieth century, that is that "as controlling circumstances are always changing, as social life is ever unfolding, the moral law never remains the same for any considerable period, and is hardly twice alike in its application. . . . An absolute and unchanging right in action is illusory."[22] Thus, the idea that there are unchanging and permanent duties, "what is right in and of itself," had to be jettisoned.[23]

Darwin's revolution led not only to a transformation of scientific methodology, but of moral pedagogy as well. Indeed, according to Douglas Sloan, Darwinism "represented the extension of the mechanical, materialistic philosophy to everything—to life, to consciousness, to human ideals and values."[24] Taking his cue from Darwin's theory that organisms adapt to their environment through natural selection, John Dewey held that the human mind adapts its ideas to its environment according to how successful those ideas are, much as a genetic modification is "selected for" by how well it enables the species to reproduce successfully. Since the mind's environment is evolving, the mind's content must evolve as well. This holds not only for our ideas about the world of facts, but also and especially for the world of values. A moral value, like an organ, is only as good as its efficiency in enabling an organism's survival. "Are the conditions of modern life so clear and so settled that we know exactly what organs, what moral habits and methods, are necessary in order to get the maximum of efficiency?"[25] Consequently, moral education cannot consist in defending and conveying static moral absolutes; rather, each generation of students must be given the opportunity to discover for itself which values work best in a constantly changing environment.

Dewey and his followers distinguished stages of moral reasoning that would lead to the determination of norms. Appropriate learning processes would provide validation for these norms, not their correspondence to an objective order of eternal verities. So the moral educator should not interfere directly with the process of validation, nor seek to guide the process of moral discovery to a predetermined outcome, nor critique or judge what issues from the process; at most, his efforts to guide, elicit, and mediate are only for the purpose of insuring the process moves forward and to provide a foundation for "social improvement." Thus, reflecting the new approach to scientific research, neither the "wisdom of the past" nor "established texts" should be emphasized. Rather, the point of moral education, according to Dewey, was to promote critical thinking and to make students more aware of their social obligations, "to use [students'] own experiences rather than classical theories as the building blocks for their moral and civic education."[26] As progressive moral education developed over the twentieth century, these assumptions led to such familiar practices as the use of moral dilemmas to demonstrate the inadequacy of the student's moral framework, typically obtained from home and church, and the heavy emphasis upon discussion rather than lecture, since communal discovery of value is at the heart of the process.[27]

In keeping with the tradition of moral philosophy, the progressives saw a direct link between their approach to moral education and democratic citizenship, yet with a distinct twist: the emphasis was no longer on the defense of timeless moral truth with application to current realities in the service of a healthy republic, but on the *adaptability* of moral values for the improvement of society. Combining Darwinian evolution, political engagement, and moral education, the progressives hoped to inculcate critical thinking skills that would make students as adaptive as possible in order to remedy social ills.[28] By the 1930s, George S. Counts was explicitly calling for teachers to employ the techniques of progressive moral education in order to begin "controlling the evolution of society."[29] It was not enough to propose a new approach; traditional forms of moral education had to be attacked. The progressives eschewed traditional approaches to education, especially character education, which Lawrence Kohlberg would later famously dismiss as the "bag of virtues" approach. The progressives not only argued that traditional character education was ineffective, a position which they supported through the famous Hartshorne and May studies of the 1920s, but they insisted that in a modern age characterized by rapid change, the stodgy moral absolutism of the past must be replaced with moral flexibility and an assertion of the relativity of values. The emphasis on technique and civic engagement over knowledge led to the neglect of matters of personal conduct in favor of an emphasis upon the processes of moral reasoning and social issues. Writes McClellan:

> Rejecting the notion that the school should teach specific moral pre-
> cepts or encourage particular traits, progressive educators hope to
> cultivate in students both a quality of open-mindedness and a gen-
> eral ability to make moral judgments. . . . Character in this view was
> not a matter of adhering to some set of rules of upright conduct—
> that was mere Victorianism. Instead, character had to do with the
> ability to contribute to the creation of a more humane and demo-
> cratic society.[30]

Adding to these powerful intellectual movements were other forces, some of which I describe above and some which I shall only mention in passing: the growing emphasis upon research, which diverted professors' attention away from general moral concerns; increasing specialization in ever-more-cloistered academic disciplines; the intensification of individualism in culture and law and the growing divide between public and private life; and, of course, the rise of and increasing popularity of professional studies.[31] This spelled the demise of the course in moral philosophy, and in many ways, any hope for a unified curriculum. McClellan concludes:

> For more than a hundred years, moral philosophy had put the fin-
> ishing touch on the education of all college students and had set the
> tone for the whole curriculum; in the late nineteenth century, it
> largely disappeared, leaving students without a capstone course
> and colleges without a formal way to complete the process of moral
> education.[32]

What is of first importance in understanding the impact of this momentous shift in the way morality was conceived and taught is that because the pedagogy of profession assumes an unchanging, normative account of human nature and moral absolutes, it is a pedagogy of *reminding, reinforcing, elaboration,* and *exhortation* of universal and necessary moral truths.

Thus, in today's cultural climate, it requires as well a pedagogy of *recovery*. And because the pedagogy of mediation rejects belief in an unchanging, normative account of human nature or the existence of moral absolutes, it is a pedagogy that stresses *adaptation, discovery,* and *open-ended application* of particular and contingent moral truth. This means that the quantitative modes of knowing and proof are ill-suited to a moral theory that is committed to both moral realism and teleological eudaimonism, since the ways we know these are not primarily via quantitative methods, but through qualitative modes of awareness, which are elicited via a pedagogy of profession.[33] Thus, as we will see, an attempt to harness moral realism and enduring moral norms to a pedagogy of mediation in the (faint) hope that a combination of a survey of options, case-study dilemmas, and open-ended dialectic in a context of instructional neutrality will produce the "discovery" of enduring moral values is fraught with peril for the simple reason that the methods employed are designed to produce completely opposite results.

MORAL EDUCATION AS CRITICAL THINKING: THE PEDAGOGY OF MEDIATION

The idea that moral education has only to do with teaching certain reasoning skills and character traits, not with professing specific beliefs about good and evil, or drawing specific conclusions about moral controversies, is pervasive in the moral education literature stretching between the 1960s and 1990s. Despite important theoretical differences, the dominant approaches of this period—values clarification, the cognitive developmentalism of Lawrence Kohlberg, the ethics of care of Carol Gilligan, and neo-classical approaches to character (or virtue) education—share a heavy reliance upon the assumptions and concepts of modern psychology, which itself displays an affinity with progressive ideas of moral education and rejects the systematic exposition and application of moral doctrine.[34] A fairly typical statement of purpose of more progressive approaches supposes that the object of moral education is first to help students identify moral issues, and second to enable them to reflect upon them in a rational and moral manner. The instructor's role is to help the students in the process, not to give them specific instruction in the nature and grounding of morality and what moral conclusions should follow from it.

Ideally, as a result of this extended engagement with critical-ethical reasoning, the student becomes a more mature moral reasoner who can think for him- or herself and in the process become a more responsible citizen. (That rigorous ethical reasoning automatically produces moral decency and good citizenship is a widespread but typically unexamined, undefended, and thus highly debatable assumption, which I will critique below.) The instructor of an ethics course explains in a nonjudgmental fashion various concepts such as "ethical egoism" or "moral relativism" and describes normative ethical theories—typically modern ones such as Kantian deontology, utilitarian consequentialism, and Rawlsian contractarianism—and then leads the class in group discussion in analyzing case studies, usually involving moral dilemmas.[35]

One of the more emphatic versions of this view may be found in *Moral Education in Theory and Practice*, by Robert Hall and John Davis. According to the authors,

our goal is not to teach youngsters to hold any particular moral values or principles. Our objective is, rather, to teach young people
what a moral value or a moral judgment is so that they can identify
moral considerations when they meet them and become aware of
the place of moral values in their own decision-making.[36]

So adamant are the authors that moral education must avoid conveying
substantive moral doctrine, they insist that instructors should refrain
from urging their students to adopt any moral perspective:

teaching the skills of moral thought and giving experience in decision-making are not the same as insisting that students adopt any
particular perspective; nor for that matter is it the same as insisting
that they adopt a moral perspective at all.[37]

This resistance to professing a moral theory can also be seen in the
1980 Hastings Center Report, *Ethics Teaching in Higher Education*. The
emphasis is again on process and modes of moral reasoning, with the
goal of enabling students to arrive at their own set of values while avoiding the transmission of a specific theory about the nature of morality, or
the drawing of specific moral conclusions. Instead, the focus is upon having the students adopt a rather vague attitude of moral earnestness. The
report's conclusion essentially identifies the profession of a moral theory
with indoctrination:

The general purpose of the teaching of ethics ought to be that of
stimulating the moral imagination, developing skills in the recognition and analysis of moral issues, [and] eliciting a sense of moral
obligation and personal responsibility. . . . Courses in ethics ought
not explicitly seek behavioral change in students. They should seek
to assist students in the development of those insights, skills, and
perspectives that set the stage for a life of personal moral responsibility reflecting careful and serious moral reflection. . . . Indoctrination, whether political, theological, ideological, or philosophical, is
wholly out of place in the teaching of ethics. Although students
should be assisted in developing moral ideals and fashioning a
coherent way of approaching ethical theory and moral dilemmas,
the task of the teacher is not to promote a special set of values, but only
to promote those sensitivities and analytical skills necessary to help
students reach their own judgments.[38]

More recently, Derek Bok contrasts the applied ethics courses that rose
to prominence in the wake of the social upheavals of the late 1960s with
the old moral philosophy course of the nineteenth century. Whereas the
latter sought primarily to "foster belief in commonly accepted values"
and to "form moral character," the former stresses "think[ing] carefully

about moral issues" and "discuss[ing] practical questions that arise in personal or professional life. . . . The principal aim [in applied ethics courses] is not to impart 'right answers,' but to make students more perceptive in detecting ethical problems when they arise, better acquainted with the best moral thought that has accumulated through the ages, and more equipped to reason about the ethical issues they will face in their own personal and professional lives." But in the typical case, this occurs "without attempting to dictate answers."[39]

Bok recognizes the force of the objection conservative critics lodge against contemporary "mediatorial" ethical instruction—that it *inter alia* tacitly endorses relativism and does more to encourage moral skepticism than moral conviction. While he endorses the common assumption that if the university imposes its values, it violates the spirit of free intellectual inquiry, he acknowledges that a pedagogy of mediation runs a risk of forming students who are sophistical moral reasoners able to argue skillfully any side of an issue without conviction. Yet while Bok is insistent that the university has a profound responsibility to inculcate moral seriousness in its students, he never really addresses conservative critics' concerns about the content of mediatorial applied ethics instruction, other than to express his faith that such courses do in fact make students more tolerant and respectful of others' opinions, and that despite critics' concerns, students will see that moral issues do have "reasonably clear solutions, given basic premises that almost all persons share."[40] However, Bok does not explain how or why he believes this will happen. Left unaddressed are legitimate doubts that students will somehow arrive at "reasonable" solutions simply from their having discussed alternatives, or that a genuinely consensual "solution" will emerge without the distortion or intimidation that can easily occur in such discussions, and without the instructor framing discussion in such a way that students are inadvertently herded into his own positions.

CRITIQUING THE PEDAGOGY OF MEDIATION

Space does not allow for a comprehensive critique of progressive moral education pedagogy, yet I believe its major weaknesses can be made apparent with even a cursory treatment.[41] First, there is good reason to question whether so-called ethical reasoning either can or should be separated from a substantive understanding of the human good and distinct moral limits. If one begins from the premises that the supreme good is avoidance of pain and pursuit of pleasure, whether human or animal, and maximization of these for the greatest number is our highest moral obligation, few can question that Peter Singer is engaging in critical reasoning of the utmost rigor when he infers from utilitarian premises that animal rights must be protected, but that unwanted infants may be killed by their parents, or that Adolf Jost's *The Right to Death*, which argued for the involuntary extermination of the mentally unfit, is "an exercise in cool rationality."[42] A progressive may respond, "Well and good, but this is all we can do, since knowledge of the human good is no longer possible. We may only encourage moral reflection, not specific conclusions." But this is itself a profoundly theoretical claim informing their supposedly neutral pedagogy. It assumes or at least implies that: (1) it is not important to know which of the various theories regarding the human good, if any, is true, (2) the instructor does not believe any of them strongly enough to endorse one, (3) which one a student chooses is a matter of indifference, (4) students already have the resources and wisdom to make moral decisions without knowing the nature of the human good, and thus (5) having a theory of the human good is unnecessary to the moral life.[43]

Even when stark neutrality is abandoned and supposedly generic civic virtues such as *justice*, *fairness*, or *integrity* are allowed into class discussion, without specific elaboration, definition, and defense, these terms will most likely be defined by the instructor's own moral views, or simply deteriorate into meaningless abstractions. It is a commonplace among communitarian and conservative critics of liberalism that the supposed neutrality of secular or liberal definitions of *justice*, *tolerance*, and *neutrality* is anything but.[44]

Typically, these definitions assume an ahistorical, autonomous "unencumbered self" whose commitments, identity, and metaphysical beliefs are mere disposable contingencies, so emphasis upon liberal verities to the exclusion of all others hardly achieves anything resembling a neutral classroom.[45]

To see more clearly what supposedly generic definitions obscure, consider that in medieval natural law theory, the centrality of a substantive understanding of the human good was recognized in the distinction between *synderesis* (the basic knowledge of good and evil, conscience, the application of this knowledge to specific circumstances), *right reason* (the knowledge of the human good), and *prudence* (the ability to apply that knowledge in a wise manner). On this model, if one does not possess right reason, though he may know on some level the basic premises of moral action, his conscience is bound to err in their application. For example, a Mafioso may define the principle of justice, which he knows through synderesis as giving each person his due, as doing harm to one's enemies and good to one's friends, and since a further principle of synderesis tells him that loyalty to family comes before loyalty to the common good, his corrupted conscience will instruct him to engage "courageously" in vigilante justice against rival gang members. For those who believe justice and fairness require the sanctity of human life, freedom of choice and autonomy may be valuable things, but they cannot trump the duty not to kill a helpless fetus. Precisely the opposite will be the case with a rights-oriented, secular liberal: while he may value human life, autonomy and equality imply that a woman has a right to choose whether or not to end an unwanted pregnancy. This is precisely why right reason is so critical: without a rightly ordered understanding of the human good, prudence—the consistent application of the correct moral principle at the appropriate time—is impossible, not because people without it will be nihilists, but because they will inevitably go wrong in the ranking of moral principles. So the assumption that so-called "generic" values, norms, virtues, and critical thinking can be taught without a comprehensive theory begs what was the first question of moral reflection for Plato, Aristotle, Augustine, and Aquinas: What is the good life for man?

Finally, we must ask with Stanley Hauerwas what effect it has on students to imply that they sit in judgment over morality itself, rather than being judged by it. To imply that students have a "choice" as to which theory they select implies that moral norms require the endorsement of the chooser for their validity. Thus they are uncoupled from any sense of the transcendent, the given, that to which one is obligated *independently* of our choosing, which is the very nature of the moral law.[46] This attitude eviscerates the force of these norms.

According to Hauerwas, forgoing the "disciplined discovery of the good" assumed by traditional approaches in favor of an exclusive emphasis upon autonomous choice and dignity produces an ephemeral, vacuous sense of personal identity. Since the self requires a foundation external to itself to define itself, and finally, its connection to others, individual identity itself is undermined. Mere dignity "erode[s] the essential sociality of the human on which any sense of dignity is possible.[47] Furthermore, a Socratic dialectic that focuses exclusively on moral dilemmas and critical reasoning ignores the obvious fact that dialectic for the purpose of building the character necessary for, say, moral courage, can only occur among those who seek virtue, that is, those who have been habituated to at least desire the good. One can, after all, engage in dialectic with nihilists, moral charlatans, and those who simply wish to impress the instructor and fellow students with their verbal and mental acuity (as is often the case in the Socratic dialogues themselves). This is why it is virtually out of the question not to begin the study of ethics with an inquiry into the nature of the human good and what constitutes good character and moral decency, as Aristotle does in his *Nichomachean Ethics*.[48]

THE PROFESSION OF A NORMATIVE ETHICAL THEORY: ELABORATION

To profess a normative ethical theory is to present it as true, to defend it against objections, and to apply it to moral questions. Yet the precise pedagogy of the old-time college presidents cannot be adopted without serious qualification. One problem with their approach, afflicted as it was by an overreliance upon quantitative modes of knowledge, was their reluctance to place their theory in historical context, and to locate moral inquiry within a living tradition. Treating moral philosophy as a deductive science independent of the past is not only a distortion of historical reality and of the nature of moral inquiry, it reinforces the unfortunate myth that we are mere self-constructed social atoms with sufficient resources within ourselves to know and to act on our moral commitments without benefit of community or external authority.

Whether this was ever true of the natural sciences, which is itself doubtful, it has never been the case with moral philosophy, and the application of an ahistorical, individualistic methodology to ethics seriously distorts sound moral reasoning. Moral philosophy therefore requires an overarching historical context, which can be achieved in large part through a chronological survey of texts drawn from the classical, medieval, and modern traditions. Ideally, the requirement should seek to reinforce and strengthen the living traditions of which the students are a part, not to demean or devalue allegiance to them as somehow antithetical to the spirit of inquiry. At the same time, a too-heavy emphasis on locating moral inquiry in "traditions of inquiry" has an inevitable tendency toward relativism—a consequence the many admirers of Alasdair MacIntyre, who to my mind has never fully resolved this problem, would do well to consider. In my own teaching I find it sufficient to profess, as it were, an ethic of natural law and Thomistic-Aristotelian virtue theory within a broad Christian theism. Students are then encouraged to adapt the broader theory to their own theological traditions, as I do with Reformed theology.

What, then, are the benefits of this approach? Among them, one cannot number the expectation that profession of a theory will consistently result in its adoption. The human mind is too multifaceted, and students too diverse and skeptical, to expect this to be the case in every instance. Consequently, the justification for a requirement in moral philosophy is not that students will adopt the instructor's views, regardless of how much the instructor would wish this to occur. The justification is rather that when a moral theory is professed, students learn to view morality as a serious and intellectually legitimate sphere of human inquiry, and thus are far more likely to recognize that there are moral and civic responsibilities that they do in fact have, which is a chief goal of the requirement. Secondly, students will learn something of the nature of sound moral reasoning (*phronesis*) by observing the example set by the instructor as he lays out his position, defends it, and applies it. Third, the profession of a theory endorses the idea that there are indeed answers to moral questions, and that however debatable these may be, inquiry and the application of sound moral reasoning can assist in determining the proper thing to do. In other words, the course will reinforce moral realism and impress upon students that there is a good that overarches all human affairs, regardless of whether they endorse the particulars of their instructor's views.[49]

Furthermore, a primary virtue in teaching is a commitment to what the instructor believes to be true. This entails that if the instructor in moral philosophy takes his subject matter seriously, what he owes to students is first and foremost his considered view of the nature of morality itself and its implications for their lives and their moral commitments. Morality is hardly less important than other fields. If professors are expected to impart what they believe to be knowledge in other fields, why should ethics be any different? As Charles Scriven has written, "intellectual accountability allows, and indeed requires, commitment to a particular point of view."[50]

It is doubtful that there is significantly less consensus in ethics than there is in sociology (pluralists vs. power-elitists vs. Marxists vis-à-vis power distribution), psychology (the behaviorists vs. the psychoanalytic school vs. the self theorists, etc.) economics (the Keynsians vs. the classical theorists), or natural science itself, the paragon of consensual inquiry (punctuated vs. gradual evolution). But even if there were clearly less consensus in regards to morality, this reason alone should not deter the profession of a moral theory. After all, if some degree of consensus on moral issues is possible and desirable through a cogent set of arguments, especially regarding the demands of justice and the achievement of the common good, all else being equal, professors should strive to form that consensus if this is in their power.

Just as importantly, the moral obligation to instruct a person in what is right, or in how to avoid wrongdoing, will in many instances be greater than other goals of teaching. If an instructor is firmly convinced that government-sanctioned racial discrimination in the American South was fundamentally unjust, then the obligation to address lingering racism among his students would be higher, in my view, than any obligation to refine their thinking skills or to nurture their autonomy for participation in democratic institutions. The same is the case if an ethics instructor believes there are ethical teachings that can help students take better control of their lives, transcend their momentary appetites in order to plan better for their futures, and handle life's disappointments with circum-spection and wisdom. If the instructor is able to impart such wisdom in a winsome and convincing manner and so motivate his students to improve their lives, this should take precedence over the development of, for instance, autonomous thought, particularly as without self-control no one can be autonomous in the first place. Yet when all is said and done, the notion that critical thinking and profession of a moral theory are in conflict is simply a false dichotomy. If care is taken to facilitate discussion, to invite criticism from students, to explain and justify one's premises, there is no conflict between encouraging critical thinking and professing moral doctrine.[51]

Another positive reason is that the moral life requires more than higher-level thinking, earnestness, and a briefcase full of concepts. It requires a theory so that students have a foundation to handle the profound complexities of modern life. As William Starr puts it:

> [A] systematic theory allows one to make moral decisions in a consistent manner. It allows one to live a life with moral standards which one can practice over a lifetime. It allows one to be a seriously morally reflective person. In the absence of theory, all ethical decision making becomes situational. There is no systematic way for a person to make moral decisions over a long span of time. This will lead to an ad hoc nonsystematic way of doing ethics which is likely to result in inconsistent moral behavior. From here, it is a short step to ethical relativism . . . and for some, another step to moral cynicism and despair. This is why moral theory is worth teaching. The stakes for university undergraduates are high.[52]

So, provided a professor is confident that his moral beliefs and his approach to moral questions are intellectually sound, his first responsibility is to teach the truth as he sees it; that is, to propound what he regards as true regarding morality and moral controversies. What is owed to students is not intellectual agnosticism and Socratic ignorance, but the opportunity to question and to critique the instructor's viewpoint, and the intellectual freedom to believe contrary to the instructor without concern for negative evaluation.

Failure to espouse one's own point of view can have several negative consequences. First is Starr's worry that students will quite plausibly infer moral skepticism from the constant bombardment of opposing theories, almost all of which have plausible arguments in their favor, yet no one of which is presented as superior to its rivals. Such an approach constitutes a kind of negative profession of moral doctrine, which of course defeats the purpose of supposedly value-neutral pedagogy, aside from running a considerable risk of implying moral relativism and even nihilism.[53]

Second is the issue of unacknowledged bias. Experienced and honest ethics instructors should know that a certain tendentiousness is unavoidable in their presentation of moral issues. The examples one chooses, the themes one raises, and even the moral issues one selects will inevitably reflect one's moral priorities and commitments. The belief that our class discussions can be entirely open-ended and effectively neutral ignores our tendency to steer through emphasis or avoidance, to affirm or to close off options through body language or simply through silence. On the other hand, if an instructor exposes his own view to evaluation and critique by the students, they will be in a far better position to question the assumptions, both spoken and unspoken, that have informed the directions taken in class, and led him to his conclusions.

As an example of the sort of unwitting tendentiousness that can occur when ethics instructors assume what they believe to be a theory-neutral, mediatorial role, C. David Lisman recommends that ethics instruction consist solely of instructor-mediated class discussion of ethical dilemmas and the neutral introduction of various theories and concepts to students. Students should be encouraged to examine the moral concepts they already have "with a view toward attaining a more informed understanding of those concepts or even replacing unquestioned concepts that do not survive critical scrutiny." At the same time, Lisman describes adherence to Divine Command theory on the part of his students as "a problem," and so when a student expresses his commitment to this theory, Lisman says he provides "fairly trenchant criticisms" of it, though he assures students that he is only trying to get them "to stretch a bit," and ends by telling them he is approaching ethics from a "secular basis" so that they can appreciate "that ethics can be founded on non-faith grounds." Elsewhere, Lisman rejects what he calls "religious absolutism" because it "resist[s] an open and reflective approach to discussing ethical issues," and so he lists ethics based upon religious belief in a chapter titled "Counter-Ethical Theories" alongside "ethical egoism," "subjectivism," and "individual ethical relativism." He then goes on to relate in greater detail how he attacks the moral beliefs of what are almost certainly conservative Christians in his classes by employing Bultmann to undermine the inspiration of Scripture, appropriating Plato's *Euthyphro* dilemma to attack Divine Command theory (presumably without discussing the views of Thomas Aquinas, Richard Mouw, or Robert M. Adams in this regard), and even citing the existence of unbelievers as raising difficulties for the epistemic status of religiously based ethics, as if there were universal agreement on any ethical theory.[54]

I suggest that a direct challenge from a professor in a supposedly "neutral" class discussion is more intimidating, and thus far more inhibiting to free inquiry, than a lecture-presentation addressed to all, with openings for questions, where students are free to ask hypothetical, yet critical questions. Moreover, it is disingenuous to portray oneself as neutral, yet in practice discourage a viewpoint that many students are likely to embrace.[55] Far better if secularist instructors would explain to students their reasons for rejecting religious belief as a basis for ethics and open their views and assumptions to criticism from students, rather than assume the posture of a neutral, unbiased mediator.

OBJECTIONS TO A PEDAGOGY OF PROFESSION

If one surveys progressive literature, the most common objections to a pedagogy of profession is that substantive profession amounts to indoctrination, and as such, is opposed to a spirit of open and free inquiry. According to John Holder, indoctrination "sacrifices ethical intelligence for the security of the absolute"; it "robs individuals and society of the possibility of moral growth. Trying to teach ethical values without teaching students how to think, how to creatively engage ethical situations, would be like training a painter with no more than a walking tour of the world's great art galleries." For Holder, a liberal arts education should foster a "community of inquiry" without masters and disciples, where everyone, including the instructor, the students, and the major figures, are fully equal "co-inquirers."[56] Throughout its history, progressive theorists have accused more didactic approaches of indoctrinating students; rarely, however, is their criticism accompanied by a definition of the term. Rather one finds that the typical definition of indoctrination is either assumed in a question-begging manner, or is self-contradictory. In the early 1980s Ruth Macklin concluded that there is no uniform definition of what actually constitutes indoctrination.[57] Observations of this kind have been a continuing embarrassment for those who would wield the charge of indoctrination at anyone whose teaching is more content-oriented than their own.

A prime example of the sort of confusion resulting from systematic attempts to discredit profession of a moral theory as indoctrination can be seen in Robert Hall and John Davis. They reject the profession of moral theory because it constitutes indoctrination, yet they face a serious problem at the outset: how does one define indoctrination in such a way that profession of a substantive moral theory is indoctrination, but profession of, say, quantum mechanics or evolution is not? If one defines indoctrination as having to do with content—teaching something as rationally justified that is not—one would have to provide a clear definition of what is rationally credible, a project they view as philosophically suspect and practically impossible. An alternative holds that indoctrination occurs when the instructor purposefully demands acceptance of his views without allowing opportunity for critique. The problem with this view, according to the authors, is that indoctrination must be intended, so if the instructor does not intend to indoctrinate, by definition, he is not indoctrinating. Furthermore, there is simply too much academic content that is rarely subject to critique, such as the multiplication table, the periodic table of the elements, the conjugation of verbs, etc. Hence on the "intent" interpretation, what is for them unobjectionable content in the standard college curriculum would constitute indoctrination.

In order to impugn the profession of moral theory as indoctrination in the absence of an epistemological justification, Hall and Davis are forced to rely on moral considerations: they maintain that it is simply unjust and unfair to represent a view as true if it lacks "credibility," which they then define as widespread agreement regarding the truth of a theory.[58] And in order to rescue the concept of credibility from epistemology's muddy waters, they bring it to the sparkling sunlight of empirical analysis. Defining *credibility* as "enjoying widespread acceptance in a particular field," indoctrination is essentially "misrepresentation of the credibility of a subject"—that is, making a theory look as if it is the only alternative, when in fact it is not.[59]

Unfortunately, this move does little to solve the problem. First, if they structure their classroom so that no substantive ethical theory is taught for ethical (as opposed to epistemological or pedagogical) reasons, they are violating their own principles by infusing moral values into a supposedly value-neutral classroom. Second, given the widespread penetration of postmodern ideas in most of the disciplines, it would appear that very few theories can now be taught without indoctrination as defined above without lengthy and ultimately distracting discussion of alternatives. Still, the idea that students are being treated unfairly if they are not allowed to consider widely held or serious alternatives is fairly intuitive. This is precisely the sort of plea made by proponents of intelligent design when they ask that their theories be included as part of science instruction. Significantly, however, they do not ask that the instructor somehow suppress his allegiance to mainstream Darwinism, only that intelligent design be presented as an alternative. If indoctrination is avoided when credible alternatives are presented respectfully, this does not exclude the profession of a moral or any other kind of theory.

Following Gerald Paske, Macklin asserts that an instructor indoctrinates when he tries to forge a certain identity in the student with the "doctrine" in question, so that the student responds to threats to the doctrine as if they were threats to his own worthiness.[60] Whatever the merits of such a view, indoctrination should not be confused with inspiration, which is a quality of the finest teaching. When they are not used in the service of evil, exhortation and inspiration are valuable pedagogical instruments, and often necessary in conveying a sense of earnestness to moral questions, which have always required the assistance of moral emotions such as reverence, pity, indignation, and shame. If because of the rhetorical abilities of an instructor a student passionately embraces and identifies with a moral theory, this should not be construed as a violation of the educator's duties to the student.

More serious, however, are cases in which students' reasoning abilities are circumvented or short-circuited in the process. Bernard Rosen defines indoctrination more economically as "when someone attempts to inculcate a view without the intended learner's exercising his or her own reasoning ability."[61] In light of the setting of a college classroom, the instructor has indeed inculcated belief in a theory in an inappropriate manner when he fails also to engage the students' rational faculties. Comparing Rosen's against Macklin's view, we can say that students cannot be victims of indoctrination if their rational faculties have been sufficiently engaged. Indoctrination does not occur when arguable premises are conceded to be such, and alternatives are presented fairly, even when students identify so strongly with the doctrine that attacks upon it can affect their sense of self-worth.

Putting aside the highly relevant question as to whether some forms of indoctrination are always such a bad thing (many moral issues such as overt racism or sexism are never treated as open questions, though historically, there would be numerous, and thus a "credible" number of exponents of such views), perhaps we can make do with a more commonsensical definition of indoctrination. An instructor indoctrinates, and thereby violates his pedagogical duties, when he professes a normative ethical theory to students, yet at the same time:

1. does not introduce plausible or credible (defined as above) alternatives to his own theory where there are such; or—to avoid criticism—intentionally conceals assumptions and questionable premises upon which his conclusions rest;
2. makes adoption of his views part of evaluation; and
3. either forbids class discussion and criticism, or conducts class discussion in such a way that alternative views and objections are not given a fair hearing.[62]

Notice that if I wish to profess a normative ethical theory, I can do this without indoctrinating if I do the opposite of what is described above;

that is, provide alternative views, do not make adoption of my view part of the course evaluation, invite criticism from students, and take care to engage the students' reasoning abilities. In point of fact, Hall and Davis eventually come to a similar conclusion, albeit without recognizing that this would allow room for profession of a moral theory: "*indoctrination can be avoided if equitable consideration is given to existing alternatives.*"[63]

The second part of the standard objection, that profession is inimical to the highest ideals of liberal (free, unfettered) education, is somewhat indirectly espoused in this volume in Warren Nord's excellent contribution. Liberal education should enable students "to think critically about the fundamental beliefs and values that define the commitments of their discipline, school, or tradition." Moreover, character education fails to be genuine education if "it does not raise critical questions about the moral and civic traditions into which it socializes students."[64] It is not entirely clear whether Nord is recommending that, say, a Catholic instructor would provide trenchant criticisms of Catholic moral teaching to his Catholic students without providing a response. But there appears to be a suggestion that to profess a moral theory systematically within a context in which alternatives are shown to be inferior may be inimical to the highest ideals of what he defines as liberal education. Interestingly, Nord also makes a solid case that the recognition of the validity of religiously informed moral theory as a "live option" must be allowed by academic freedom, yet he is not entirely clear as to whether he believes open profession is compatible with liberal education.

So even if we agree that a pedagogy of profession must be allowed by academic freedom, does it stifle free inquiry and intellectual creativity? I suggest the answer to this question must be given historically, and not merely assumed. Nord traces the origins of what he describes as "liberal-free education," which I would categorize cautiously as a pedagogy of mediation, to Socrates and the philosophy of the "high Middle Ages," though he recognizes that its full flowering occurs only with the development of the late nineteenth-century research university. With all due respect, I would suggest that the pedagogy of mediation discussed in this essay has few antecedents in Western educational practice prior to the late nineteenth century, with the debatable exceptions of Socrates and the skeptical tradition, though of course the latter taught skepticism through its pedagogy.[65]

If history tells us anything, however, it is that profession in itself, certainly without the sanctions of physical or material reward and punishment, seems to have little effect on freedom of inquiry. Judging by Plato's espousal of substantive metaphysical and normative doctrine in the *Republic*, despite the example of Socrates' studied profession of ignorance, and Aristotle's critique of Plato's account of the good in book 1 of the *Nichomachean Ethics* after spending eighteen years as his student—not to mention Aristotle's (qualified) rejection of idealism in general—neither profession of a theory or the lack of the same encumbered these erstwhile students' ability to think for themselves. Intellectual history is fairly brimming with such examples: Albertus Magnus's replacement of Platonism with an Aristotelian basis for Christian theology; the failure of the Jesuits at La Fleche to make Descartes an Aristotelian; Herder's rejection of Kant's abstract moral universalism; Gilligan's reformulation of Kohlberg—not to mention the fact that moral philosophy was radically reconceived in the nineteenth century after decades of systematic instruction. These examples demonstrate that profession of a theory does not preclude creative and free inquiry, and in fact may just as easily serve to inspire, if not indeed aggravate it.

It is especially noteworthy that none of the great moral philosophers of the Western tradition—Aristotle, Aquinas, Kant, and Mill—spend time on ethical dilemmas and "help[ing] students develop their capacity to engage in critical thinking about ethical issues" in the *Nichomachean Ethics*, the *Treatise on Law*, the *Foundations of the Metaphysics of Morals*, or *Utilitarianism*, but rather spell out a theory of the human good (or the moral will, in the case of Kant), and defend it against objections. Yet is there serious reason to believe their students and readers were thereby prevented from engaging in critical thinking?[66] The assumption that the profession of a normative ethical theory, if taught in a context avoiding indoctrination as outlined above, is incompatible with the development of critical thinking skills, creative imagination, or intellectual freedom, frankly ignores both Western intellectual history and the common experience of those of us who have bristled and rebelled against our professors' ideas. At a minimum, the claim that theory profession inhibits liberal education must explain why theory profession so often results in innovation and repudiation.

REQUIRING MORAL PHILOSOPHY IN THE STATE UNIVERSITY

May a requirement in moral philosophy wherein a substantive moral theory is propounded be instituted in state universities, given commitments to pluralism, diversity, and academic freedom? It goes without saying that this problem is vastly more acute in a secular or state university than in a private Christian liberal arts college. Yet if higher education needs to recover moral philosophy, this cannot occur only within Christian colleges, whose students constitute a mere one percent of the U.S. student population.[67] Gouinlock rightly warns against "the appalling hazards of establishing an authority who will determine just what morals are to be taught." The immediate consequence will be the "politicization" of the curriculum: "When an itemized list of 'correct' moral positions is to be taught, struggle for political control must follow, and the university as a citadel of honest inquiry and learning collapses." This represents a "descent into barbarism."[68]

Gouinlock's concerns are valid, yet the result of any sober assessment of the present situation is that the academy is already hopelessly politicized, especially through its obsession with the politics of an extremely narrow definition of *diversity*, as anyone outside of it, and certainly those inside it, can readily see.[69] This is due to a simple fact of human nature mentioned before: moral concerns and the expression of moral belief in whatever we do, including teaching and scholarship, are irrepressible. There is no such thing as "value-neutral" education, and there never has been. So the question is not whether someone's morals will be taught, but how and to what extent they will be taught fairly and responsibly, with a generous sampling of alternatives duly represented. If this is the goal, it is obvious that if the state university strives for balance and equal representation, the presence of religiously informed moral belief would have to be significantly increased.[70] For all the reasons cited, the reigning assumptions and attitudes of the contemporary secular state university are almost exclusively hostile to substantive religious belief.

One obvious way of correcting this, and also a good way of challenging the insidious dogmas of naturalism and positivism, would be to have the requirement in moral philosophy staffed with Ph.D.s in religious studies, or by philosophers with backgrounds in theology—that is, with instructors who are both moral realists and who view religious perspectives as capable of generating knowledge claims, and who will either tolerate or openly encourage their students to draw from their religious traditions. Moreover, since moral theories always reflect a social and cultural tradition and broader epistemological and metaphysical commitments, a moral philosophy requirement is the ideal setting in which to stage the agon of worldviews proposed in Alasdair MacIntyre's *Three Rival Versions of Moral Enquiry*. Indeed, without a context in which these debates are made explicit and related to other areas of human inquiry, there is arguably no way in which our cloistered, overly specialized, and self-protective academy might conduct such an argument.[71]

But how could this happen, since the universities are redoubts of postmodern political correctness, Enlightenment liberalism, and secularism? The short answer is that under current circumstances it probably cannot. The longer answer is more optimistic, though certainly ambitious, and it holds the promise of enabling the university to address many of the things discussed in this volume.

Consider that in the typical case, when university presidents are selected, the committee is composed not just of faculty and administrators, but members of the local community. The reasons for this practice are various, but surely one of them is that it reflects the belief that the university is central to the life of the community, and the community should have a voice in the person who is chosen to educate its sons and daughters. I suggest that this should also be the case with the person selected to teach a capstone requirement in moral philosophy. Even if a majority of the student body is not from the local community, it is only fair that the community has a say in what is taught regarding the nature of good and evil to those dwelling within it. The search committee should be composed of a majority of faculty lest the faculty view the person chosen with suspicion and ostracize him (a fate one would wish on no one), and also because the responsibility for academic quality is properly the purview of faculty. However, with the search committee composed in part of members of the community selected by trustees or, if need be, the Board of Regents, this would help insure that the person is not so outside the mainstream that he or she is incapable of respecting regional moral traditions and mores. Nonuniversity people are also perhaps more likely to recognize that *ensuring genuine diversity* means hiring people who think differently, regardless of how they look, not hiring people who look different, but think alike. Granted, the type of people selected in Madison, Wisconsin or Berkeley, California, might differ considerably from the sort of person selected in West Lafayette, Indiana, or Fayetteville, Arkansas, but this may help give otherwise colorless state universities some sort of identity that does not depend upon the success of their athletic programs or their comparative rankings in *US News & World Report.*

To the extent that governors and legislators desire public universities to address the needs of civil society for moral decency and civic responsibility, and to the extent they desire that publicly funded university faculties not neglect the need for solid undergraduate education in favor of building the prestige of graduate and athletic programs, they may be willing to earmark funds or subsidize such positions in moral philosophy for a mere fraction of the millions they spend every year on higher education. Faculty can demonstrate that they are willing to meet the taxpayers' legitimate concerns halfway by adding or carving out a semester-length course in what are typically meager, cafeteria-style general education requirements. Besides, faculty are typically more than happy to expand the ranks if such hires do not directly compete against their own programs, as would be the case here.

I am not suggesting this would be an easy sell either to faculty, administration, or the statehouse. But given the widespread dissatisfaction with directionless, indifferent state universities, and the recognition that moral formation in higher education cannot simply be ignored, it may be time we relearn something the American university forgot barely a century ago: that a capstone experience in moral philosophy is integral to solid undergraduate education in a participatory democracy.

Chapter 4

Pro Ecclesia, Pro Texana

Schooling the Heart in the Heart of Texas

—Stanley Hauerwas

THE CHALLENGE OF THE PRESENT

I believe that we live in dark times. By "we" I mean we Christians. We live in a country that is quite literally out of control. Possessed by power unchecked, Americans think we can do whatever we want to do. After September 11, 2001, moreover, Americans seem ready to do anything to return the world to normalcy. By "normal," Americans mean simply a state of affairs in which they feel safe, something that we are attempting to restore no matter what the cost securing our safety imposes on the rest of the world. The American desire for security, to have our lives protected not only from the reality of death but the recognition that we will die, is clothed in the language of the highest ideals. America does not go to war in its own interest, but to make the world more democratic.[1] Americans believe that we are what anyone anywhere would want to be if they had our money and education. In short, Americans believe that America is the world's first universal society. Americans' most benevolent ideal is that someday the whole world will be America.

I believe we live in dark times. By "we" I mean we Christians. We find ourselves in churches that are hardly distinguishable from Rotary Clubs. The church has accepted her bargain with America, allowing herself to become sequestered into the private. So sequestered, we are not even doing well in the so-called personal side of life. Our churches are torn apart by questions about sexual behavior, while our lives are in fact dominated by greed. Indeed, one of the most disturbing developments in our time is how lust has become a form of greed. So the church in a time of war accepts the devil's bargain and elects to focus our lives on genitalia. As a result, our sexual ethics becomes incoherent because Christians have forgotten that how our lives are formed by singleness and marriage is intelligible only if we remember that the church exists to offer the world an alternative to war.[2]

I believe we live in dark times. By "we" I mean we Christians. In particular I am speaking of Christians who work in universities. If we have learned anything after September 11, 2001, it is that universities have abused their privileged position by doing little more than confirming for our students that the way things are is the way things have to be. September 11 is obviously an event not quickly absorbed or understood. The first response rightly must be one of silence.[3] Yet nowhere has the failure of the university been more apparent than in our inability to provide truthful descriptions for the sorrow that should grip our lives in response to September 11. "We are at war" are not words of appropriate sorrow. They are merely the words necessary to make Americans feel safe in an unsafe world.[4]

If universities are about anything, they are about the careful use of words; but the response to September 11, 2001, surely suggests that the universities of America have failed to form those they graduate to be concerned about word care.[5] Universities that claim to be shaped by Christian convictions seem, like their secular counterparts, not only to have produced students who are unable to recognize when they are serving powers foreign to the gospel but, even more discouraging, students who in fact desire to aid the rule of those powers. That desire, moreover, is only enhanced by what students learn during their time at the university.

My litany is not meant to create despair. I certainly have no interest in making the world darker than it is. I realize some suspect my negative characterizations of American society are overdrawn and my characterizations of the church are too romantic. In effect, I am accused of making the church look good by making American society look bad. I hope that is not the case. If I am guilty of such a strategy, I would certainly be making a theological mistake. After all: for Christians, despair is a sin. Moreover, as apocalyptic people, Christians must not assume that the times in which they happen to live are more dark than other times at which Christians have lived. For Christians to get in the game of "my time is worse than your time" can only be a sign of self-righteousness. Yet the darknesses do differ.

For Christians the discovery of the difference requires attention to that which makes us an apocalyptic people. In his important book, *Paul among the Postliberals: Pauline Theology beyond Christendom and Modernity*, Douglas Harink observes that

> most simply stated, "apocalypse" is shorthand for Jesus Christ. In the New Testament, in particular for Paul, all apocalyptic reflection and hope come to this, that God has acted critically, decisively, and finally for Israel, all the peoples of the earth, and the entire cosmos, in the life, death, resurrection, and the coming again of Jesus, in such a way that God's purpose for Israel, all humanity, and all creation is critically, decisively, and finally disclosed and effected in the history of Jesus Christ.[6]

Harink notes that the language of apocalyptic puts the emphasis on God's action, which means that Christians cannot help but understand our existence as a conflict with enslaving powers from which we have been freed by God's action in Christ. Accordingly Christians believe that what has occurred in Jesus Christ is cosmic, "unsurpassed and unsurpassable," revealing what was previously hidden.[7]

No small set of claims—claims moreover that meant that Christians from the beginning had no choice but to develop a robust intellectual tradition. For, Christians, however, thinking was not a speculative enterprise; rather, as Robert Wilken contends, it always reflected their attempt to understand what had happened in Christ. Accordingly, Christian thought has always been governed by the facts of revelation, by the language and imagery of the Bible, and by how "the life and worship of the Christian community gave Christian thinking a social dimension that was absent from ancient philosophy."[8]

This is but a reminder that Christians did not need the creation of universities to establish a Christian intellectual tradition. Indeed one might well ask that if one of the tasks of the Christian intellectual tradition is to help Christians discern how the darknesses differ, is the university as we know it not more of a hindrance than a help in such an endeavor? That is particularly the case in American universities, whose wealth seems to require us to educate our students to believe that they are the end of history. What alternative did the United States have but to go to war against terrorism? Just to the extent that most students who graduate from the universities of America, whether they be Christian or not, think the answer to that question is "none," we have an indication that the American university, whether the university is Christian or not, serves the state.

The modern university and the modern state are by design mutually supportive projects.[9] For example, consider the legitimating story, a story reaffirmed in numerous disciplines in the university, about the rise of the state. The state—that is, the peculiar institution developed over the last four centuries characterized by a centralized and abstract power exercised through a monopoly over physical coercion within a geographically defined territory—was necessary to end the religious wars of Europe, we are told.[10] The only problem with this story, a story at the heart of most defenses of liberal democracy, is that it is not true. As William Cavanaugh argues in his book *Theopolitical Imagination*, the state as we know it began before the rise of the so-called religious wars. Indeed the states that were aborning at the time of the so-called religious wars found it quite useful to play different religious loyalties off one another in order to concentrate power.[11] The legitimating story the state uses to justify its existence is the same story used to create the thing called "religion" that is now acceptable only if it is kept private.

The state so constituted now replaces the church as the exemplification of universal values.[12] Cavanaugh observes, "The rise of the modern state is marked by the triumph of the universal over the local in the sovereign state's usurpation of power from the Church, the nobility, guilds, clans, and towns."[13] We should not be surprised, therefore, that the sciences become the paradigm of knowledge in the modern university just to the extent that the various sciences characteristic of "higher learning" are able to repress their particular histories. Moreover the results the sciences promise (e.g., "soon we will cure cancer")—results crucial for the support they receive from the state—can be used by the state to satisfy the desires of the populace, something so necessary for the legitimation of state power. The state's support of research to delay death now becomes the necessary condition to sustain the work of the university.

What, you may ask, does this highly contentious diatribe have to do with the schooling of the hearts of our students in the universities of America? At the very least, it should make clear that American higher education is an extraordinarily successful system of moral formation. The loyalty college graduates have toward the state of America is remarkable. Of course I am well aware such loyalty is half-formed before they come to the university; but through the education students receive, their loyalty to America is made unquestioned just to the extent that they learn "to be critical thinkers." Any society that produces "critical thinkers," they are confident, must be superior to those societies that still require conformity. I believe few developments more determinatively confirm this analysis than the popularity of "ethics" in colleges and universities. This is a remark I must now try to explain.

WHY "ETHICS" MALFORMS THE HEART

I begin with a story about the development of ethics at Duke. A North Carolina philanthropist decided that, as one of his last great philanthropic acts, he would give Duke University twenty million dollars to develop a center for ethics. He wanted to do so because he was concerned that our society was losing its "Jewish-Christian" heritage. His trust company told him that to give the university that much money would be a mistake because "all they do is sit around and talk." So a modest three million dollars was given to the university to give us an opportunity to plan and develop the center. When I was told about these developments, I observed that such a center faced two obstacles: namely, that the two most distinguished ethicists at Duke, Alasdair MacIntyre and myself (not that I am in Alasdair's league), did not believe in ethics, and that we certainly did not believe in ethics centers.

Sure enough when they told Alasdair about these developments, the first thing he is alleged to have said is that he was on the side of the trust. Then he asked whether anyone had observed a correlation between those that teach ethics and the quality of their lives. He suggested that if the philanthropist really wanted to do something to enhance the moral character of Duke as a university, he should give the money to address the inequity of pay between those who clean our classrooms and those who teach in the same classrooms. Suffice it to say, his comments did not prevent the center from becoming a reality.

I want to be clear. I am not denying that much good may be done by such centers. I serve on the board of the center at Duke and I admire the people that head it as well as many of the programs that the center develops. I even think some good may come from service learning, but I worry that the down side of such programs is that they encourage undergraduates to believe they should take themselves seriously as moral agents. I assume that the most important lesson undergraduates should be taught is that they are not yet well enough formed to know what they do and do not do nor what they should and should not want.[14]

I am, moreover, extremely sympathetic with those who try to teach ethics to undergraduates. It is not their fault that they find themselves in an impossible position. That position is quite simply that they lack the authority to teach ethics in the manner that any serious teaching of ethics should be taught, that is, with the aim of changing lives. Because they lack the authority to change lives, too often they must teach in one form or another what I call "the standard course in ethics." The standard course begins by helping the students understand the importance of the distinction between meta-ethics and normative ethics. Students are told this is a very important distinction because if they are not able to sustain some account of the status of the right or the good, then relativism is right around the corner and we will all go to hell in a hand basket. After spending six weeks doing metaethics, the students cannot make up their minds whether they will be nonnaturalist about the good or naturalist about the right. They are relieved to learn, however, that whatever metaethical position they think most defensible does not necessarily entail the normative alternative they think most defensible. The normative alternatives are usually identified as teleological or deontological. Basically that means you choose between Mill or Kant. After some weeks of discussing the weaknesses and strengths of these normative positions, most students discover they would like a little of each.

Finally the course begins analysis of cases, which piques the students' interest. So they are asked to imagine what they would do if they are among a group of students exploring a cave. They are on their way out, but the first one exiting the cave turns out to be the largest of the group and gets hopelessly stuck in the entrance. He or she cannot go forward or back. Whether the one stuck is a he or she will provide an opportunity for gender analysis. Suddenly the group notices the water is rising in the cave at an alarming rate. They are all going to drown except fatty, who will only get his butt wet. They search the area that is still dry and discover a stick of dynamite and matches. Do they blow fatty out of the mouth of the cave to allow them to escape? The utilitarians argue "'greatest good for the greatest number' so blow the big one up." The deontologists hold fast to "never do an evil that a good may accrue" and decide it is better to die than to kill fatty. Students love this kind of game because they understand such exercises are no threat to their lives.

Indeed these kinds of ethics courses, and I am willing to acknowledge that some courses may be more substantive, are designed to underwrite the presumption the students have prior to taking such courses. Students assume that ethics names that part of life in which you have to make up your own mind. The kind of course I have described legitimates that assumption by simply giving students names to describe the choices they are going to make anyway. Often such choices are said to be about the fundamental values that should guide our lives, which means students never entertain the thought that the very idea of "values" underwrites the presumption that when it comes to what we care about, it is finally up to us to decide what we "value."

Please note, I am not trying to make anyone who has taught this kind of ethics course feel guilty. What choice do they have in the absence of any background of shared practices sufficient to sustain argument? Yet I think it would be better that such courses not be taught. They should not be taught because such courses hide from ourselves and our students the moral debates we ought to have in America. Alasdair MacIntyre suggests that one of the tasks of the

> moral philosopher is to articulate the convictions of the society in which he or she lives so that these convictions may become available for rational scrutiny. This task is all the more urgent when a variety of conflicting and incompatible beliefs are held within the same community, either by rival groups who differ on key moral questions or by one and the same set of individuals who find within themselves competing moral allegiances.[15]

The ahistorical character of the ethics courses I have just described can be put down to the desire to avoid MacIntyre's understanding of the task of the moral philosopher. It is important to note, moreover, that the abstract character of such ethics courses is not accidental but rather the outworking of the attempt of modern universities to be ahistorical institutions that can serve anyone anywhere. Of course in trying to serve anyone anywhere, it turns out that the universities turn out people educated to be willing agents of the modern state.

Moreover, this is not just a problem for courses in ethics, but for most of the humanities in the modern university. Indeed I think one of the great moral crises confronting the university is the crisis in the humanities. In many ways the challenges represented by postmodernism and multiculturalism could not have come at a worse time. Such challenges only confirm the judgment of our colleagues in the sciences that the work done in the humanities is finally a matter of opinion. Anyone who has served on the Appointment, Promotion, and Tenure Committee of a research university can testify to the difficulty those in the humanities have when we try to explain to our colleagues from the sciences why certain forms of research in the humanities are significant. I shall never forget one of the meetings of the committee at Duke at which a statistician with the best will in the world asked, "What is modernity?" A good question with many good answers, but where do you begin to answer that question if universities now produce highly educated people who have never encountered the notion of modernity prior to serving on the Appointment, Promotion, and Tenure Committee?

I suspect the only difference between courses in ethics and, for example, history is that students assume historians know something the student does not, so they defer to the authority of the historian.[16] So history, as well as the social sciences, seems to have greater veridical status for students because in such courses you gain information otherwise unavailable.[17] That is why history courses are of greater moral significance than courses in ethics for most students in the university. For in history courses students gain the descriptions necessary to assume that the way things happened were inevitable, which means there is no alternative to the way things are. For example, I suspect, even at Baylor students graduate with the presumption that an entity called the United States of America is more important than Texas.

In truth I suspect the best moral training that occurs in the contemporary university is in the sciences. At least in those disciplines the student is educated to acquire habits necessary to participate in ongoing research. I think "negative results are as good as positive results" is an impressive form of moral training. That the highest praise one mathematician can give another mathematician—that the work the other does is "deep"—is a lovely indication of the moral character of mathematics. In like manner, the highest compliment a physicist uses to describe the work of another is that the work is "elegant." I think the aesthetic character of these judgments suggests that the moral formation the sciences require can teach us a great deal about how we should live in other aspects of our lives. The difficulty, of course, is that the very language of "other aspects of our lives" means the disciplinary divisions of the contemporary university reflect as well as contribute to the fragmentary and compartmentalized character of modern life.[18]

Therefore we should not try to school the hearts of our students by teaching ethics as a desperate attempt to supplement what we fear students do not get as part of their general university education. If the hearts of students are not formed by the work they do in all their classes in the university, then teaching ethics will not and cannot be any help and in fact may do much harm. As MacIntyre contends,

> Insofar as education has moral import, it is not in and through the teaching of morality or values or religion or anything else as a separate and additional set of subjects; it is rather that there is a moral import in the whole structure of education, in everything that we teach, and that morality is not primarily about constraints upon how we pursue the various goals which we pursue, it is primarily about the nature of these goals themselves.[19]

PRO ECCLESIA, PRO TEXANA

I am aware that what I have had to say about "the schooling of the heart" has not exactly been an upbeat message. Surely I should have some suggestions to make about how universities like Baylor (which are after all Christian) ought to go about schooling the hearts of their students. I do have some modest suggestions, but before making them I need to express a worry about the language of the "schooled heart." I confess when I first saw the title of the conference I thought the Baptists had finally given up and become Methodist. We Methodists are heart people. Baptists have no hearts at all; instead Baptists have the Bible, which they use as a club to beat one another into submission.

In this respect I am on the side of the Baptists. I am so because I think Jim Burtchaell is right in *The Dying of the Light* to see one of the reasons Protestants were not able to sustain the Christian character of their universities was because they were pietist. I am sure he is right about this, which makes it all the more remarkable that, at least as far as I know, the many reviews and reactions to his book seldom discuss his argument concerning the role of pietism. Of course there were and are many kinds of pietism, but I think Burtchaell rightly identifies the movement's stress on the all-sufficiency of scripture, insistence that the laity should not be subject to the clergy, and elevation of spontaneity as an alternative to liturgy.[20] I think, moreover, that Burtchaell is right to suspect that though pietism seemed to oppose rationalism, in fact the pietist critique of dogmatism, clericalism, legalism, and formalism well prepared the ground for rationalism. Certainly the name Immanuel Kant is enough to suggest that there is something to the connection between pietism and rationalism.

One of the great deficiencies of pietism was the belief that the Christian intellectual tradition could be left behind. No more did Christians need to quarrel about the two natures of Christ. Moreover, pietists often had little use for the church. Christian doctrine as well as an overemphasis on the church, from the perspective of pietism, only leads to conflict, if not religious wars. Of course, pietism did develop an intellectual tradition. It is called Protestant liberalism, which means Protestants became advocates of the universalism that the growth of the modern state found so useful.

Burtchaell argues that pietism in one form or the other was shared by most of the Protestant denominations that founded colleges and universities in America. As a result, these denominations thought

> that religious endeavors on campus should be focused upon the individual life of faith, as distinct from the shared labor of learning. Religion's move to the academic periphery was not so much the work of godless intellectuals as of pious educators who, since the onset of pietism, had seen religion as embodied so uniquely in the personal profession of faith that it could not be seen to have a stake in social learning.[21]

So the Christian character of the college or university was no longer thought to be found in the academic subjects of the university, except possibly the department of religion, but instead "had to live an eccentric existence in chapel, in volunteer service, and in clean living and all-around manhood."[22]

I fear the language of the "schooled heart" can reproduce this understanding of the relation of church and university. Hopefully Baptists are just too mean (and I mean that as a compliment) to make the mistakes the Methodists have made. At least I would hope to save the Baptists from becoming Methodists, though I suspect given the current turmoil in Baptist life that the so-called "Moderates" are well on their way to becoming Methodists. Soon Baptists will find themselves saying, like the Methodist Board of Higher Education, that the religious task of Baptist colleges and universities is to sensitize their students "to intellectual, moral, and value-centered issues . . . to affirm a universal gospel for a universal community."[23] If Baptists are to avoid such drivel, then it becomes all the more important for the church as well as for Baylor that Baptists rediscover that what they believe is unintelligible without the resources of the Christian tradition usually called catholic.

In fact, I think Baylor is wonderfully positioned to school the hearts of her students. Barry Harvey recently reminded me of a comment I made at Baylor several years ago that explains why I think Baylor is well positioned to be a research university in which Christian practice actually makes a difference for what is taught there.[24] I was, I believe, at a conference at the Institute of Church-State Studies. (I should say I have never approved of the Baptist fetish about the separation of church and state. The separation usually means: the state is free to do anything it wants to do and the church should keep its mouth shut.) I was given a cup of coffee with Baylor's shield, and so I discovered Baylor's motto is *Pro Ecclesia, Pro Texana*. I exclaimed, "What a great university. Your life is determined by the only ontological realities that count."

Harvard's original motto was *Veritas: Christo et Ecclesiae*. I do not know when Harvard shortened the motto, but now *Veritas* is quite enough for it. I noted I feared that Baylor might go the way of Harvard.[25] As soon as a university begins to talk about excellence, you can kiss Christianity goodbye. But I noted that if Baylor shortened its motto, you would still be in a better position than Harvard because you would still have "Texana." The attempt to make truth qua truth the purpose of the university results in the failure of those at universities dedicated to the "search for truth" to acknowledge whose truths they serve because they have come to think they serve no one's truth in particular.[26] The questions that are seldom asked at universities (because we do not know how to answer them) are: "What is the university for?" and "Whom does it serve?"

What a wonderful thing it would be if Baylor could say it served Texas. At the very least, such service might offer some resistance to service to the nation state. Of course Baylor must be on guard that it serves the Texas of dust storms and barbed wire because, as Cavanaugh points out, in a world dominated by global markets the local and the particular can be prized because they have now become a novelty and are thus valuable as scarce commodities.[27] Nor am I suggesting that what it means to be a Texan does not require knowledge that is not Texas's knowledge if we are to live well as Texans. Texans will understand better what it means to be Texan after they have read Plato's *Republic*.

In *Goodbye to a River*, a book given me by Kyle Childress, as John Graves makes his way down the Brazos, he observes,

> The provincial who cultivates only his roots is in peril, potato-like, of becoming more root than plant. The man who cuts his roots away and denies that they were ever connected with him withers into half a man. . . . It's not necessary to like being a Texan, or a Midwesterner, or a Jew, or an Andalusian, or a hybrid child of the international rich. It is, I think, necessary to know in that crystal chamber of the mind where one speaks straight to oneself that one is or was that thing, and for any understanding of the human condition it's probably necessary to know a little about what the thing consists of.[28]

I read this passage in Graves as a reminder that Texans are only able to be Texans if we remember that *Pro Ecclesia* precedes *Pro Texana*. The history of Texas, like all the histories of the world, is a bloody history. Such a history cannot and should not be denied, nor should it be forgotten. Such a history threatens to entail further violence, however, if there is not a more determinative community that can acknowledge that the history is ours without trying to justify such violence as necessary. We believe that community is called church, whose practice of forgiveness makes possible the truthful telling of the story of Texas.[29] The Christian story, like the story of Texas, is also a parochial story, the story of a Jew who turned out to be the Son of God. That we believe the One called Jesus is the One who moves the sun and the stars makes the story of Jesus no less parochial.

But we also believe that any university shaped by the story of Christ is also a university that is peopled by those that would rather die than lie.[30] Such people, such parochial people, rightly expect that they should hold themselves, their colleagues, and the students they teach accountable to speak truthfully in the face of the lies that would dominate our lives. Schooled hearts require training by schooled speech, hopefully beautiful speech, that makes possible the exposure of those powers that would have us kill in the name of "universal values."[31]

I believe we live in dark times. By "we" I mean we Christians. But I do not believe that there is nothing we can do. We can take the time God has given us to speak truthfully to one another. Such speech is hard and takes time. Yet Christians believe we have been given all the time in the world to do the work necessary to discover the difference between the false and the true—discoveries as wonderful as why the wings of butterflies are differently colored or why Dante's poetry burns with truth. I believe the university can be and sometimes is one of the institutions of God's time. As Christians who have the privilege of being called to do the work of the university, we must do our work with the confidence and joy that comes from having good work to do. If we do our work with joy, I do not think we will have to think about schooling hearts. Such hearts cannot help but be schooled by the wonderful world opened by learning to see that all that is is God's burning bright creation.

Part II

Christian Resources for Moral Formation in the Academy

Chapter 5

Wisdom, Community, Freedom, Truth

Moral Education and the "Schooled Heart"

—David Lyle Jeffrey

Shema Yisrael, adonai elohenu, adonai echad . . .

You shall love the Lord your God with all your heart, with all your soul, and with all your strength. And these words which I give you today shall be in your heart and you shall teach them diligently to your children, and shall talk of them when you sit in your house, when you walk by the way, when you lie down, and when you rise up.
—Deuteronomy 6:4-7

Suppose it to be true that virtue could not be taught; that no firm principles could be deduced from any exemplar, that all learning was irreparably circumstantial, personalistic, autobiographical. Suppose further that the hard-core relativism of the literary theorists accurately described both an ethical and an epistemological limit, that there is therefore no objective truth to be had from texts, or, for that matter, from other persons. Suppose our ego-centrism really is so thoroughly prophylactic that likewise nothing of the past—no artifact, no record, calculus, or testimony—can achieve for us the status of an authority, or even be received as much more than a mere curiosity. Then in what would acceptable education consist?

In improved techniques, apparently, for the heightening of self-consciousness, for the increase and extension of physical—especially sexual—vigor, and the passive mastery of "useful" mechanical knowledge by sophisticated technical means.

None of these technical innovations, we are regularly assured, has been without its value. But the displacement of *theoria* by *praxis*, of the *logos* in learning by the *techne* in technology, has been more radical in twentieth-century public education than at any previous time in the history of higher education.[1] A consequence of this complex is a corresponding diminishment of concern amongst educationists to set as a goal the development of virtue. In so ardently pursuing various and multiform "values" at the expense of common virtues, individual self-expression at the expense of communal wisdom, private gain at the expense of common profit, is it possible that we have made the phrase *moral education* almost an oxymoron?

No one seriously doubts that even a Christian college or university can entirely evade the necessity of technical training and a certain fashionable cachet in the packaging and marketing of educational products. The academic marketplace is more highly competitive than ever, and professional education, with its predisposition to focus on specific technologies and methods, has grown proportionally as part of the work we do.

On the other hand, when even a Christian college or university finds that money and market-fashion eclipse the historic rationale for a liberal education, then serious questions about the institutional identity, justifiability, and even viability of these institutions are likely to arise. It is no accident that this kind of conversation is taking place in church-related colleges and universities. But in many cases, our institutions have found it commercially easier to imitate the wisdom of the world, if I may be permitted this phrase, than to do the tougher work of invigorating in our curricula something of that wisdom which Scripture tells us is ultimately "from above."

In my title I have identified four educational desiderata, which I take to have been perennially central to moral education in a *Christian* context. All are elsewhere—to say the least—contestable. In the context of a secular education, I suppose that even to conjoin them in this way would be to risk being thought of as belaboring an archaism. Yet each remains foundational to Christian moral education, and because each has a biblical meaning at variance from normative cultural usage, it seems to me that a situated reflection is appropriate.

WISDOM

In the Old Testament, wisdom (*chōkma*) implies an educated discipline of mind coupled with a skillful practical discernment (*binah*) in daily affairs. It involves thus both *theoria* and *praktika*, and is never purely one or the other (Exod 28:3; 31:1-5; Deut 34:9; Prov 1:2-7; Isa 10:3). "Wisdom" concerns all kinds of possible human knowing, up to but not necessarily including the knowledge of divine revelation. As such, the term sometimes becomes idiomatic for those books of moral instruction in the biblical anthology which, taken together, have obtained the designation "wisdom literature": Job, Ecclesiastes, Proverbs, and so on. Proverbs, for example, presents itself explicitly as a manual of moral instruction, offered to the student that he might seek wisdom in a full life, becoming so intimately familiar with wisdom as to be said to be "married" to her (Prov 3:13-18; 4:1-13).

The Venerable Bede, greatest of the early Anglo-Saxon biblical commentators, is representative for Christian tradition in the way in which he insaturates this particular text at the heart of Christian moral education. The proverbial aphorisms are directed, Bede says, toward five representative goals of biblical wisdom-teaching: how to believe rightly, how to live properly, how to perceive others truthfully, how to give sound direction to the intentions of one's own heart and, finally, how to define responsible objectives for teaching others.[2]

It is pertinent to our topic that in biblical Hebrew the seat of wisdom is the heart (*lēb; lēbab*). Thus one applies one's heart to knowledge (*da'at*; Deut 29:4), and to the skills of understanding (*binah*; Prov 2:2; Exod 31:6). To have acquired wisdom is to be "wise-hearted" (*chokma–leb*). Solomon was granted his request for wisdom with the divine words: "See, I have given you a wise and understanding heart" (1 Kgs 3:12; cf. 4:29). In this way, expressions involving the heart signify a range of intellectual processes: to "consider carefully" or to "take seriously" is literally, to "lay to the heart" (Deut 4:39; 1 Kgs 8:47; Eccles 7:2). To pay attention is, literally, "to give the heart" (Prov 23:26; Ezek 4:4); to "take [something] to heart" is still a familiar biblicism in English (Deut 8:5; Prov 8:5; Eccles 1:13, 17); and in the Psalms as well as the New Testament the heart ponders (Ps 4:4; 77:6; Luke 2:14, 51), meditates (Ps 19:14), and is the locus of considered belief (Rom 10:9ff.)—as well as of considered doubt and disbelief (Mark 2:6-8; Luke 5:22; Mark 11:23). The heart, moreover, remembers (Isa 44:19; Deut 30:1), and when something is forgotten, it is said in Hebrew to have been "turned aside from the heart" (Deut 4:9; Ps 31:12). It is no surprise, then, that in the Old Testament it is the heart which acts as the seat of conscience: persistently, into the New Testament, whenever "our hearts condemn us" (1 John 3:20ff.), memory, intellect, and discernment of the will are all involved (1 Sam 25:31; 2 Kgs 22:19). "To learn something by heart," as we say in English, invites and conveys all three aspects of mental discipline.

As we have seen, the Deuteronomic commandment to love God with "heart, soul, and strength" (Deut 6:5-6) similarly privileges the heart. This makes fulsome Hebraic sense. But not so evidently in Greek: when Jesus reiterates this command, focusing it toward the second commandment to "love your neighbor as yourself (Matt 22:37-40), on Matthew's account he substitutes "mind" for "strength." One reason may be that the Greek equivalent for Hebrew "heart" (*lēb*), *kardia*, has other, more purely emotional connotations for its hearers. Something more is needed to indicate intellectual affection as a connective for moral education leading to social action. In Matthew Jesus amends his text from "strength" to "mind," permitting his translation of the great *shema* to bear the full weight of Hebrew "wisdom." Perhaps more deeply than we have registered it, the Great Commandment remains thus a précis of moral education in the Christian tradition.

"Of course!" we might respond: "Who does not remember this teaching?"

Yet memory itself has not for a long time been fashionable in early education, Christian or otherwise. Those who by disciplined training of their memories in youth possess capacious memory are thought by some educational theorists to have an "unfair advantage," as do even those who speak several languages. Tacitly, the drive of American higher education in the late twentieth century has been, in part, to make both attainments—the cultivation of a disciplined memory and the discipline of foreign language acquisition—unnecessary, or even perhaps undesirable. But these two forms of forgetful neglect, I would suggest, have been unwise, and that particularly in respect of moral education. Each of these impulses is antisocial: the one rejects the *socius* or neighbor of the past, the other the *socius* or neighbor of the present. We have not loved these neighbors as ourselves.

The biological inexactitudes of Hebrew "heart" language in respect of the life of the mind are not at all infelicitous from the perspective of education—at least not wherever education has as part of its purpose the nurture of the affections for the sake of building maturity and character. "Thy word have I hid in my heart, that I might not sin against Thee," sang the psalmist (Ps 119:11); the pregnant virgin Mary, considering the revelation vouchsafed to her, "pondered all these things in her heart" (Luke 2:19). The connection between the word taken to heart and the Christian doctrine of the Incarnation is, of course, direct and profoundly far-reaching in its implications.

Like many of my generation, when still a child I memorized both poetry and Bible verses. The discipline of memorization in both cases was one presented as a practice propaedeutic to the acquisition of wisdom. Included in my own childish repertoire (and wisely so, I reckon), were these words attributed to Solomon: "The fear of the Lord is the beginning of wisdom" (Prov 9:10). But I soon learned that the Scriptures in particular abound in such counsel. "The fear of the Lord is the beginning of wisdom," repeats the psalmist, who then adds: "all those who *practice* it have a good understanding" (Ps 111:10). As we have seen, it is this capacity to express knowledge through principle with practical or applied intelligence which is the real hallmark of moral education on the biblical view. Knowledge is Wisdom's servant, and not the other way round. So then, in the commentary of St. Thomas Aquinas it is unsurprising to find that

> a wise man in any branch of knowledge is one who knows the highest cause of that kind of knowledge, and is able to judge of all matters by that cause; and a wise man absolutely is one who knows that cause which is absolutely highest, namely God. Hence, the knowledge of eternal things is called wisdom, while the knowledge of human things is called knowledge.[3]

With or without the benefit of philosophy, the continuity of Christian reflection on this distinction reinforces the point with persistent application to embodied wisdom, or practice of the virtues. Four centuries after Aquinas, John Bunyan in his *Pilgrim's Progress* has his character Faith observe that "[t]here is . . . knowledge and knowledge. Knowledge that resteth in the bare speculation of *things*, and knowledge that is accompanied with the grace of faith and love, which puts a man upon doing even the will of God from the heart."[4]

Yet there has long been some play—even tension—between intellectual abstraction and embodied application in Christian discussions of wisdom. The Renaissance philosopher Descartes, for example, believed that "the sciences as a whole are nothing other than human wisdom."[5] Indeed, following in the wake of Descartes and Francis Bacon, the identification of human wisdom with the sum of scientific knowledge has become more or less the "conventional wisdom" of the secular university.

It is more typical of Christian formulations, on the other hand, to suggest that the intellectual disciplines, each of them, in some manner flow forth from the wisdom of God and best make sense when referred to their ultimate cause.[6] Knowledge of that cause is therefore regarded as indispensable to the pursuit of all other knowledge, and all other knowledge, when rightly referred to him, is an enrichment of that primary knowledge which the Scriptures call wisdom. On this account, wisdom is a *plenum*, a property of the whole person. Speaking of Christ as the incarnate exemplar, St. Anselm of Canterbury will say, he "is the understanding of understanding, the knowledge of knowledge, the wisdom of wisdom, and the truth of truth."[7] It is for this deeper reason, I think, that Augustine expects the Christian scholar to speak "more or less wisely to the extent that he has become more or less proficient in the Holy Scriptures," for he adds, "I do not speak of the man who has read widely and memorized much, but of the man who has well understood and has diligently sought out the sense of the Scriptures."[8] For Augustine, there is a plenary sense in which all of Scripture reveals the mind of God, and it is in this sense that one receives it as the "word" of God made flesh in the incarnation. Moral education in the Christian tradition has always implied a conversation which begins with biblical wisdom—the *totam integrum* of the Scripture as centered upon the person and praxis of Christ—and in the light of this wisdom proceeds to explore the words and works of men.

The great African bishop and teacher of the universal church was among the early Christian writers who identified the wisdom spoken of by the book of Proverbs (especially the personification of wisdom in chapter 8) with the *logos*, the word from the beginning of John's gospel.[9] In its amplitude, Augustine's pedagogical conviction was that one might also approach this discovery from "without" the text, that reason possessed of truth would ultimately reveal the source of *all* wisdom to be Christ, the eternal logos.[10] The best approach would be, however, to combine both methods simultaneously. On Augustine's view, the flow of insight from Scripture to rational inquiry and back again to Scripture gains increments of insight with each sweep of the widening gyre. Thus, he says, the wisdom of Christ in its turn confers a special order and necessary formation for moral discernment, for, unless God's wisdom in Jesus had condescended to adapt himself to our weakness, we could not properly differentiate between the high wisdom of God and the low cunning of men.

Consistently with the Apostle James in his epistle, Augustine encourages the learner to anticipate progressive refinements of understanding as part of the benefit of reading Scripture in community. Greater maturity enables one to distinguish between wisdom which comes "down from above" and that which is "earthly, unspiritual," even "devilish." But it is definitively the wisdom incarnate for us in Jesus—his example—which shows us the way to approach that which we try to understand in the world. He quotes the Apostle James in his summary of the Sermon on the Mount in such a way as to identify spiritual wisdom with moral virtue:

> For where there is envy and selfish ambition, there will also be disorder and wickedness of every kind. But the wisdom from above is

first pure, then peaceable, gentle, willing to yield, full of mercy and
good fruits, without a trace of partiality or hypocrisy (Jas 3:16-17).

One cannot avoid recognizing that these are requisite virtues for the
community in which such wisdom is to be nurtured. But the source of
wisdom by which understanding is to be tested is the community of
interpretation we call the church—that wisdom which is Christ. By
allowing for persistence in our conversation with the exemplar, moral
education in a Christian context will be a perpetually self-correcting
course in intellectual navigation.

And thus, as Augustine puts it, "Although He is our native country, He
made Himself also the Way to that country."[11]

FREEDOM IN COMMUNITY

Moral education in a Christian context is thus intrinsically, even
inescapably, a corporate function. Whereas great knowledge may be
acquired by solitary study, and individualized tutorial mentoring may
further sharpen both wit and skill development, moral education
requires for its proper Christian practicum a wider communal context.

The Latin word *collegium*, from which we get the English word "college," is appropriate to our situated reflection on moral education in several ways. Originally it signified a partnership or a body of associates
engaged in a common enterprise: this could be a guild, a fellowship, or
any kind of civic association. But in the time of the early church it came
especially to apply to Christian religious foundations. The fourteenth-
century English translator of the Bible, John Wyclif, refers to "Christ and
his colage, the Apostles" (1380); this much older idea of an original apostolic college composed of Jesus and his disciples gives rise also to the
name of the college of cardinals in the Roman Church. But the firm connection with Christ's teaching as foundation is definitive for the common
use of "college" to signify, in the earliest days of university history, a society of scholars incorporated within or without a university. Such a college
was dedicated especially to Christ-centered learning—not in the sense
that it was always formally theological, but in the sense that it sought the
radical exemplar of wisdom within whatever sphere of knowledge. The
College of the Sorbonne of the ancient University of Paris and the ancient
colleges of Oxford and Cambridge began in precisely this way. Their
many descendants typically also began, in Cardinal John Henry Newman's words, as a response to the desire of the churches that "their people should be taught a wisdom, safe from the excesses and vagaries of

individuals, embodied in institutions which have stood the trial and received the sanction of the ages."[12]

Newman's sentence admirably captures two of my four perennial desiderata—*freedom* and *community*. Here, in the United States, a large number of denominational colleges from across the Christian spectrum have been founded on similar principles. And though many of these have sadly lost their original identity and been absorbed into the secular public university, their names and mottoes still bear muted testimony to a once lively commitment to apostolic obedience and evangelical witness. A few colleges, let us be grateful for it, have not forgotten their apostolic roots.

The purpose of such colleges is *not* primarily to critique secular university education nor to try somehow to prove its inadequacies. Nor, on the other hand, do we intend to compete with the more pastoral work of Bible schools, convent schools, or seminaries. Rather, we want to offer a type of rich and foundational education which, from the earliest days of the university, has characterized Christian higher learning, and yet to do so in such a way as to fit our graduates to be singularly productive in the life of the church and in their work in the world now. Our desire is for fit training for the "mind and the heart," a rigorous and profitable diet for maturing young minds which want—and can already see that they need—a dimension of richness, integration, and unshyness about pursuing matters of truth and consequence. What is required for this task, as my colleague Stephen Prickett has said, is the construction of a certain quality of mind in a collegial setting.[13] We must be willing to run counter to that drift in higher education which has allowed it, as Ernest Boyer has observed, increasingly to be seen as "a private benefit [rather than] a public good."[14]

To that end our curricula ought, in the view of many of us, to be weighted toward the more generous liberality of foundational disciplines, historically and pedagogically integrated, and grounded, however modestly, in the apostolic faith that gave rise to the first universities and the formation of those disciplines. Further, we think we should endeavor to teach these disciplines by intensive shared reading and direct intellectual engagement in seminar and discussion, not by mass lectures or lectures on video-tape such as invite the student to be a passive consumer of "educational products." Our librarians, chaplains, visiting faculty, and artists-in-residence should all be invited to take up their part in keeping the spiritual priorities of our learning together before us by active engagement in community conversation. We believe we must resist the commodification of education by refusing to treat our students as clients, but welcoming them rather as neighbors and collaborators, members with us in what the Christians of an earlier age were pleased to call an *enkuklios paideia*, a circle or community of learning in which professors are an integral and self-correcting part of the student body—in that they, too, continue to learn. Inasmuch as is possible we should be reading together from the works of the great thinkers of the ages, considering their scientific discoveries, learning to understand the complex beauty of their paintings and singing their music of praise to God until these things become, in the end, our own, "taken to heart" as we say—or as we might equally say, until they become fit furniture for the habitation of lively minds.

If, on many campuses, the intellectual and spiritual fare is not always so communally rich as that which we attempt, that too can be at least a passing subject for our thoughtful reflection. Perhaps we can, with sympathy—and as a warning to ourselves—try to imagine why it is that universities and colleges once founded upon principles like our own departed from them so far as to be thoroughly opposed not only to Christ and the church, but in some cases opposed even to cultural remembrance of their own historic witness to Christ and, at last, to the very idea of communal learning in search of universal or self-transcending truths. For the sake of an accountable moral education, I would argue, far too much of the actual history and practice of our predecessors has been "turned aside from the hearts" of our colleagues and students alike.

One must have a certain sympathy for the desire of late twentieth-century educators in particular to be "free" from the burdens of the past. But for such a preoccupation with "freedom from" our connectedness to others, one always pays a price. Freedom has become for our culture a debased term, and in its debased assertion, a contradiction, in many cases, of community. Contemporary notions of Christian freedom can too easily reflect the modern secular connotation of autonomy and license instead of the biblical idea which is their contrary rather than their source. As late as the Reformation, the word *freedom* signified something much more like "liberty of spirit" than "independence from others," or being *auto-nomos*—a law unto the self. In bilingual dictionaries of that earlier period, for example, English *freedom* was glossed by the French word *largesse*, or generosity. That is, while in contemporary secular parlance freedom typically implies self-directedness, with little if any sense of corporate responsibility, the older word typically implied other-directedness, a certain generosity. This older notion, perhaps unsurprisingly, is a much better translation of the biblical notion: even where liberation from bondage is intended in Scripture, the context is one of relationship to God and to others (e.g., Exod 20:1-2). When Jesus famously said, "you shall know the truth and the truth shall make you free" (John 8:32), we may rest assured that he did not mean "independent" or "autonomous." When the Apostle James spoke likewise of the "perfect law of liberty" (Jas 1:25; 2:12) it was as a condition ideally suited to "visiting orphans and widows in their trouble," and to keeping oneself "pure and unspotted from the world" (1:27).

From the point of view of the biblical writers then, and of those who still choose to give them credence, *other-directed freedom* is an indispensable condition of a moral education. We should acknowledge that non-Christian writers of antiquity have contributed powerfully to this understanding. Seneca, for example, like Aristotle before him, located this kind of generous freedom in the meaning of *liberal studies* itself, even as he insisted that "there is really only one liberal study that deserves the name—because it makes a person free—and that is the pursuit of wisdom."[15] Yet for freedom to be generous, we must be taught its self-transcending moral cadences. That, too, is a function of wisdom.

Augustine, who so magnificently championed the pursuit of knowledge for the sake of Christ's kingdom, warned that in order for one to

> arrive at some useful knowledge and regulate his life and morals according to that knowledge . . . he has need of divine guidance, which he may obey with confidence, and of divine aid, so that he may obey it freely. Otherwise, in his zeal for knowledge, he may fall into some deadly error because of the infirmity of the human mind.

Freedom itself, Augustine representatively thought, depends upon the perdurability of authority, of objective Truth.[16]

On this view one of the most productive things we can do to keep from being conformed to the bondage of this world—to preserve a generous liberality—is to walk away from any merely licentious notion of freedom. If from that selfish individualism we are to be, as the apostle urges, transformed by the renewing of our minds, it will be precisely so that we "discern what is the will of God—what is good and acceptable and perfect" (Rom 12:2). For those of us who call ourselves "Christian," a key measure of our acquisition of Christian wisdom will be that we ourselves understand how to "freely obey" our sovereign Lord, and accordingly to be self-effacing among our colleagues as we practice this freedom together.

TRUTH

It is important for the sake of truthfulness, and thus for health in our own perspective, that we see that the impulses which oppose witness to Christ today are not at all a peculiar feature of either modern or postmodern culture. More than a century-and-a-half before Jesus was born, the Roman slave and playwright, Terence, alluded to the anarchic and subjectivist character of human nature when he wrote (more succinctly than I can match in translation) *Quot homines, tot sententiae*—there are as many notions of wisdom as there are people with opinions. Or, as the book of Proverbs has it, centuries earlier, "Every way of a man is right in his own eyes" (Prov 21:2; cf. 16:2). True, the biblical wisdom writer adds, as the cynical Terence does not, a stiff corollary: "Every way of a man is right in his own eyes, but the Lord pondereth the hearts." That is, for the biblical writer there is a perspective of extrapersonal truth which judges mere opinion—even searches beneath it right down to motive. On the biblical view we are therefore self-deceived when we pretend to be relativists.

But the Roman poet still has something irrefragable to contribute. He knew how much even the suggestion of possibly objective truth can infuriate those whose central motive, even in what they call the pursuit of knowledge, is actually self-justification. *Veritas otium parit*, observes Terence, "Truth engenders hatred."

If it is a reflex of self-interest to deny that there is a universal fact which might oblige us to the interest of others, denial can become vehement when we confront a wisdom which suggests that we cannot be, in Kant's or Nietzsche's or anyone else's sense, our own creators. Few cultures, perhaps not even that of imperial Rome, have outdone ours in our glorification of the "self-made" man or woman—our pursuit of self-interest at the expense of all other interests.

In his *Christian Critique of the University*, Charles Habib Malik reminds us that as important as what is taught in secular universities is what is *presupposed* by them, "because what is presupposed is often far more subtle and potent than what is explicitly taught; what you are silent about will pass as something so much taken for granted that you do not need to say a word about it; while what you explicitly put forward may be arguable." Therefore, he sagely adds, "seek first what the university is silent about, and then you know the secret of the university."[17]

Well, let us think about this for a moment. It used to be, during the middle decades of the twentieth century, that the public university was silent about its post-Christian presupposition that there was no such thing as what used to be called "objective" truth. Now it is no longer silent on this point, because justifying and providing for relativistic lifestyles—"personal freedom"—has become finally a more pressing therapeutic concern than mollifying the mathematicians and hard scientists, most of whose work depends upon some working postulate of "objective" truth (or extramental reality). But there remains another related and possibly deeper silence in the university that has not been rhetorically justified. This is because, for the very institutional survival of publicly funded universities, it probably cannot be. I refer to the cherished modern idea that higher education would solve most of our social problems, that the right sort of "liberated" and thus morally neutral education would usher in utopia.

One of the chief apostles of this view, a man once widely celebrated in the university for his educational philosophy and perhaps especially for his book, *Why I am Not a Christian* (1957), was Lord Bertrand Russell. Now Russell advocated for and against many issues on which we might agree with him. But within his confidence in the sufficiently salvific power of utilitarian knowledge, there is an educational messianism finally corrosive of moral education as we have been considering it. Here is one example: in his *Education and the Good Life* (1926), Russell argued that

> [a] community of men and women possessing vitality, courage, sen-
> sitiveness, and intelligence, in the highest degree that education can
> produce, would be very different from anything that has hitherto
> existed. Very few people would be unhappy. The main causes of
> unhappiness at present are: ill health, poverty, and an unsatisfying
> sex life. All of these would become very rare. Good health could be
> almost universal and even old age could be postponed. Poverty, since
> the industrial revolution, is only due to collective stupidity.[18]

Russell's cure for sexual dissatisfaction I forebear to quote, but it will suffice for you to know that it has had many less philosophical proponents.

Russell's optimistic antirealism has become a humanist credo for many in the post-Christian university, a credo upon which many have based their curricula, written their books, and staked their institutional futures. But in the intervening years, despite a twentyfold increase in the percentage of our young people being given more or less the kind of education Russell envisioned, it has not, of course, turned out to be the case that "very few people" are unhappy. Sexual liberation has created its own dystopia, the gap between the rich and poor widens worldwide, and in the richest culture the world has ever seen, most of the resources of medical advance go into trying to control (or mask) the wages of sin, which is still death. And never has there been less empirical evidence to suggest that education qua education, even amongst those vital, sensitive, and intelligent "in the highest degree that education can produce," has produced adequate resistance to the degradation of human freedom, community, and the will to discover self-transcending truth.

Arguably the best-educated generation in the history of the modern world was that which came to maturity in Germany during the Third Reich. Yet these "intellectuals" could march men, women, and children into gas chambers and ovens and within hours attend concerts with music by Mozart and Brahms. Afterward they could discuss Goethe and Nietzsche with a critical competence that many a professor might envy. They were fully attuned to the "will to power," but they had a correspondingly diminished will to truth. Nor has it been noted of late that Rhodes scholarships or higher degrees from Oxford, Harvard, Yale, or Cambridge have not prevented political leaders in our generation from approaching almost surreal levels of ignominy and disgrace. That there is little value in analytical intelligence without the cultivation of moral intelligence may be perfectly apparent to the cobbler, the bus driver, or the Iowa farmer in his combine bumping along in the frosty night.[19] But it has not been socially acceptable to say so, at least officially, among the disciples of Bertrand Russell, or by those whose heavy burden includes maintaining his myths in the public university. That is, there continue to be some crucial evidential truths about which public education continues to be largely silent.[20]

We, who have set out to build on a different foundation, ought not to look on this wobbly edifice so much in judgment as in compassion, and with much self-scrutiny lest we also should be tempted by whatever gradualism to forget the most basic lessons of educational history. At the risk of appearing to speak indelicately, let me offer, on the basis of this history, an imperative hypothesis for moral educators: we all need a Truth which is bigger than ourselves.

In Shakespeare's comic play, *As You Like It*, the witty character named Touchstone echoes both Socrates and St. Paul when he says, "The fool doth think he is wise, but the wise man knows himself to be a fool" (5.1.34). Touchstone should be our touchstone too, for in his own way he also points us to the Rock. As we pursue truth we, of all people, need most to remember, with the faithful of all ages, the wise counsel of Scripture, that it is folly to "claim to be wiser than we are" (Rom 12:16), to be, even for a moment, "wise in our own eyes" (Prov 3:7).

After many years of reflection and practice, I have come to think that Augustine was surely right about another of his "incarnational" analogies; namely, that for moral education to be efficacious, the teacher himself/herself must be a "touchstone," a vital exemplar.[21] Few today really want this accountability, which is, I suppose, why the apostles thought that few among us should be teachers (Jas 3:1; cf. Rom 2:21). But where a sense of calling is confirmed as authentic, it is yet one more instance in which those virtues, which are our goal, are indispensably also the means by which we attain the goal.

Who is not inspired, and yet also admonished, by the stirring passage in Thomas Hughes's *Tom Brown's Schooldays* in which Hughes describes the effect of Thomas Arnold's intellectually rich sermons upon his students:

> [Arnold] stood there Sunday after Sunday, witnessing and pleading for his Lord, the King of Righteousness and love and glory, with

whose spirit he was filled, and in whose power he spoke. . . . There always were boys scattered up and down the School, who in heart and head were worthy to hear and able to carry away the deepest and wisest words there spoken. But these were a minority always. . . . What was it that moved and held us, the rest of the three hundred reckless, childish boys? . . . We couldn't enter into half that we heard: we hadn't the knowledge of our own hearts and the knowledge of one another; and little enough of the faith, hope and love needed to that end. But we listened, as all boys in their better moods will listen (aye, and men too for the matter of that), to a man who we felt to be, with all his heart and soul and strength, striving against whatsoever was mean and unmanly and unrighteous in our little world. It was not the cold clear voice of one giving advice and warning from serene heights to those who were struggling and sinning below, but the warm living voice of one who was fighting for us and by our sides, and calling on us to help him and ourselves and one another. And so, wearily and little by little, but surely and steadily on the whole, was brought home to the young boy, for the first time, the meaning of his life; that it was no fool's or sluggard's paradise into which he had wandered by chance, but a battle-field ordained from of old, where there are no spectators, but the youngest must take his side, and the stakes are life and death.[22]

Hughes's account and, we may expect, Arnold's sermons, were each a living reification of the Deuteronomic *shema*. (It is a sobering reflection that Arnold's own son Matthew, the literary critic, apparently had not quite the ears to hear it.)

CONCLUSION

It is my growing conviction that to do the work of moral education in the Christian university accountably we will need to recover the sources of antique as well as modern wisdom, the wisdom of others as well as that which makes us "seem wise in our own eyes." As one who is trying to take the Christian revelation and tradition seriously, I believe that we must learn to love "with heart, soul, and mind" both God and our neighbor, whether the *socius* of the past or the *socius* of other cultures, and that no learning that neglects either of these can be meaningfully moral. These loves will require the twinned disciplines of a trained memory and linguistic self-transcendence, and by these means a significant widening of the circle of those we are pleased to call "neighbor." Students who learn alongside us—not merely in front of us—will, in apprenticing to these disciplines of the schooled heart, experience thus something much more of the true meaning of their freedom and grow deeper in wisdom, truth, and love. Moreover, if we do our part wisely, what they will have learned they will be able to pass on, because they will know it "by heart." But if acquisition of wisdom, a deeper knowledge of freedom in community, and the love of truth are to be the goal of our moral education, their deep and principled practice must also, if I may paraphrase Augustine once more, become the means by which we reach our goal. We, who are teachers, must "freely obey," in a fully thoughtful yet vigorously practical way, the Great Commandment. We are the ones who must now, with all urgency, take these things to heart—if in the end mind itself is to matter.

Chapter 6

Tracking the Toxins of *Acedia*

Reenvisioning Moral Education

—Paul J. Wadell and Darin H. Davis

Charles Taylor's influential little book, *The Ethics of Authenticity*, describes how modernity's peculiar twist on the notion of authenticity has led people to deny their connection to something or someone that transcends them—what Taylor calls the inescapable horizons of significance.[1] In particular, Taylor expresses worry about the dark side of individualism: though individual liberty is an undeniably great achievement, people have privileged the self over family, civic and religious community, and the common good. People who misunderstand authenticity, and thus pursue a debased form of the ideal, live lives that are flatter and poorer in worth precisely because they fail to realize that something independent of the self provides the background of intelligibility that gives the self its meaning. One's identity—indeed, the very significance of one's life—is defined in relation to someone or something other than self.

Taylor's explanation of how the modern self became dislocated from its horizons of significance has resonated with many, but whereas Taylor focuses on a certain conceptual confusion about the notion of authenticity to explain the malaises of modernity, we explain the disconnected modern self by pointing to a pervasive vice in contemporary culture—

acedia—traditionally classified as one of the seven deadly sins.[2] Thus, in what follows we first explore the nature of *acedia* and what in the culture both exhibits it and encourages it. We contend that *acedia* naturally accompanies the enervating individualism Taylor rightly deplores and, more seriously, that the young increasingly succumb to it. Second, we offer a possible way for confronting and overcoming the problem of *acedia* within the context of higher education by suggesting that *vocation* become a central theme in the moral education of students. More specifically, we argue that the fundamental vocation of every human being is to respond to the call of goodness, a call that requires one to seek and be engaged with a purpose greater than one's self and, ultimately, with God. It is only by seeking excellence in goodness—and for Christians, in holiness—that genuine authenticity is achieved. But such authenticity is both difficult to accomplish and fragile because it requires the transformation of one's most deeply entrenched attitudes and desires and the development of new habits conducive to human well-being. Thus, precisely because answering the call to goodness is challenging and difficult, one's moral development is imperiled without acquiring the skills that only the virtues can provide.

Although the virtues needed are many, three strike us as particularly important: hope, courage, and perseverance. We examine the nature of these virtues and why they are indispensable for the moral life before closing with a modest proposal about how moral education in universities and colleges might be reconceived along these lines.

THE TOXIC POWER OF *ACEDIA*

According to Aquinas, *acedia* is more than straightforward sloth or lethargy.[3] For him, *acedia* describes an expansive indifference toward moral and spiritual excellence due to the conviction that such excellence either does not matter or, even if it does, cannot possibly be attained. In the first case, *acedia* captures the person for whom moral and spiritual excellence hold little appeal; such a person, Aquinas says, has "lost a taste" for spiritual things.[4] Goodness no longer attracts him because, compared to other possible pleasures, it has little significance; indeed goodness may disgust him because pursuing it would demand renouncing the pleasures he has come to desire.

In the second case, however, people succumb to *acedia* not out of disgust for the good, but because they believe that moral and spiritual excellence, however admirable, is impossibly beyond them. For these people *acedia* is a paralyzing spirit of dejection that robs them of hope, a toxic, diffusive sadness that gives rise to despair. The dejection they suffer is so pervasive and so oppressive that they lose all aspirations for excellence, lowering their sights to lesser goods and purposes.[5] *Acedia* characterizes persons who move through life engaged by nothing hopeful or worthwhile because they have come to believe such goods, no matter how alluring, are beyond a human being's grasp. They focus their lives not on "lofty and joyous things,"[6] such as goodness, service, holiness, or friendship with God; but on trivial distractions that not only corrupt, but will eventually make them oblivious to the hope they have lost. As Aquinas summarizes, "To look upon some worthwhile good as impossible to achieve, whether alone or with the help of others, stems from extreme depression, which sometimes can dominate someone's affections to the point where he begins to think that he can never again be given aspirations toward the good."[7] This "lowering of one's sights" away from aspirations toward the good, whether out of disgust of the good or despair of achieving it, is the essence of *acedia*.

One literary treatment of *acedia* is given in Walker Percy's *The Moviegoer*, a novel that is prefaced with this quote from Kierkegaard's *The Sickness Unto Death*: ". . . the specific character of despair is precisely this: it is unaware of being despair."[8] Through Binx Bolling, the novel's central character, Percy probes Kierkegaard's insight. About to celebrate his thirtieth birthday, Binx has little sense of what to do with his life, but his uncertainty hardly troubles him.

"For years now I have had no friends. I spend my entire time working, making money, going to movies and seeking the company of women."[9] Working, making money, going to movies, and seeking the company of women are all good things; but Binx invests himself in them precisely because he has no idea that life might involve something more, something better, something ultimately all-encompassing. He is, as Paul Elie writes, "an admirable nihilist, whose main virtue is integrity—a refusal to believe what others believe just because they believe it."[10] Binx's life moves from one activity, one distraction, one titillating triviality to the next. The "realist" settles for less, renounces great hopes and grand ambitions, because there is no surpassing good and no remarkable promise to be had. "Life goes on and on we go, spinning along the coast in a violet light, past Howard Johnson's and the motels and the children's carnival," Binx explains to his secretary. "It is not such a bad thing to settle for the Little Way, not the big search for the big happiness but the sad little happiness of drinks and kisses, a good little car and a warm deep thigh."[11] Binx recognizes the emptiness and meaninglessness of life in ways others do not. He sees the artificial, contrived, and manipulated quality of everyday life and recognizes how contemporary society alienates us from one another as well as ourselves.[12] But his knowledge hardly matters because it offers him no way out of the malaise that suffocates hope in him and everyone else.

THE PERVASIVENESS OF *ACEDIA* IN OUR CULTURE

Binx Bolling is no exception, for there is no shortage of people in contemporary culture for whom life is little more than a series of entertaining distractions and novelties. But might this seemingly unquenchable thirst for the new and the different, as Kierkegaard and Percy suggest, mask a deeper, albeit unconscious, despair? *Acedia* is a dejection of soul—a moral and spiritual torpor—that leads to the trivialization of oneself and one's relation to others. Consider the recent proliferation of "reality" television. Though some of these programs seem silly and harmless, certainly something seems amiss when people agree to choose their partners in marriage based upon the results of a viewers' poll; or when couples in supposedly committed relationships venture to "Temptation Island" to be seduced by attractive, unattached members of the opposite sex. *Acedia* abounds when the story lines of such programs continually push the envelope with more outrageous behavior; but *acedia* rules when the once sacred (marriage vows, respect for persons, fundamental human dignity) becomes a trivial source of distraction. Have the creators of these programs, those who view them and those who profit from them, embraced the nihilism Kierkegaard and Percy rightly feared? Do they fear boredom more than meaninglessness because they long ago concluded there was no meaning, no purpose to be had? Those who exhibit *acedia* are committed to distracting themselves through the rest of their lives because there is nothing beyond a cascade of distractions to, if only momentarily, enliven them. *Acedia* dominates because anything truly magnanimous seems not only out of reach, but unthinkable.

The young, including the students we teach, are no strangers to *acedia*. This may seem surprising since young people normally exhibit a natural sense of wonder and joy at life, and deep hope about life's possibilities. But the world adults have created and bequeathed to the young has in many ways stifled their wonder and silenced their hope. Students may begin their educational journey seeking something better, something truly magnanimous, but along the way disenchantment and disillusionment settle in because they have taken to heart society's message that economic success and social acceptance matter more than moral and spiritual excellence.

Students are malleable and impressionable, quickly absorbing and taking on the form of what is handed on to them. That their magnanimity is replaced by *acedia*, their idealism by expedience, reflects not an inevitable adjustment to reality, but the unfortunate transformation suffered by those who are taught to aim for nothing more than "comfortable survival."[13] One of our own students recently remarked on a course evaluation that while the course material was mildly interesting (surely not a ringing endorsement), "I just want to live my life and not waste it questioning everything." Like this student, there are many others who, by the time they reach the college classroom, have wholly imbibed the casual nihilism and calculated indifference characteristic of *acedia*. The problem is not that they seek job security, professional certification, and economic survival, but that they often seek nothing more. Like the adults who have formed them, these students, armed with cell phones and iPods and X-Boxes in their dorm rooms, "float on an ocean of pleasant distraction."[14] Thus, while the young are in some ways quite connected to the world around them, many are unplugged, at least morally and spiritually speaking.

Brian Mahan offers a compelling example of how *acedia* has invaded students' thinking.[15] He tells the story of Pam, a college senior who, after much struggle and uncertainty, turned down acceptance to Yale Law School for service in the Peace Corps. Mahan shares Pam's decision with his students, asking them to evaluate her choice: Yale Law School or the Peace Corps? What should Pam have done? What would they do? At first, the students' responses shined with the individualism and relativism that dominates our society. "Well, if that's what she wants . . . you know . . . why not? Who's to say what's the best thing for somebody else?" they opined. As one student summarized, "Well, I'd probably have gone to Yale. I'd like that. But it's fine that Pam chose the Peace Corps. More power to her."[16] Mahan's students were baffled that he even raised the question. In a society where freedom of choice has become the sovereign, indisputable good, why ask what path anyone should choose? Why examine motives if everything is arbitrated through the lens of personal preference?

But as the discussion moved on, "the polite veneer of nonjudgmental acceptance" faded and a tone of cynical suspicion prevailed.[17] Students who at first were reluctant to judge anyone's choices became harshly dismissive of Pam's. It seemed incredible to them that anyone would choose the Peace Corps over Yale Law School, and once unassailable motives had to be deconstructed and exposed. Some concluded that Pam chose the Peace Corps not out of a desire to serve others, but because she was afraid to go to Yale. The Peace Corps would allow her to feel superior to those she served, but the tough, competitive atmosphere of Yale might reveal that Pam was not as bright as she thought. By going to the Peace Corps, the students reasoned, she could maintain the honor and prestige of having been accepted at Yale without being tried and tested by actually going there.[18] Many wondered if Pam had lied to Mahan about her acceptance into Yale Law School. She must have lied, they concluded, because anyone who had been accepted surely would have gone there.[19]

In reflecting on this discussion, Mahan concludes that the students' responses revealed how deeply they had "assimilated our culture's scripted expectations for success and failure."[20] Instead of praising and being inspired by Pam's decision, they found it incredulous because of their belief that it is dangerously naïve to choose a life of dedicated service over one of calculated self-interest and economic success. But Pam's choice also troubled them because she saw and responded to something more costly, something dramatically more challenging, but perhaps ultimately more hopeful. Her decision to forgo Yale for the Peace Corps was unsettling for Mahan's students because she showed there was another way to go about life, a path to follow that was defined not by desires for pleasure, self-interest, power, or wealth, but by compassionate service on behalf of others. Pam showed that the way out of *acedia* is through *magnanimity*, a way of life that helps one aspire "to things that are great simply and absolutely."[21]

To help students aspire "to things that are great simply and absolutely" ought to be the primary aim of moral education, but that teachers frequently do not attempt to help students aspire to great things reveals that the moral and spiritual dejection of soul that is the handiwork of *acedia* runs rampant in the academy. Brian Hook and Rusty Reno echo this assessment when they write that "our age is allergic to heroic ambition and inured to the attractions of excellence."[22] We see this verified when we ask students in our own classes questions about the justification of their moral views or the reasonableness of belief in God. Frequently students respond with the all-too-familiar line, "Who's to say? It's just a matter of opinion." Though such responses may reveal a rather unsophisticated form of relativism at work, more often than not they bespeak a deeper and more dangerous indifference about questions that traditionally have been regarded as ultimately important for life. If this is so, the greatest challenge is not, as is often alleged, to rescue students from the incoherence of relativism, or conversely, their dogmatic slumber. The real test, revealed through the torpor of *acedia*, is convincing them that these questions matter at all, and that a life that fails to wrestle with them is morally and spiritually impoverished. Though wanting in coherence, at least the passionate relativist is engaged; though lacking the intellectual virtue of humility, the dogmatist is at least committed. Those who suffer from *acedia* are neither.

THE CAUSES OF *ACEDIA*

How can the affliction of *acedia* be explained? What accounts for the dwindling belief in the supremacy of a magnanimous life? Why are we reluctant to judge one way of life better than another? Why do ambitions for excellence trouble us? Hook and Reno suggest three reasons. The first is an "egalitarian piety" that is dismissive of excellence.[23] In this milieu, a person's desires, needs, choices, and beliefs are beyond judgment. What matters is not whether those desires and needs are worthy, those choices good or those beliefs true; rather, all that matters is that they are one's own. Personal identity and authenticity are secured not through a way of life capable of making one wise, honest, and good, but through self-expression, even though how we choose to express ourselves may change everyday. What matters is that we are "true to ourselves," no matter how vapid and fluid our sense of self might be. "Our lives are vindicated by our choices," Hook and Reno explain, "and in the grip of egalitarian piety, we clear away invidious distinctions and objective standards that might impede self-expression. . . . Existence itself becomes heroic."[24]

In an atmosphere of egalitarian piety, the only way to fail is to be inauthentic. But this is virtually impossible because authenticity comes not by following a normative ideal or submitting one's life to a moral or religious exemplar. No, authenticity is inherently self-bestowed because it consists in nothing more than following one's own truth and honoring one's own experience.[25] It is unthinkable that one's truth might be little more than fantasy or one's experience impoverished, much less morally dangerous. After all, there is no higher truth by which all truths must be judged and no accounts of human excellence that might reveal some experiences to be shallow and foolish. This is the harvest of *acedia*, a collapse into a relativism and individualism so encompassing that few stop to consider the absurdity and despair to which they lead us. If there is nothing more than "one's own truth" and no meaning to be found in any experience other than the stultifying realization that it is one's own, nothing finally matters. As Hook and Reno observe, "the demands of egalitarian piety force a renunciation of surpassing excellence. The horizon of heroism must be domesticated and the range of achievement constrained so that all might think themselves worthy, actually or potentially, of the palm of victory."[26] But with no notion of excellence, no account of a truly worthy and admirable life, what is there to achieve? And what could it possibly mean to "win" at such a life?

For Hook and Reno, a second explanation for the loss of aspirations for excellence (and for us an explanation for the pervasiveness of *acedia*) is a cynical suspicion that results in widespread distrust of and disenchantment with anything that is noble, heroic, or magnanimous.

When cynicism conquers, motives that at first appear to be purely benevolent are unmasked to reveal a calculating self-interest. Lives that seem dedicated to serving others are exposed as reinforcing structures of domination and oppression. If cynicism prevails, every saint is a stooge, every hero a rascal in disguise. Nothing good, nothing excellent, nothing holy is as it seems. No wonder Mahan's students were skeptical of Pam. No one would really ever prefer a life of disinterested service over a life of self-advancement. No heart can be that good, no soul that untarnished. And so instead of being inspired by those who want to give themselves in service to others, we ridicule them. Instead of emulating the good, we work to unmask them as frauds. This too is the harvest of *acedia*, a cynical disenchantment with anyone who strives to be heroic in goodness or holiness. But the result of a loss of belief in high ideals and noble purposes is sadness and emptiness because after having exposed all aspirations toward excellence as fraudulent, we are left with a humanity held hostage to its worst impulses.

A third explanation for the diminishment of magnanimity (and for us the triumph of *acedia*) is captured in Hook and Reno's account of "supine indolence." By this they mean lives marked by puny ambitions and insufficient hopes. Supine indolence describes persons who never risk anything for the sake of a greater good, who refuse the "danger" of grand commitments and extravagant dreams. Their lives are measured by such extreme caution and calculation that anything that might make existence more than sheer survival seems wildly imprudent. In this expression of *acedia*, the fundamental imperative is to conform, to be ordinary, and never to reach out for more. As Hook and Reno write, "We compact our souls; we pour ourselves into jobs and projects—but with a defensive purpose. . . . We do not extend ourselves in the risks of ambition governed only by the lure of excellence and blind to the dangers of failure."[27] This failure to extend oneself on behalf of some transcendent purpose is what makes the Christian life of discipleship incomprehensible to anyone captive to *acedia*. What is the point of surrendering one's life to an adventure that begins with repentance, is lived through sometimes heroic virtue, and may culminate in martyrdom? Those who succumb to the rigors of such a demanding and seemingly impossible life are to be shunned, not imitated, precisely because they dared to be something other than ordinary.

Hook and Reno's account closely resembles Taylor's depiction of the narrowing and flattening of the self. The notion of self-determining freedom as freedom from external imposition loosened the individual from precisely those sources of identity that gave meaning to his or her life; family, civic, and religious ties—even the great chain of Being—have yielded to the primacy of the purely autonomous individual. But while Taylor's diagnosis of the ills of contemporary culture rests ultimately on what he considers a misconstrual of the demands of authenticity, our view is that the loss of purpose that Taylor so rightly illuminates—and the loss of aspirations for excellence that Hook and Reno describe—is perhaps more revealingly understood as evidence of the ubiquity of *acedia*.

It is important to note that Thomas Aquinas said *acedia* was fundamentally a sin against charity.[28] For Aquinas, a person of charity is not one who practices a safe and predictable love, but one who sets his or her life on the most unsurpassable possibility available to human beings, namely, to live in friendship with God and to enjoy intimacy, even union, with God. Thanks to God's goodness and God's grace, human beings can risk grandiose hopes; they need never to settle for anything less than their most exalted possibility: to grow in likeness to God by being continually transformed in the goodness of God. This is what God's love wants for us, and if we truly love ourselves, it is what we should want as well. In this respect, *acedia*, expressed through "supine indolence," is a failure in love, a failure to love both God and ourselves as we ought. To turn away from the most graced possibility of our lives—to renounce that excellence—is to deny ourselves the only happiness (Aquinas' *beatitudo*) that can ultimately fulfill us. This loss of belief in the very excellence necessary for human flourishing and perfection is what makes *acedia* toxic for the soul, a truly deadly sin. To surrender to *acedia* is to turn away from the good that is most properly and exquisitely human exactly because in pursuing it we become more than we already are. To surrender to *acedia* is to renounce the blessedness God both offers us and wants for us. In the most absolute sense, it is failure to be who we are called to be.

OVERCOMING *ACEDIA*: MORAL EDUCATION AND VOCATION

If we are right in our analysis of both the pervasiveness and the toxicity of *acedia*, there must be a way for this deadly condition of soul to be confronted and overcome. And if the young are dangerously susceptible to it, then moral education must provide a response to *acedia*; that is, it should suggest how a life of meaningful engagement and commitment is decidedly better than its alternative. Accordingly, vocation must become a central theme of moral education because it is only in hearing and responding to the call of goodness that the young develop the excellence most proper to human beings. Unlike *acedia*, which collapses us in on our selves and bottoms out in despair, goodness calls us out of our selves and into relationship with others—most of all into relationship with God. A life spent seeking, responding to, and being fulfilled in goodness culminates in joy because it is through goodness (a goodness Christians call holiness) that human nature reaches its highest possibility.

Human beings are created to seek what is best, fashioned to hunger for what is true and good and beautiful. We are programmed to respond to the lure of goodness and love and compassion. This is the fundamental human vocation, namely the call to move out of ourselves by seeking a relationship with goodness, love, and beauty primarily through friendship with God, but also through lives of love and service with others. Put differently, to be human is to be on a quest; it is continually to search for the goodness and love in which we are completed. In *The Moviegoer*, Binx Bolling discovers that the only way out of the despair wrought by *acedia* is by taking up a quest—and by the end of the novel he finds his purpose in love and devotion for Kate Cutrer and the rest of his family. In many of Percy's novels, the main characters break free from the malaise gripping their lives by allowing their disillusionment to propel them on a search for something more and something better. Just as Binx eventually discovers the point and purpose of his life, we find ourselves not by turning in on ourselves, but by moving out of ourselves by beginning to search for the love and goodness that seem to be missing.[29]

A human being is a wayfarer, a pilgrim on a journey. But the metaphor of journey, perhaps most profoundly expressed in Augustine's *Confessions*, suggests that none of us is the answer to the incompleteness of our lives. *Acedia* abounds because we focus our attention in on ourselves instead of outward on something better and greater. Instead of taking up a quest for goodness and love infinitely greater than ourselves, we tragically lower our sights by falling in love with ourselves instead of falling in love with God. Surely this was Augustine's discovery in the *Confessions*: the fundamental human error is not that we hope for too much, but that we settle for so little. Instead of doing what we are created to do, namely, seeking and worshiping the highest good, we turn in on and worship ourselves. Like the first human couple in the original sin, we deify ourselves instead of praising God.[30] In doing so, we misunderstand happiness. Consequently, overcoming *acedia* hinges on transforming desires and redirecting ambitions.

Instead of being primarily ambitious (even obsessed) about wealth, consumer goods, status, security, or celebrity, teachers need to foster ambitions for virtue, goodness, honor, and integrity—but especially, for Christians, an ambition for God. Moral formation, thus, should help students to nurture the right desires, to become passionate about the most promising purposes. Mahan argues that students, despite displaying all the signs of *acedia*, actually "seem to desire something deeper, something more idealistic, something different from what they were told constituted success American style."[31] They want to believe that lives devoted to service, compassion, justice, and goodness are better than lives centered on gratifying the whims of the self. They distrust what they have been taught about what constitutes a good and successful life because they recognize "how alienating and constricting were the images of success and failure that the ascendant culture had bequeathed to them."[32] In fact, Mahan suggests, many students fail to seek another way not because they have been seduced by the dominant philosophy of a good and successful life, but because they are continually told that a life devoted to selfless service and love is dangerously unrealistic. At best, giving oneself in service to the needs and well being of others is a passing fancy, a fad embraced in adolescence when one can afford to be idealistic. But becoming an adult, the standard script tells students, demands leaving such idealism behind because in a world where only the self-centered survive, putting others first is recklessly irresponsible.

Mahan says there is a " 'shadow government' of compassion and idealism" in all of us, particularly the young.[33] Accordingly, moral education must draw that desire for compassion and idealism out of the shadows and into the light. Teachers must appeal to the too often silenced belief of students that fulfillment and happiness are found not in lives of calculated self-interest, but in lives spent seeking excellence through virtue, service, goodness, and love. It is what Aristotle, Augustine, and Aquinas understood when they said happiness for human beings comes from the ongoing seeking of, and participating in, what is best for us—the life of virtue for Aristotle and the life of goodness formed through friendship with God for Augustine and Aquinas. Unlike the message trumpeted by our culture, neither Aristotle, nor Augustine, nor Aquinas envisioned happiness as the freedom to pursue and satisfy one's desires regardless of what those desires might be, a path guaranteed to lead to *acedia*. Rather, they agreed that happiness requires the satisfaction of desires, but only on the condition that one's desires and inclinations had first been transformed.[34] If happiness comes to the person who loves and possesses the consummate good—who seeks what is best for human beings—then *acedia* is overcome and authenticity assured only when one's desire for the comfortable and pleasurable is replaced by a desire for the good. In a culture obsessed with consumerism, trivialities, and endless distractions, Aristotle, Augustine, and Aquinas suggest that the way out of *acedia* begins with a reordering of our loves.

But how can this be done? How can teachers encourage students to refocus their attention on goods and purposes that can help them break free from the tentacles of *acedia* and instead find freedom and flourishing in a genuinely good and hopeful life? One way is to appeal to what Mahan calls "an epiphany of recruitment."[35] All of us have moments in our lives where we experience being drawn beyond ourselves, moments where we are called to devote ourselves to something challenging and costly, but also compelling. An epiphany of recruitment is an experience in which we realize to be human is to be summoned to live for the sake of something demanding and heroic; indeed, it is to pursue a life of "epic proportion" not only because of what such a life will ask of us, but also because of what it promises. It is what happened to the disciples of Christ when Jesus invited them to "Come and see."

But an epiphany of recruitment also is a kind of revelation because it opens our eyes to see that the conventional messages about success and fulfillment are counterfeit, moral and spiritual dead ends. Instead of repressing or fleeing from such moments, students should be encouraged to embrace them because an epiphany of recruitment is always a summons to pursue what is best. As Mahan writes, "An epiphany of recruitment is not an end in itself; it is an invitation to a different kind of life."[36]

To respond to that invitation is to become part of a quest. For Christians, it is the quest of the disciple who falls in behind Jesus and follows him precisely because of what the "cost of discipleship" promises. To take up the quest, whether it is described as a life of discipleship or, for Aristotle, an apprenticeship in virtue, will be initially disorienting because it sets us on a path utterly at odds with what we have been taught will make us happy. Becoming part of a quest for moral and spiritual excellence—for Christians the *summum bonum* who is God—is upending because along the way our attitudes, habits, inclinations, and desires are transformed. We learn that what we thought we wanted does not matter nearly as much as we believed and certainly is not worth the gift of our hearts. We discover that happiness and fulfillment demand unlearning so many of the messages we have imbibed and then being trained in new wants and new desires. And on the quest, so much that we have been taught constitutes achievement and success is unmasked as trivial and banal; in fact, we wonder how it ever appealed to us, why it ever fascinated.

In this respect, breaking free from *acedia* requires being reeducated about happiness. Consider the beatitudes. Usually dismissed as impossible eschatological ideals or, at best, a perfectionist ethic for a special elite, one learns in the quest for discipleship that Jesus' Sermon on the Mount is simply a radically different (and disruptive) understanding of happiness.[37] In the beatitudes Jesus did not teach what he thought would be impossibly impractical; rather, he proclaimed the true path to happiness and well being, however shocking and unthinkable that path first appears. Being poor in spirit, thirsting for holiness, practicing mercy, being single-hearted about God, and even risking persecution hardly blends with our customary understandings of happiness. But that is the point: in any quest, but perhaps especially the quest of discipleship, everything is changed. We learn to embrace ideas and ways of being we once would have abhorred because through the quest we have been transformed.

In the Christian moral life, the beatitudes are not utopian ideals but the concrete practices by which one is initiated into a life of goodness, happiness, and excellence; in other words, for the Christian the beatitudes are the antidote to *acedia*. In his first pastoral work, a commentary on the Sermon on the Mount, Augustine argued that the beatitudes are not hopelessly impractical; rather, they are precisely the new attitudes and actions a person must acquire if he or she is to know happiness by becoming like God. Augustine believed "the beatitudes give us Christ's answer to the primary human question about happiness" because by practicing them and living according to them one is continually conformed to the goodness of God and participates more completely in the life and love of God.[38] And as Augustine's *Confessions* powerfully illustrates, it is only by seeking and being conformed to the goodness of God that human beings can overcome the self-absorption that constitutes despair. Such a radical reorientation in our thinking about happiness also must become a central element in the moral formation of students.

BEING EQUIPPED FOR THE JOURNEY: THE NEED FOR HOPE, COURAGE, AND PERSEVERANCE

If happiness comes from seeking, participating in, and being changed by a way of life that continually orientates one to the greatest possible good, then it is important for students to realize that the moral life must take the form of a quest or a journey. Aristotle, Augustine, and Aquinas saw that because happiness is goodness, it is not something we instantly and fully possess. In fact, happiness (Aquinas' *beatitudo*) is gradually, and often painstakingly, attained as we participate more fully in the best possible life, for Aristotle the life of virtue, for Augustine and Aquinas the life of *caritas* or friendship with God. Such a life is inherently magnanimous (in Taylor's language, rich with horizons of significance), but it is precisely the transcendent character of such conceptions of happiness that makes them open to disappointment and discouragement. As with any good quest, there is no guarantee that one who undertakes Aristotle's journey to *eudaimonia* or Aquinas' pilgrimage to heavenly beatitude will successfully achieve his goal. Goodness can lose its attractive power when there are things that distract us from its beauty or convince us it is not worth the effort that securing it requires. Indeed, when we are surrounded by so many conflicting understandings of human fulfillment and prosperity, we need ways to remain focused on and devoted to what truly is best for us. If we are not to be sidetracked or defeated by hardship, adversity, discouragement, temptation, fear, or fatigue, we need to be especially skilled in three virtues: hope, courage, and perseverance. Other virtues are surely important, but if the moral life is an ongoing and often perilous quest toward goodness and excellence, these three are crucial. And given the interconnectedness of the virtues, each of these three absolutely depends on and is strengthened by the others; hope cannot be sustained without courage and perseverance, and courage and perseverance are unintelligible without hope. Moral education must give an account of these three virtues.

First, then, is the virtue of hope. Hope is the virtue that orients us to fulfillment, the virtue by which we consistently seek, despite hardships and discouragement, our most magnanimous possibilities in life. If human life is a pilgrimage toward the good or goods in which we are completed, hope sustains us on that journey by keeping us focused on what is best and most perfecting. For Christians, hope is the truly theological virtue, rooted in grace, by which they turn their lives toward God and each day seek goodness and holiness through friendship with God. It is through hope that we never lower our sights, never give up on God's great promises to us. Hope, Josef Pieper writes, is the "steadfast orientation toward a fulfillment and a beatitude that are not 'owed'" us, but that God in his goodness has promised us, namely, "a real, grace-filled participation in the divine nature."[39] In short, it is through hope, along with all the other virtues, that we participate, however imperfectly and incompletely, in that fulfillment each day.

But because we move toward a goodness and happiness that we never perfectly possess, the moral life has the character of a quest, what Pieper calls *status viatoris*, the "condition or state of being on the way."[40] It is this tension between the *telos* of Aristotle's *eudaimonia* or Aquinas' *beatitudo* and our always imperfect realization of it now that makes hope necessary. In fact, Pieper calls hope "the virtue of the *status viatoris*; it is the proper virtue of the 'not yet.'"[41] Put differently, it is precisely because it is so easy to be disillusioned about one's capacity for goodness or disheartened by one's growth in love for God, that the lure of *acedia* is so strong and, therefore, the need for hope so clear. Pieper says *acedia* is a species of sadness—a deep sorrow of soul—that flows from the loss of conviction in anything truly worthwhile and promising, anything genuinely ennobling and good. "Acedia is the signature of every age," Pieper says, "that seeks, in its despair, to shake off the obligations of that nobility of being that is conferred by Christianity and so, in its despair, to deny its true self."[42] This is, from our perspective, an apt description of our times. We are created for perfection in a love and goodness we either no longer believe can possibly be attained or else no longer believe exists. The work of hope is to resist this fatal disillusionment and to keep us resolute in our quest to become one with the love and goodness for which we were created.

But none of us can sustain the hope necessary for exquisite goodness and resilient happiness alone. Writing about hope, Aquinas said it is the virtue by which we believe something difficult is nonetheless possible to attain. But he immediately added, "usually only with the help of others." We are "much more inclined to be hopeful," he wrote, "when we have friends to rely on."[43] Aquinas knew hope is not a solitary virtue, because we always hope together; hope is not something we can achieve for ourselves. Instead, Aquinas said, it is a gift we receive, first from a befriending God in grace, Christ, and the Spirit, but also from those friends who share our commitment to goodness and who participate in the quest for it along with us. Precisely because of the challenges and difficulties inherent in the quest, we cannot endure it alone. And precisely because of the deep and often painstaking changes that seeking and sharing in the good demands of us, we need others not only to support us, but also to remind us that a quest for excellence in goodness is the only life truly worthy of human beings. As Aquinas realized, we need companions in hope. We need friends bonded to us by a shared commitment to authentic goodness and the special way of life that seeking and growing in goodness demands. None of us can navigate the virtuous life alone. We are bound to lose our way in discouragement or else give up the quest altogether if there are not others journeying with us who remind us of the value of our quest and who delight in it with us.

The second virtue that students should come to understand as particularly important is courage, a virtue that works in partnership with perseverance to sustain hope. Courage helps us deal with all the things in ourselves, in others, and in society that hinder our pursuit of moral excellence. Unless we learn to deal with these impediments to excellence, hope diminishes because we no longer believe we can overcome the temptations, setbacks, and failures that beset us on the quest. Aristotle connected courage with the battlefield—it was the virtue most needed by the soldier in war.[44] Employing the metaphor of the battlefield, we can see why we must be armed with courage if we are to battle with, and not be defeated by, our fears and weaknesses, or be seduced by beguiling, if ultimately counterfeit, notions of life. Courage is not needed to sustain one in a trivial conception of life because trivial narratives of life require nothing of us. It takes no courage to remain steadfast in ways of life that demand no sacrifice, no generosity, no transcending of one's self. But narratives characterized by ambitions for moral and spiritual excellence cannot be embodied without courage, precisely because they demand the transformation and transcending of one's self.

Aquinas saw courage as a quintessential virtue for nurturing and sustaining the Christian's quest for excellence through the life of *caritas* or friendship with God. But for him courage meant not only *endurance* amidst suffering and adversity, but also *daring*.[45] If one is to share and grow in the holiness and goodness acquired through a life of friendship with God, one must not only deal with weaknesses, temptations, and adversity, but also look for ways to overcome them. This is the role of daring, the element of courage by which one attacks, in order to conquer, all that stands in the way of the good. Daring captures the energy, imagination, insight, and determination necessary to overcome all the things that stand in opposition to a genuinely magnanimous life. As Aquinas reflected, "But courage ought not merely to endure unflinchingly the pressure of difficult situations by restraining fear; it ought also to make a calculated attack, when it is necessary to eliminate difficulties in order to win safety for the future. Such action appears to belong to daring."[46] The "future" Aquinas had in mind was eternal beatitude with God and the saints in heaven.

An essential part of courage, daring helps one battle with and overcome anything that might diminish one's participation in that unparalleled good. Put another way, daring is the capacity not only to remain steadfast in one's pursuit of authentic happiness and goodness amidst the lure of more immediately gratifying possibilities but, more especially, to overcome those things that can deter, and even redirect, our growth in happiness and goodness. As an expression of courage, daring is the ability to see counterfeit narratives of human fulfillment as the illusions they truly are and the commitment to continue one's initiation into goodness with joy.

The third virtue we see as important in moral education is perseverance. Aquinas described perseverance as "prolonged endurance in any good which is difficult."[47] This aptly describes the contour of both his and Aristotle's conception of the moral life. For Aristotle, *eudaimonia* may be the best possible life for humans, but it is hardly easily achieved because it essentially consists in uprooting the vices that stand in the way of the virtues needed for human flourishing, and such a thorough rehabituation of the self takes considerable time. Even more so, friendship with God may be the most perfect and promising possibility for human beings, but it requires a transformation and reordering of the self through grace and the virtues that is not only daunting, but also prolonged. Closely related to courage, perseverance is the virtue that helps us "persist to the end of a virtuous undertaking," to strive to achieve an end that is not easily accomplished. Knowing that we will neither easily nor quickly accomplish the exquisite goodness that we seek can defeat us; accordingly, we need to learn how to persevere in hope lest discouragement, impatience, or fatigue permanently deflect us from what is best. Perseverance is the virtue or *habitus* by which we remain resolute in our zeal for, and steadfast in our orientation to, excellence in goodness despite how long acquiring it may take.

Regarding perseverance, Aquinas said its "action should continue through life," not only because seldom are we without the challenges and obstacles that make remaining steadfast in the good difficult, but also because the quest for goodness is by its very nature of long duration.[48] Along with hope and courage, moral education must attend to perseverance because without it, the ambition for goodness that is the quintessential element of the moral life easily dies. Although the human vocation is to respond to the lure of goodness, goodness (as well as holiness) can lose its initial attractiveness when achieving it is the work of a lifetime. As Aquinas pithily commented, perseverance is an essential virtue in the Christian life because it is "difficult to continue firm in great enterprises."[49]

MORAL EDUCATION IN THE UNIVERSITY: A PROPOSAL

Throughout this chapter we have suggested that a liberal arts education, particularly a Christian liberal arts education, must recognize the deep need and significant opportunity for the moral formation of students. If the toxins of *acedia*, both personally and institutionally, are to be overcome, colleges and universities must realize that moral formation is an inherent and irreplaceable part of their mission. As educators, our aim should be to form students who are not only skilled in their professions, but who are also good, truthful, and wise. The primary goal of a liberal arts education should not be that its students are "marketable," but that they are virtuous and astute about what it means to live a flourishing life. Accordingly, we want to conclude with some brief suggestions about what moral education—particularly in Christian colleges and universities—might look like.

First, if we are ever to break free of the stranglehold of *acedia*, moral education must recover an understanding of life as a truly "great enterprise," one that will help students achieve their utmost possibilities in human excellence. Thus, moral education must foster in students an ambition for goodness instead of an ambition for wealth; likewise, virtue must be shown as more compelling than celebrity, service more attractive than self-aggrandizement. The essayist and novelist Wendell Berry once noted that no person was ever "called" to be rich or powerful.

Though one may become rich and powerful, that is never one's vocation. What we are called to be is magnanimous, people who aspire to what is best, people who are unstintingly attracted to what is true and good, and who through love actually become good. Christian colleges and universities, then, must emphasize that the fundamental aim of ethics is not making up one's mind about complex moral issues, much less choosing which values one wants for life; rather, ethics must focus on learning how to live a flourishing life. Morality is not essentially about choice, but about excellence in goodness. As educators, we misconstrue the moral life and seriously shortchange our students if we have nothing more to offer them than support for whatever values and desires they might finally endorse. No life is morally praiseworthy simply because we have chosen it; rather, it is morally praiseworthy because by growing into it and embracing it we actually become good.

Thus, moral education begins with the question, "How should I live?" rather than "What should I do?" Contrary to the dominant assumptions of our culture—and contrary to the spirit of *acedia*—answering this question about the good human life is no private matter about which we can afford to remain neutral. Some ways of life clearly are better than others. Some ways of life, for instance, initiate us into the traditions and practices conducive to excellence and flourishing while other ways of life diminish and deceive. There should be something distinctive about a Christian liberal arts education, but perhaps nothing should distinguish it more than its commitment to showing students what it means to live a happy and good life, and what might be required of them to achieve it. At the very least, we should teach them that being smart (or rich or powerful or famous) is not enough.

Second, if Christian colleges and universities are to contribute effectively to the moral formation of their students, they must recover a rich and vibrant sense of vocation. As we have suggested throughout this chapter, Christian theology envisions men and women not fundamentally through the lens of free choice, but through the lens of vocation. To be human is to be called to something greater and more expansive than ourselves. The one vocation every human being shares is to respond to the call of goodness, because it is only in hearing and responding to this call, particularly the goodness who is God, that we grow, develop, and are fulfilled properly as human beings. It is easy to begin to live inauthentic lives, and many smart, talented people go wrong because they silence the call to goodness. A good education is one that teaches students to be captivated by truth, goodness, and beauty. Human beings are called to care about what is true and good and beautiful because these are the things— each an attribute of God—that draw us beyond ourselves and ultimately perfect us. Put differently, if *acedia* leads us to "lower our sights" by turning away from what can transform and complete us as human beings, a renewed sense of vocation invites us to "raise our sights" to what is best.

As educators, we should want our pupils to be more than excellent students: we want them to be excellent human persons—to dazzle us with their knowledge and expertise but, more important, to amaze us with their commitment to justice, their compassion for others, their sense of fairness and honor, their trustworthiness and courage. This is how the great English theologian, Cardinal John Henry Newman, envisioned a "liberal education." He argued that such an education is "useful" precisely in the measure that it "*tends* to good, or is the *instrument* of good. . . ." In Newman's words, cultivating the intellect is "not only beautiful, perfect, admirable, and noble in itself, but in a true and high sense it must be useful to the possessor and to all round him; not useful in any low, mechanical, mercantile sense, but as diffusing good, or as a blessing, or a gift, or power, or a treasure, first to the owner, then through him to the world."[50] Like Newman, we believe part of the vocation of Christian colleges and universities is to nurture in students not only a desire for increasing goodness in themselves, but also for diffusing it in the world.

Third, any attempt to restore the fundamental place of moral education in Christian universities and colleges will succeed only when these institutions are committed to affirming and pursuing a coherent vision of the moral life *and* equally committed to providing a place where meaningful initiation into that life can occur. Schools that possess a vibrant religious identity—those that understand their mission and how their moral and theological commitments should inform the lives of their students—provide the most hospitable settings where the moral quest for goodness can be identified, celebrated, and collectively pursued. It is particularly important that all of the faculty see the moral education of students as an integral dimension of their vocation and, consequently, their professional responsibilities. A concern for the moral formation of students must infuse every discipline within the curriculum, and educators must realize that the classroom, just as much as the chapel, is a fitting setting for initiating students into the practices and traditions of virtue.

How might our general point about moral education be applied to a particular course? As a provocative example, consider how a business ethics course taught through the lens of happiness, vocation, and virtue might look different from the more common approach to applied ethics in which students are presented with an assortment of moral theories and then confronted with difficult cases and instructed to "solve the moral problem." On the latter approach, a business ethics course—like other applied ethics courses—bears resemblance to a cafeteria lunch: a little Kant, some consequentialism, a side of rights and justice. Perhaps some attention is given to virtue ethics, though it is sometimes wrapped up in an ethics of care. Then students are presented with difficult case studies about specific issues that arise in business practices; the aim is to show

how each theory can be applied to the given case. But the risk is that students come to view such hard cases as intellectual puzzles requiring only intellectual ingenuity to solve. Moreover, if the moral theories themselves are presented in such a way as to suggest that no moral theory is better than another—since each provides an internally coherent account of what ought to be done in the case at hand—students receive a badly distorted picture of the moral life. Instead of being invited to think about whether and how a life in business is their calling, students are asked to grapple with incredibly tough cases while simultaneously assuming the view that no normative theory is really better than another. This method of teaching ethics leads precisely to the brand of cynicism we described earlier.

A course in business ethics taught as an initiation into happiness should be decidedly different, for it should place the question of vocation front and center. Students can be led to encounter such questions through a variety of historical texts—Augustine and Aquinas are but two—but there are contemporary authors who speak to the question of vocation in business more specifically.[51] Having students explore texts like these focuses their reflection on the right sorts of questions, but it also provides students a place from which to stand when they reflect. Since moral deliberation, judgment, and action do not proceed from a neutral standpoint, there is no need to pretend that they do. Encouraging students to confront these foundational questions in a business ethics course may seem quite beside the point to some, but to those who think that academia somehow must respond to the recent proliferation of corporate scandal, we maintain that there is no more fitting or effective way to educate morally those who are about to enter the American business culture. They need to encounter questions about happiness and vocation. Obviously there will be other features of such a course that will make it different than the standard business ethics course. Students should learn to speak the language of the virtues to see how hope, courage, and perseverance matter—as well as other virtues like prudence, justice, honesty, and temperance. Again, a variety of texts can acquaint students with a robust conception of the virtues, but novels and film also can show students how a consideration of character is fundamental to ethics. For example, some twenty years after its release, *Wall Street,* the movie starring Charlie Sheen and Michael Douglas, still holds up well as an intriguing depiction of Sheen's character, Bud Fox, and his struggle to understand his place in the world as he pursues the counterfeit notions of happiness modeled by Douglas's character, Gordon Gekko. But what will make a course like this distinctively Christian—and for us particularly powerful—is the way that it provides an alternative to Gekko's famous line: "Greed is good."

Students should be challenged to think how the Christian faith offers a radically different notion of happiness than the one so often supplied by contemporary culture. Again, there are a variety of resources to draw from to engage students' moral imaginations—the Scriptures, texts in the history of philosophy and theology, the rich resources of Catholic social teaching—but more important than the choice of a particular text is the approach taken in the course by its instructor. Students are quick to discern whether their professors are actually committed to the ideas they profess. Again, we think it imperative that college and university teachers recover their vocation as moral educators.

In conclusion, our discussion here has been an attempt to diagnose more accurately what we see as an insidious vice in the culture and to suggest in detail a way to reenvision moral education to respond to its threat. More particularly, we have suggested why three virtues—hope, courage, and perseverance—are so integral to the moral life and therefore crucial to any moral education effort. If *acedia* is the ill that we think it is, and if the young are especially vulnerable to it, then helping initiate students into a quest for goodness is the most important work that we as educators can do. There is no more noble aim than to encourage students to see that moral and spiritual excellence is not impossibly beyond their reach but is, as a matter of fact, what they were made for. Indeed, we believe that helping students to imagine such greatness and to heed the call to excellence is precisely what we were made for, too.

Chapter 7

Could Humility Be a Deliberative Virtue?

—Shawn D. Floyd

For much of the twentieth century, academic orthodoxy proclaimed that colleges and universities were not conduits of moral pedagogy. Here academic convention follows the tradition of John Stuart Mill, who said that the task of the modern university is not to tell students what to believe or how to live, "but to give [them] information and training, and help [them] form [their] own beliefs in a manner worthy of intelligent beings."[1] In order for students to make informed choices about important philosophical, ethical, and social matters, the academy must refrain from advocating substantive conceptions of the good life. Moreover, a professor cannot allow her prejudices to interfere with students' intellectual autonomy. Instead, she must help students cultivate those skills that will prepare them to make choices *they* deem necessary for a well-lived life.

Today, however, the idea that moral advocacy has no place in education is not as widely shared as it once was. Even self-described liberal theorists have come to reject the idea that moral neutrality in education is something for which educators ought to strive. According to Amy Gutmann, all theories of education will involve substantive moral conceptions, and those conceptions will not be neutral with respect to the kinds

of virtues students ought to develop.[2] Instead of devising impartial pedagogical practices, many liberal theorists encourage a forthright endorsement of their most cherished ideals. For them, a salient objective of
education is to prepare students to contribute to—and flourish in—a
society in which its citizens collectively embrace the foundational principles of democracy. For this reason, our educational institutions ought to
promote distinctively democratic virtues.

While it may be difficult to develop an exhaustive list of democratic
virtues, we can at least call attention to those that recur in the literature:
tolerance, civility, honesty, the ability to engage in rational inquiry,
respect for persons, and any excellence that enables one to function well
in a socially and intellectually diverse environment.[3] These excellences
rightly enjoy a privileged position among liberal theorists' moral repertoire. After all, the strident nature and large number of moral disagreements in public life constantly threaten to undermine productive debate
and political consensus. In an effort to offset the contentious nature of
these disputes, we need habits that promote goodwill, cooperative
inquiry, and respectful disagreement. Gutmann refers to these habits as
"deliberative virtues" and suggests that democratic education is an ideal
environment in which to cultivate them.[4] Thus she advocates a model of
pedagogy that encourages "rigorous, honest, open, and intense intellectual discussions, both inside and outside the classroom."[5] For it is by
means of respectful disagreement and patient adjudication of opposing
views that one comes to embody democracy's most prized ideals.[6]

I profess some camaraderie with those liberal theorists who reject the
myth of moral neutrality in education. I also affirm their efforts to identify virtues central to democratic education. As a Catholic Christian who
is heavily invested in these issues, I am naturally interested in the role *theological* virtues might play in democratic education's pedagogical repertoire. Could virtues that are traditionally aligned with or emerge from
religious commitments be placed alongside the virtues of the liberal academy? Responses to this question will range from ambivalence to
incredulity. According to some liberal theorists, theologically oriented
ideals are unduly sectarian and unlikely to produce civility, respect for
rational inquiry, and similar traits thought to strengthen democratic practices. I wish to challenge this claim. I will argue that the virtue of humility, although inspired by the Christian moral tradition, is necessary
(though perhaps not sufficient) to foster and sustain the practices Gutmann claims are central to democratic education. More specifically, I will
argue that humility should itself be considered a deliberative virtue.

In developing my argument, I will focus primarily on Thomas
Aquinas' understanding of humility.[7] Aquinas provides one of the most
thorough accounts of humility one can find within the Christian tradi-

tion. Also, that account is especially illuminative for my general thesis. Aquinas' account of humility not only complements the democratic virtues extolled by the academy, it seems necessary for their realization. The modesty of this claim ought not to minimize its apparent implication: in an effort to achieve the ends to which democratic education aspires, the liberal academy would do well to take seriously those intellectual habits whose roots reside in the Christian tradition.[8]

TWO INITIAL OBJECTIONS

Those committed to the principles of democratic liberalism are sometimes suspicious of those who advocate views on the basis of staunchly held religious ideals. In fact, the claim that religious ideals are congruent with the aims of democratic education may strike some as entirely counterintuitive. For this reason, I will begin by addressing two objections to which the underlying assumption of this chapter might seem vulnerable.

First, colleges and universities play host to a variety of divergent views, commitments, and traditions. For this reason, those institutions must actively promote an environment in which people can discuss their differences in respectful and noncoercive ways. Yet the putative certainty of religious claims—as well as the uncompromising posture of those who assert them—seems inimical to an environment of respect and openness. As he puts it in one fairly notorious expression of this view, Stanley Fish claims that "the trouble with Christianity . . . is that it lacks the generosity necessary to the marketplace's full functioning" and is "insistent upon the rightness of its perspective and deaf to the perspectives that might challenge it."[9] By contrast, the liberal mind loathes and avoids any expression of certitude. Furthermore, it purports to be "open to all thoughts and closed to none."[10] On Fish's view, liberalism is inextricably tied to skepticism, or at least some form of it. For it eschews recalcitrant commitment and embraces intellectual tentativeness. That one should be "ready at any moment to jettison even [one's] most cherished convictions, is the very definition of 'reasonable' in a post-Enlightenment liberal culture."[11] Such openness is contrary to the unconditional allegiance required of religious believers. For this reason, he argues that "a person of religious conviction would not want to enter into the marketplace of ideas, but to shut it down, at least insofar as it presumes to determine matters that he believes have been determined by God and faith."[12]

Why think that intolerance of the sort Fish describes is a necessary constituent of religious commitment? Nothing in the Christian tradition requires people to behave in intolerant ways when confronting opposing views. In fact, many Christians insist that a commitment to civility, tolerance, and peaceful dialogue is an extension of, not a departure from, their religious views.[13] To this extent, Christians will want to abide by the principles of liberal dialogue. As George Marsden points out:

> It is perfectly possible . . . to hold . . . an Augustinian view that faith in God, rather than faith in self or material contingency, should shape one's essential vision of reality and yet to support the rules of liberal society as a God-given means for accomplishing some limited but immensely valuable goals.[14]

Michael McConnell offers a similar corrective to Fish's account:

> A Christian does not want to "extirpate" liberalism "root and branch," as Fish asserts, because it is only under conditions of freedom that genuine conversion and worship can take place. Indeed, a religious believer feels no more need or desire to "shut down" the marketplace of ideas than anyone else who is convinced of the persuasive power of the truth. The believer is confident that a full and fair consideration of the evidence can only promote his cause. Error may need the power of state coercion, but truth, never.[15]

Indeed, only by describing Christianity as closed to argument can one conclude that it is an ideological enemy of liberalism. Most Christians will reject Fish's account of what Christianity requires of them, and they will in turn deny that they cannot be good democratic citizens.

Moreover, most liberal theorists are likely to deny Fish's claim that skepticism is a necessary component of liberalism. But suppose for a moment that Fish is right about this claim. Such skepticism is not more likely than religious belief to encourage tolerance. Skeptical attitudes can be just as dogmatic as religious ones, and they are likely to forestall nontrivial discussions about issues such as abortion, foreign policy, affirmative action, and the establishment clause. In fact, I would submit that the sort of skepticism Fish has in mind is likely to undermine civil debate about such issues. A person willing to abandon her convictions so quickly is not likely to invest much confidence in them in the first place. Because of her incredulity toward all philosophical and religious viewpoints, it is doubtful she will consider them as serious contenders for her allegiance. Moreover, her incredulity may breed condescension toward people who are persuaded by those views. As a result, the sort of skepticism Fish describes may inhibit a person's ability to converse sincerely and civilly with those who challenge whatever views she does happen to hold, however tentatively.

A second potential objection is as follows. The liberal academy is well known for its skepticism of virtually any expression of religious belief in argument or conversation. This problem concerns not so much the unconditional loyalty religious beliefs demand of their adherents. The problem, rather, is that the claims that express those beliefs are not likely to garner much support in an environment where claims and arguments are assessed on the basis of more widely shared standards of evaluation and judgment.[16] Why so? To put the matter as starkly as possible, religious claims are believed by the academy to defy public scrutiny. While those claims are no doubt meaningful to those who utter them, they are no more than quaint expressions of deeply held convictions and personal affections.[17] How can these claims be assessed? And on what grounds? Even if such claims are true, they cannot be appraised and embraced on the basis of what Amy Gutmann and Dennis Thompson call "publicly acceptable reasons or methods of inquiry."[18] Their private nature puts them beyond the scope of open examination and debate. This is why introducing religious beliefs into the academy would, according to Marsden's account of this objection, "violate rules essential for promoting fruitful public discourse."[19] While there may be nothing inherently wrong with religious commitments, the liberal academy is simply the wrong forum for their expression.[20]

The preceding objection clearly rests on a woefully inaccurate portrayal of religious belief. Far from being mere personal affections, religious beliefs are more akin to philosophical beliefs in that they reflect one's fundamental assumptions about the world, the good life, and human nature. Like philosophical beliefs, religious beliefs have important implications for the kinds of intellectual and ethical positions people are willing to support. For this reason alone, it seems reasonable to suppose that religious considerations may occasionally find legitimate expression in the academy. Marsden puts the matter in the following way:

> Even though religious people should honor the rule that they cannot offer their special revelations as the public evidence of their views, they can still reflect on the implications of such revelations within the bounds of the mainstream academy by talking about them conditionally. That is, it is perfectly legitimate to ask an academic question in the form of "if this religious teaching were true, how would it change the way we look at the subject at hand?"[21]

It is difficult to see how appealing to religious beliefs in this way would violate established norms of dialogue and inquiry. Besides, to insist that such appeals are contrary to "publicly acceptable reasons or methods of inquiry" assumes that there is a consensus about the kinds of reasons people tend to accept when debating contentious issues. The problem, however, is that there is no such consensus. In fact, one could argue that there is considerably more disagreement in the academy about such reasons than some would prefer to admit. As Michael Baxter argues:

> Beneath an apparent consensus, there often lurks a much more sub-
> stantive set of disagreements, as there is regarding [for example] the
> morality of parents killing their offspring and the adequacy of nar-
> rating human events with naturalistic explanations—and also
> regarding, I might add, the nature of genuine consensus and thus
> the conditions under which it is proper to use such descriptions as
> "agreement" and "disagreement."[22]

But even if there were such a consensus, whether it would be an ideal
basis for argument is still an open question. For the claim that any legitimate form of public inquiry precludes religious (i.e., "private") considerations presupposes an obvious cleft between the public and private—a
distinction not only rooted in a contentious philosophical doctrine, but
that seems tailored to root out religious claims in advance.

I realize that a religious person may not wish to appeal to her religious
beliefs when engaging nonreligious colleagues, although it would be per-
missible for her to do so. Religious appeals are not usually effective in
winning over nonreligious audiences. If, however, one's religiously
inspired views are true, then it is reasonable to suppose that there are
nonreligious considerations that corroborate their truth. As Marsden
notes, even if a person's fundamental reasons for endorsing a position are
religious, there may be "other, more widely accessible, grounds" to which
she can appeal when arguing on its behalf.[23] Yet to offer such arguments
is not to appeal to some broadly agreed upon standard of inquiry, nor is
it to capitulate to the view that one's religious beliefs are ultimately private. Rather, it is to adopt what Nicholas Wolterstorff describes as an ad
hoc strategy of deliberation—a strategy whereby we appeal to reasons we
think are likely to convince those we are trying to persuade.[24]

So far, I have addressed what I take to be two possible objections to
making room for religious ideals in the liberal academy. I now wish to
make a positive case for including at least one such ideal. Liberal theorists insist that the practices of civility, mutual respect, and reasoned
debate are central to democratic education. But such practices can only
be sustained by those who are shaped by more fundamental dispositions.
In the absence of those dispositions, appeals to civility, rational dialogue,
and mutual respect collapse into vapid abstractions and platitudes. One
of those dispositions is the virtue of humility. To borrow a description
offered by Mark Schwehn, humility is a "precondition" for achieving the
ideals of democratic education.[25] In other words, humility ensures that
one will be favorably disposed to engage in the deliberative practices of
the academy. Aquinas' account of humility can help us understand why
this is the case.

AQUINAS ON HUMILITY

The fact that Aquinas esteems humility as a genuine human excellence is no surprise. Those unfamiliar with the details of his view, however, might be surprised to learn that he takes humility to be a part of temperance. According to Aquinas, temperance is a virtue that restrains the immoderate desire for physical pleasures.[26] Yet he also thinks that any virtue that restrains or suppresses immoderate desire is a part of temperance, and humility is the virtue which restrains the insatiable impulse to achieve great things.[27]

By associating humility with temperance, Aquinas seems to be offering a view of humility that is different from our understanding of the term. We often think of humility as an awareness of our moral frailty, intellectual finitude, and limited abilities. On this view, humility is primarily a cognitive state—one that consists in a particular kind of self-understanding. How, on this view, could humility be a matter of temperance, which involves the restraint of concupiscible appetite? Aquinas addresses this worry:

> It would seem that humility concerns not the appetite but the judgment of reason. For humility is opposed to pride, which concerns things pertaining to knowledge. . . . Therefore it would seem that humility is chiefly concerned with knowledge whereby one thinks little of oneself.[28]

In answering this objection, Aquinas would have us ask why human beings are inclined to think highly of themselves. While it is true that the proud person is deceived about her own goodness and/or abilities, that deception involves a crucial appetitive element. Her self-appraisals are informed by a *desire* for praise and recognition, the strength of which may cloud her self-understanding and, in turn, inhibit her ability to judge herself accurately.[29] Aquinas therefore insists that pride—a vice often contrasted with humility—not only consists in an inaccurate self-appraisal, it also involves inordinate desire. For "pride is the appetite for excellence in excess of right reason."[30] By contrast, the humble person is characterized by a sense of restraint with respect to those things she is unable to achieve. She has a judicious view of her capacities which, in turn, serves "as a rule for guiding the appetite."[31] In other words, the humble person does not desire that which lies beyond her ability because she has a more reasonable understanding of what she can achieve.

But while it may be true that humility involves restraining a certain kind of desire, it is still unclear why Aquinas insists on subsuming humility under *temperance*. After all, humility denotes a restrained desire for what lies beyond one's abilities, whereas temperance denotes a restrained desire for physical pleasures. In short, humility and temperance restrain different things. But what Aquinas wishes to convey here is that humility restrains a certain kind of desire *in the same manner* as temperance. He puts the point in the following way:

> [I]n assigning parts to a virtue, we primarily consider the likeness that results from the mode of the virtue. Now the mode of temperance . . . is the restraint or suppression of the impetuosity of a passion. Hence whatever virtues restrain or suppress, and the actions which moderate the impetuosity of the passions, are considered parts of temperance.[32]

On this view, temperance and its subsidiary virtues concern the restraint of appetite in its various manifestations. Because humility consists in restraining the impetuous desire for great things, it more closely resembles temperance than some other virtue. This account would also explain why Aquinas thinks meekness and clemency are parts of temperance. They, too, restrain certain appetitive drives, namely anger and the inclination to punish, respectively.[33]

By locating humility in the appetite, Aquinas rejects the notion that humility is an external expression of modesty.[34] If humility is primarily a matter of outward behavior, then a person who has a high opinion of herself can nevertheless be humble. Daniel Statman endorses a view roughly along these lines.[35] He argues that humility is a behavioral disposition that flourishes among those "who are of high merit and outstanding character."[36] Yet he also says that such people have good reasons to be proud. As a result, they may have to combat an ongoing desire to boast, demean those of lesser achievement, or behave in other ways that offend or belittle others.[37] Great persons would therefore do well to exercise restraint by not calling attention to themselves and by treating others with respect. According to Statman, this is precisely what humility consists in. It is "a disposition to avoid arrogance and boastfulness in spite of one's (justified) high self-assessment, and to be careful not to interpret one's (true) superiority as granting one extra, more permissive, moral rights."[38]

According to Statman, then, humility exists in those who justifiably think themselves great but avoid ostentatious displays of that greatness. Clearly, the cogency of Statman's account of humility depends on whether a person can ever justifiably think of herself as great. Yet Statman does not seem to appreciate the extent to which people are deceived about their putative greatness.[39] In a recent study of this subject, Stephen Moroney compiles an impressive amount of literature—mostly from social psychology—that strongly suggests that we *routinely* exaggerate our talents and abilities.[40] We also tend to overrate the quality of our character, usually by excusing our moral deficits and ignoring the self-serving nature of our putatively good actions.[41] Given our tendency to deceive ourselves in these ways, how can we ever be justified in thinking that we are great? Such high self-appraisals are rendered untrustworthy by the numerous errors that plague our self-understanding.[42] As a result, it seems as if we are rarely, if ever, actually able to be humble according to Statman's understanding of humility.

Aquinas' account of humility is sensitive to the self-deceptive tendencies of human beings. As he understands the term, humility forestalls unduly high self-appraisals, which he takes to be rooted in an immoderate desire for praise, also known as *vainglory*.[43] For Aquinas, the term "glory" refers to the display of something great or beautiful, say a commendable quality or achievement which attracts the admiration of others.[44] The term could also refer to the belief that one's own good is worthy of praise and adoration.[45] Of course, to praise one's own good is not in itself sinful. After all, one ought to praise those things that have genuine value. Yet when the praise we seek is "vain and empty" it becomes an object of vainglory. For example, Aquinas insists that the desire for glory or praise is vain when it is sought strictly for oneself and not God's honor.[46]

Moreover, Aquinas describes vainglory as a "capital vice." Capital vices are dispositions whose objects are so desirable that we may commit a host of condemnable acts in order to attain them.[47] Vainglory is such a vice because it spawns a variety of sins (Aquinas calls them "daughters"), all of which are done for the sake of others' praise and admiration. For example, *boasting* is often for the sake of gaining others' honor or approval.[48] Similarly, *discord* and *contention* are due to the belief that resisting the will of others is somehow praiseworthy.[49] *Obstinacy* is being unduly committed to one's own opinion or averse to considering better ones.[50] *Disobedience* occurs whenever one defies the command of a superior.[51] Another expression of vainglory is *love of novelty*, whereby one desires to impress others through gratuitous inventions or achievements.[52] If one misrepresents one's actual abilities or boasts achievements that are not one's own, then one commits the sin of *hypocrisy*.[53]

Humility functions as a corrective to the aforementioned sins, and thus should be of interest to anyone concerned about what virtues might sustain the deliberative practices of the academy. For who would deny that the tendencies Aquinas associates with vainglory are inherently at odds with goodwill, deference, tolerance, and civil debate? In the absence of humility, we are more likely to conduct ourselves in self-righteous ways. We may denigrate others who advocate views different from our own. Also, we may be overly confident in our beliefs and refuse to consider views that might challenge them or even help us acquire a more truthful account of the world. Insofar as humility forestalls these tendencies, there is good reason to consider it an ideal virtue for institutions committed to democratic education.

Paul Weithman addresses many of these issues in his own account of humility and its opposing vices. And while his discussion of humility is different from mine in important respects (I will return to his discussion below), his account of vainglory is helpful here. He notes that we are especially vulnerable to the sins associated with vainglory when engaged in argument:

> Arguments can, after all, be highly competitive affairs, and the winners often enjoy a sense of their own superiority. Sometimes too they enjoy the acknowledgement of their intellectual superiority by the vanquished or their auditors. Undue attachment to these spoils of victory can lead one to argue for the wrong reasons, to endorse bad arguments, to refuse to listen to the interlocutor. This is no doubt why Aquinas numbered the argumentative vices of contention, discord, and pertinacity among the daughters of vainglory.[54]

Weithman's description of vainglory's daughters as "argumentative vices" is illuminative for our purposes. Contention, discord, obstinacy, and hypocrisy aptly describe the nature of contemporary moral debate, both in the academy and the larger culture. And while calls for civility and respect are no doubt laudable, genuine exemplification of these qualities will depend in part on one's preexisting dispositions. In other words, we need certain virtues in order to listen sympathetically, to value others' contributions, and to express goodwill to those with whom we disagree. In the absence of those virtues, we will lack the motivation to participate consistently in the academy's deliberative practices.

Aquinas' account of humility addresses this concern. Recall that humility is a part of temperance. As such, it is precisely the sort of virtue that can avert those sins precipitated by an excessive desire for praise, admiration, and even intellectual achievement. In order to illustrate the significance of this point, consider Aquinas' account of *studiositas*. According to Aquinas, *studiositas* concerns the pursuit of knowledge. And while it may seem appropriate to construe *studiositas* as an intellectual virtue, Aquinas insists that it, like humility, denotes a kind of appetitive restraint.[55] Thomas Hibbs's gloss on this subject is helpful. As he explains, we are sometimes "so captivated by the objects of knowledge that we are oblivious to other relevant goods."[56] We therefore need *studiositas* because it guides our desire for knowledge to the appropriate objects and "away from less noble inquiries and objects of knowledge."[57] While it is not the purpose of this paper to explore the virtue of *studiositas*, the concept enables us to see more clearly that our intellectual practices are always governed—and often stifled—by what we desire. It is for this reason that we need humility to restrain our desire for praise and forestall any behavior that is inimical to goodwill, civility, and mutual respect. Insofar as humility accomplishes these tasks, I think it can actually promote successful participation in those practices deemed central to democratic education.

MUST HUMILITY BE A THEOLOGICAL VIRTUE?

There is one aspect of humility I have yet to address, namely, its theological nature. According to Aquinas, humility strengthens our relationship with God by expelling pride and making us more receptive to his grace.[58] Aquinas therefore says that humility aims at our spiritual welfare by tempering the desire to exalt oneself through personal achievement.[59] Participants in the liberal academy may find this aspect of humility objectionable and seek an account of humility shorn of its theological content.

There are two issues that need attention here. The first one is whether the theological aspects of humility are severable from Aquinas' account. One might think that his view is not only circumscribed by theological commitments, but that it derives its intelligibility from them.[60] If Aquinas' account of humility is irreducibly theological, then nonreligious academics may resist annexing humility into their repertoire of democratic virtues. Second, suppose we *could* excise the theological content from Aquinas' account. Should we seek to do so? There is at least one good reason for answering this question in the negative. But before I discuss that reason, I'll address the question of whether one's acceptance of humility (as Aquinas understands it) also requires that one embrace its theological aspects.

According to Aquinas' view of humility, one need not embrace any particular set of theological commitments as a condition for being humble. Nor do theological commitments bestow intelligibility on the concept of humility itself. For while it is true that humility, ideally conceived, "regards chiefly the subordination of man to God,"[61] Aquinas acknowledges that one can achieve some degree of humility simply by engaging in actions associated with it.[62] For example, "acknowledging one's shortcomings," "putting others above oneself," "refraining from stubbornness," "not being in a hurry to speak," "avoiding immoderate speech," "checking one's laughter," "avoiding haughty looks," and similar acts can restrain outward manifestations of pride and, in turn, produce a progressively better (that is, more humble) character.[63] In short, the aforementioned actions can eventuate in an internal change whereby a person is not so inclined to value her own putative excellence. From this perspective, she can be humble apart from subordinating herself to

God. And presumably she can understand and appreciate what humility requires apart from any religious reference.

Of course, Aquinas thinks that only God can provide us with the virtues and gifts necessary for perfect moral rectitude. Yet he also thinks that the natural good of human beings is not wholly lost because of sin.[64] Although the desire for virtue is diminished by the Fall, human beings can nevertheless acquire an imperfect measure of moral virtue through the proper exercise of their natural aptitudes.[65] By "moral virtue" I have in mind qualities such as temperance, justice, and courage. Since humility is a part of temperance, we should expect that those who are not particularly religious could cultivate at least some measure of humility. More to the point, the virtue of temperance seems perfectly intelligible apart from a theological context, and thus there is no good reason to think that its subsidiary virtues are not similarly intelligible. I'll have a bit more to say about this issue below. But for now, I see no reason to suppose that one's endorsement of humility requires an acceptance of the theological commitments Aquinas happens to have.[66]

The more important question now seems to be this: in the context of the liberal academy, would a nontheological variant of humility be preferable to an expressly Christian one? Some people think so. A potential worry here is that outright advocacy of religious ideals may be disrespectful to those who do not share them. Paul Weithman offers an argument along these lines.[67] On his view, we Christians ought to refrain from advocating or appealing to religious ideals when arguing in public contexts. Instead, we should adhere to the requirement of democratic liberalism and "try to cast [our] arguments in terms that others could accept even without accepting our religious views."[68] In conducting ourselves in this way, we respect those who have beliefs and reasons for acting that are different from our own. According to Weithman, such respect may serve as an ideal corrective to religious pride, intolerance, and the "belief in or desire for superiority [over] citizens who do not share [our] religious views."[69]

Weithman admits that the sort of respect he describes here is not perfectly analogous to Christian humility. For this reason, he suggests that people can seek for themselves a theologically richer account of humility if they desire. Those who want such an account, however, "must seek it in the revelation of divine greatness and in the practices of their churches."[70] In order to limit religious intolerance and disrespect, however, we can simply abstain from invoking religious ideals and adhere to the Rawlsian notion of "respect[ing] other citizens as reasonable."[71] According to Weithman, the Rawlsian idea of respect is consistent with Christian humility. In fact, it "reinforces and prepares the way for the humility Christians must learn elsewhere."[72] The primary difference between Rawlsian respect and Christian humility is that the former is more modest in scope. In other words, Rawlsian respect "aims only at inculcating habits that hold pride and contempt in check" and does not require one to embrace the commitments with which Christian humility is often associated.[73]

I think that Weithman is right to claim that one need not embrace a theologically rich account of humility in order to enjoy some of its benefits. Yet there are two aspects of his argument that should give us pause. First, despite its admirable features, the notion of Rawlsian respect is not an ideal substitute for humility, even for the purpose of treating other people as reasonable. As we have seen, humility is an appetitive state that prevents improper boasting, unduly high self-estimations, contempt for others, and so forth. As such, it equips us with the motivation to treat others with genuine respect and charity. Rawlsian respect, however, is an act of argumentative restraint whereby one refuses to argue from religious considerations. And while the latter may curtail acts of disrespect and religious intolerance, it does not necessarily assuage attitudes that yield conceit or a false sense of superiority, religious or otherwise. In short, argumentative restraint is not enough because it fails to address our extant motivational shortcomings. A more fully developed humility, however, offers something of unique and irreducible value. In contrast to argumentative restraint, humility can actually motivate us to submit to what honest inquiry and respectful deliberation require. Of course, one could argue that practicing respect can help foster a more humble character, but this claim simply underscores the need for something richer than Rawlsian respect.

Second, it is not clear how respect (as Weithman describes it) would require one to remain silent about one's religious beliefs. In fact, such a requirement seems to render the virtue of respect unnecessary. Why seek to cultivate deliberative virtues when the views most likely to generate conflict are prevented from being heard? There is no need to respect a view one never has to confront. In an environment like the liberal academy, we will inevitably encounter objectionable views. And it is for precisely this reason that we extol mutual respect as a desirable quality. Rather than asking people with divisive or unpopular views not to appeal to them, perhaps we should seek to cultivate those virtues that prepare us to entertain and discuss views we do not necessary share.[74]

Having noted my hesitations about Weithman's account, I'll now offer a reason for why we should not extract humility from its theological context. If Christianity possesses insights about humility one cannot find elsewhere, then excluding religiously inspired considerations may prevent one from gaining a richer grasp of the subject. In order to make this point clearer, I will return once again to Daniel Statman's essay. On his

view, standard accounts of humility require that, in order to be humble,
a person must (1) have an accurate understanding of her ability and character and (2) not think highly of herself.[75] But suppose a person is, as
Statman describes, "genuinely admirable and worthy."[76] Would it be
appropriate for her to think highly of herself and still remain humble?
Apparently not, since doing so would violate the second condition for
humility. For this reason, Statman thinks that humility traditionally
understood does not allow a truly great person to acknowledge her greatness *and* be humble. Statman considers a possible solution to this problem. According to this solution, a truly admirable person can be humble
so long as her self-estimations are congruent with her actual character
and abilities. She must, so the argument goes, "keep [her] accomplishments in perspective" by not misjudging or exaggerating her merit and
achievements.[77] Yet what it means to have such a perspective is not clear.
Consider a person who, as Statman describes, is a

> human being who has many of the virtues that . . . determine per-
> sonal merit; a person who is pleasant, benevolent, clever, sensitive,
> good-looking, brave, assertive, a good father [or mother], etc.; a per-
> son who is blessed with many natural qualities, and who has also
> achieved striking gains thanks to his [or her] will power, courage,
> and hard work.[78]

He then asks, "What exactly would it mean for such a person to keep
his [or her] qualities and achievements 'in perspective'?"[79] The answer
depends on the perspective of those to whom she is being compared.
Most people will think that the person just described warrants exception-
ally high praise. Yet if we compare that person to those who are singularly unique in character, ability, and intelligence, then she may not
appear all that exceptional.[80] Statman denies, however, that this should
prevent a person from ever thinking highly of herself: "The fact that one
can always be a better person in one or another respect does not rule out
the possibility that one's achievements might truly be impressive."[81]

But is there a perspective according to which one might justly refrain
from thinking highly of oneself? Whatever that perspective is, it must be
one according to which all human beings—including the most gifted and
accomplished—rightly see themselves as having comparatively little
worth. According to Statman, we can find such a perspective within the
Judeo-Christian worldview.[82] For those who take such a view as their
conceptual point of departure, " 'keeping things in perspective' . . . would
be understanding how low human worth is in comparison with God's
greatness. It would mean grasping the fact that even the worthiest man,
such as Abraham, is really only 'dust and ashes.' "[83] This view is noticeably similar to one offered by Augustine who, while considering the mag-

nificence of God's power and wisdom, sees that human beings are "sinful" and but a "tiny part" of creation.[84] Given our creaturely limits and moral frailties, it seems odd that anyone could justly think of himself as great—especially when God is the standard of comparison.

Statman treats this view with admirable deference. Yet he does not seem inclined to accept it, which is why he offers an alternative view of humility. Regardless of his attitude toward the religious view, there is, I think, an important lesson he wishes to draw from it: analyses of humility are not neutral with respect to "rival theories of human worth."[85] In other words, the account of humility one accepts will always reflect a substantive view of human nature and value. According to the Judeo-Christian tradition, human beings are valued by God but nevertheless deficient in character and ability. If anyone (regardless of religious perspective) is inclined to think that humility requires one to acknowledge that moral weakness and intellectual finitude are constituents of human nature, then one might want to consider the theological context within which such a view makes the most sense.[86]

Now, Statman thinks that we cannot make sense of humility, traditionally conceived, independently of such a context: "Humility [so construed] is intelligible as a virtue only within religion."[87] I think this claim is too strong, and I have already given reasons for rejecting it. Yet a slightly weaker version of this claim seems warranted. One could say, for example, that a theological context is *superior* to others in helping us understand *why* we should consider humility a desirable trait. If humility is central to democratic education, then considering religious accounts of the subject may benefit persons who desire to emulate humility in more consistent ways. In fact, a theological account may offer insights that *only* such an account can provide. If this is true, perhaps those insights provide better reasons for being humble and, *a fortiori*, do a better job of promoting humility as a virtue that is necessary for democratic education.

CONCLUSION

Democratic education requires people who desire to practice civility, mutual respect, and reasoned debate; it requires people who are motivated to recognize the integrity of views they do not accept. According to the account I have provided here, one cannot sustain such practices without having been shaped by the right kinds of dispositions. Humility is just such a disposition, and for this reason we should include it within democratic education's catalogue of virtues. In short, we should consider humility a deliberative virtue. Of course, a person might be reluctant to embrace the theological commitments that accompany traditional accounts of humility. And while my defense of humility does not require her to accept those commitments, her allegiance to democratic education may be measured by whether she is willing to consider and evaluate their alleged truth. At the very least, she should recognize that humility—a virtue on which the success of our deliberative practices depends—is tied to and bequeathed by the Christian tradition.

Chapter 8

Cultivating Humility

Teaching Practices Rooted in Christian Anthropology

—Stephen K. Moroney, Matthew P. Phelps,
and Scott T. Waalkes

INTRODUCTION

Christian scholars have a long history of interest in virtues and virtue ethics, rooted especially in the work of Aristotle, Augustine, and Aquinas. According to Alasdair MacIntyre, a virtue is an "acquired human quality the possession and exercise of which tends to enable us to achieve those goods which are internal to practices and the lack of which effectively prevents us from achieving any such goods."[1] We assume that the central practices of higher education are *learning* practices aimed at seeking the good called *truth*. While acknowledging that other virtues, such as studiousness and integrity, are requisite to learning and pursuing truth, in this essay we focus on cultivating the virtue of humility in students.[2]

Although humility was a vice for Aristotle, Hume, and Nietzsche, it is an essential virtue for several Christian scholars who explore the role of virtues in higher education. Mark Schwehn asserts that humility "is both a spiritual excellence and a pedagogical virtue."[3] Parker Palmer describes the nature and purpose of humility as follows:

Humility is the virtue that allows us to pay attention to "the other"—
be it student or subject—whose integrity and voice are so central to
knowing and teaching in truth. Its opposite is the sin of pride, once
defined by G.K. Chesterton as "seeing oneself out of proportion to
the universe." In the words of Karl Deutsch, humility is "an attitude
towards facts and messages outside of oneself . . . openness to experience as well as to criticism . . . a sensitivity and responsiveness to
the needs and desires of others."[4]

According to Elton Trueblood, "students who are really humble are eager
to learn because they realize how little they know."[5] Indeed, it is precisely
a lack of humility in students that Mark Schwehn identifies as a key spiritual barrier to learning:

Much of what passes for laziness or the proverbial 'lack of motivation' among today's students really involves a lack of humility, stem-
ming in part from a lack of piety or respect for that aspect of God's
ongoing creation that manifests itself in works of genius. . . . *Some
degree of humility is a precondition for learning.*[6]

If one acknowledges that a lack of humility is an intellectual deficiency
in students that keeps them from learning as well as and as much as they
could, one is then confronted with the practical issue of how to cultivate
learners who are more humble. Here we have several concerns with the
current literature. For example, James Sire relegates the cultivation of
humility to practices removed from academic life. He offers the following
advice to students:

Listening to your friends respond honestly to your best thoughts is
a relatively easy if painful way [to cultivate humility]. But rereading
the Sermon on the Mount is even better, if more devastating. Can
you do so and remain proud? Immersion in Scripture, meditation on
the mind and life of Jesus, active participation in a specific community of faith: these are the best ways to humility.[7]

While Sire's advice has merit, it does not address the cultivation of humility in the classroom. In contrast, Richard Foster's advice is directly rooted
in academic practices:

It soon becomes obvious that study demands humility. Study simply
cannot happen until we are willing to be subject to the subject matter. We must submit to the system. We must come as student, not
teacher. Not only is study directly dependent upon humility, but it
is conducive to it. Arrogance and a teachable spirit are mutually
exclusive.[8]

Foster's advice more directly addresses our focus on cultivating humility in the classroom. However, he offers little specific advice about how teachers might do so. Parker Palmer *does* offer specific advice rooted in academic practices, yet his concern is the development of humble teachers, not students.[9] Student virtues are at the heart of Jay Wood's *Epistemology: Becoming Intellectually Virtuous*. Throughout most of his book, however, he tends to focus on virtues as *preconditions* for learning rather than as *fruits* of engaging in the learning process. When he specifically addresses how virtues are acquired and why it is that some people are more virtuous than others, Wood emphasizes "personal choices" in which we detect our intellectual deficiencies and resolve to correct them, as well as the roles of "accidents of history, geography, and the natural lottery."[10]

In sharp contrast to Wood's emphasis on personal choice, Mark Schwehn enlists the view of John Henry Newman, as follows:

> Newman nevertheless insisted that a virtue like humility depended, finally, upon religious conviction. . . . [H]umility could not be, for Newman, an achievement, the result of willful exertion—that was modesty; rather, humility arose in the soul as a natural accompaniment of religious affections such as awe and reverence before the greatness of God.[11]

We agree with Newman that the "greatness of God" is a powerful, humbling force. In addition, we hold that a proper understanding of others and ourselves, rooted in Christian anthropology, should inspire humility in students. Therefore, our first thesis is that *students can be humbled by understanding others as made in the image of God and themselves as limited and sinful*. In the first half of the chapter we use a tripartite Christian anthropology—humans as the *imago Dei*; as finite, limited creatures; and as sinners—to underscore the need for humility in learning. Furthermore, we believe it is important to show how humility can and should be cultivated through teaching practices *within* academic disciplines. The cultivation of humility should not be relegated to spiritual practices outside of the normal activities involved in learning an academic subject. Hence, our second thesis is that *the very subjects we teach offer plentiful resources for cultivating humility in our students*. In the second half of the chapter we describe ways in which we try to cultivate humility in our students as we teach within the disciplines of international studies, psychology, and theology. Our aim is to provide educators with theological and pedagogical resources for cultivating humble learners.

CHRISTIAN ANTHROPOLOGY AS A FRAMEWORK FOR CULTIVATING HUMILITY IN STUDENTS

Humans as the Image of God

In a recent book, Martha Nussbaum argues that liberal education should cultivate "world citizens" who develop a "narrative imagination," in which students imagine themselves in the shoes of people very different from themselves.[12] She argues that the development of this imaginative capacity breeds compassion, which she describes as being "willing to entertain the thought that this suffering person might be me." But we need to draw lines: "which creatures am I to count as my fellow creatures?"[13] Unfortunately, Nussbaum offers little guidance about which "creatures" are to be objects of compassion, other than to commend the reading of literature.[14] While we concur that reading literature can cultivate compassion, we contend that the doctrine of the *imago Dei*—the teaching that human beings are created in the image of God—offers a clearer and firmer basis for relating to others.[15]

Why should students *care* about people different from themselves? Christians can offer an answer deeper than mere imaginative compassion, for they confess that God as Creator is the basis for our creaturely relationships. The Genesis story emphatically introduces the point: "Then God said, 'Let us make man in our image, our likeness.' . . . So God created man in his own image, in the image of God he created him; male and female he created them" (1:26-27).[16] But how does this teaching ground humility? As students internalize the doctrine of the *imago Dei*, they open themselves to hearing the voice of God or seeing the face of God in others. In the words of Herman Bavinck:

> The image of God is far too rich to be completely represented by a single human being, no matter how gifted he [or she] might be. That image can only be disclosed in its depth and riches in the whole of humanity with its millions of members. As the traces of God (*vestigia Dei*) are spread out over the many works of God, both in space and time, so the image of God can only be seen in its totality in a humanity whose members exist both after and next to each other.[17]

Richard Mouw echoes this point, writing that "there is no one human individual or group who can fully bear or manifest all that is involved in the image of God, so that there is a sense in which that image is collectively possessed. The image of God is, as it were, parceled out among the peoples of the earth. By looking at different individuals and groups we get glimpses of different aspects of the full image of God."[18] The *imago Dei*, as an ontological reality, tells us that every human person reflects in some way the glory of God, reminding students that they need to approach others with humility because those others reflect God to them.

Scripture commends at least three ways of respecting God's image in others, each of which pushes us more deeply into humility. First, Genesis 9:6 and James 3:9-10 link injunctions against killing or cursing others to their bearing God's image. Nicholas Wolterstorff neatly summarizes the idea: "An act of injury to my fellow human being is an act of injury to God."[19]

Second, the *imago Dei* defines others as neighbors worthy of love, because God loves them (John 3:16). As Thomas Merton puts it, "To say that I am made in the image of God is to say that love is the reason for my existence, for God is love."[20] As the loving God incarnate, Jesus reminded his disciples to love their enemies. He reminded them that God sends rain and sun to the just and the unjust, caring for all. He pointed out that anyone could love his or her family and friends. Even the tax collectors did that. But could people love their enemies (Matt 5:44-48)? To see our most reviled enemies—the very people we define as subhuman—as neighbors, as worthy of our love, we need to emulate God. Jesus, as God-in-the-flesh, practiced this kind of love toward Samaritans, the out-group of his day (Luke 10:25-37; John 4:7-10). Humility of this kind means emulating Christ and redefining all people, even enemies, as neighbors. As C. S. Lewis put it, "The load, or weight, or burden of my neighbor's glory should be laid on my back, a load so heavy that only humility can carry it. . . . Next to the Blessed Sacrament itself, your neighbour is the holiest object presented to your senses."[21]

Third, we reflect God's image when we practice hospitality in community.[22] Witness the story of Abraham and the three visitors (Gen 18). When three strangers approach Abraham, the text says, "he hurried from the entrance of his tent to meet them and bowed low to the ground," addressing one of them humbly as "my lord" (Gen 18:2-5). Abraham treats these strangers with care, starting with a humble bow. Unbeknownst to him, he may have been welcoming God himself; according to Eastern Orthodox tradition, the three visitors in the story point us to the Trinity. Viewing the doctrine of the Trinity through the *imago Dei*, it is possible to say that human beings were created by, and in the image of, "an Eternal Community of three fully connected persons."[23] To be created in God's image is to be created in and for community. Abrahamic hospitality—humility toward strange others—is commended throughout the Hebrew canon, where God's people were reminded that they should care especially for widows, orphans, and strangers—precisely the people most vulnerable to exclusion from the Hebrew community (e.g., Ruth; Ps 146:7-9). To foster a community of *shalom*, these outsiders needed to be made welcome. That was difficult for the Hebrews, just as true hospitality is difficult for us. It requires a willingness to welcome outsiders, which demands humility. The humbling of the prophet Jonah makes this point most strongly in Scripture, reminding us that God loved and cared even for Israel's archenemies, the Assyrians in Nineveh. Every human is created in God's image. He loves them all.

Yet when confronted with outsiders in the classroom, many of our students fail to display humility. They, like all of us, often fail to see God's image in others. They may overlook how they are connected to others in human community. And it is easy for them to interpret others' lives arrogantly. The more dissimilar the other, the more likely students are to view him or her as something less than a child of God. Thus, it is urgent to instill humility in the classroom, and one way is to cling to the truth that others reflect God and have something to teach us.

Humans as Finite, Limited Creatures

Scripture testifies that human beings are made in the very image of God. Thus, as argued in the preceding section, we should approach such image bearers with humility, being open to the truth they have to offer to us, even if, perhaps especially if, they are quite different from ourselves. This high view of others is one biblical basis for the cultivation of humble learners.

Another basis is the low view of human beings as finite, limited creatures crafted from finite elements. In Genesis 2:7 we read, "the Lord God formed the man from the dust of the ground and breathed into his nostrils the breath of life, and the man became a living being." Not only is creation from "dust" explicit in this passage, but it is implicit as well. The root of the Hebrew word for man is the color red—possibly referring to the red earth—and it bears a striking resemblance to the Hebrew word for ground. Thus, the very name given by God to the first humans and to humankind in general reminds us that we are dust (Gen 5:1-2).[24]

Because we are prone to forget our humble beginnings, reminders are scattered throughout the Scriptures. Job reminds us when he says to God, "Remember that you molded me like clay. Will you now turn me to dust again?" (Job 10:9). Psalm 90 proclaims, "You return men back to dust, saying, 'Return to dust, O sons of men'" (v. 3). Psalm 103 declares, "As a father has compassion on his children, so the LORD has compassion on those who fear him; for he knows how we are formed, he remembers that we are dust" (vv. 13-14). In the first letter to the church in Corinth we read, "The first man was of the dust of the earth, the second man from heaven" (15:47).

Humility, like *Adam*, is a word with an earthy root. It is derived from the Latin, *humus*, meaning fertile ground.[25] Richard Foster asserts that, "in one sense humility is nothing more than staying close to the earth."[26] We find the spatial metaphor of "staying close to the earth" to be an especially suitable one for capturing the essence of humility. It suggests that to cultivate humility one must simply remember one's true name. It also suggests that mere propositional knowledge of being made from dust is insufficient for growing in humility. Rather, the kind of "remembering" called for is kinesthetic. One must adopt the proper posture—a dependent, subordinate posture—under God, others, and the world.

The posture of human beings is integral to a key biblical theme: God exalts the humble and brings down the proud. God reminds his people that they are incapable of knowing and serving him from a stance of prideful autonomy and calls them to an appropriate, subordinate relationship to their Creator. For instance, we find a strong reminder and call to humility in Deuteronomy 8:2-3:

> Remember how the LORD your God led you all the way in the desert these forty years, to humble you and to test you in order to know what was in your heart, whether or not you would keep his commands. He humbled you, causing you to hunger and then feeding you with manna, which neither you nor your fathers had known, to teach you that man does not live on bread alone but on every word that comes from the mouth of the LORD.

In addition to its expression in biblical narratives, the humility theme can be found in the Psalms, Proverbs, and books of the New Testament: "You save the humble but bring low those whose eyes are haughty" (Ps 18:27); "Before his downfall a man's heart is proud, but humility comes before honor" (Prov 18:12); "Therefore, whoever humbles himself like this child is the greatest in the kingdom of heaven" (Matt 18:4); "For whoever exalts himself will be humbled, and whoever humbles himself will be exalted" (Matt 23:12); "He has brought down rulers from their thrones but has lifted up the humble" (Luke 1:52); "Humble yourselves before the Lord, and he will lift you up" (Jas 4:10).

The Scriptures clearly and strongly promote humility as a desirable character trait. Yet, one could reasonably ask, what makes humility a *virtue*? To what end, or *telos*, do the biblical teachings on humility point? From our perspective, the clearest answer to this question is found in the letter to the Philippians:

> Do nothing out of selfish ambition or vain conceit, but in humility consider others better than yourselves. Each of you should look not only to your own interests, but also to the interests of others. Your attitude should be the same as that of Christ Jesus: Who, being in very nature God, did not consider equality with God something to be grasped, but made himself nothing, taking the very nature of a

servant, being made in human likeness. And being found in appearance as a man, he humbled himself and became obedient to death—
even death on a cross! Therefore God exalted him to the highest
place and gave him the name that is above every name, that at the
name of Jesus every knee should bow, in heaven and on earth and
under the earth, and every tongue confess that Jesus Christ is Lord,
to the glory of God the Father (2:3-11).

With respect to humility, as in everything else, Jesus Christ is our *telos*.
With respect to humility, as in everything else, we are to be transformed
into his image (Rom 8:29; 2 Cor 3:18). We see in this passage that Jesus
Christ, Lord of all creation (Col 1:15-20), humbled himself in becoming
human, in serving others, and in obeying the Father to the point of death.
We see God himself not considering "equality with God something to be
grasped." We see God himself coming down to earth—taking on the form
of animate earth—taking on the limitations of human nature.[27] We see in
Jesus Christ a person with bodily limitations (John 4:6) and cognitive
limitations (Mark 9:21; 13:32) but without sins (Heb 4:15). In short, we
see in the incarnation a clear affirmation of human creatureliness and the
posture that constitutes an appropriate response to it.

Although it is relatively neglected by many theologians, human creatureliness is a dominant aspect of Christian anthropology for others, such
as Reinhold Niebuhr, who writes, "The Biblical view is that finiteness,
dependence, and the insufficiency of man's mortal life are facts which
belong to God's plan of creation and must be accepted with reverence and
humility."[28] Similarly, C. Stephen Evans states that, "[n]o Christian view
of man can afford to ignore the fact that man is solidly part of nature.
That man is dust, a bodily creature, makes this especially evident. It is
bodily existence which serves as a forceful reminder of man's general
creatureliness and the limitations which go with that status."[29] Note that
for Niebuhr and Evans human finitude and creatureliness are not evil.
Yet, Niebuhr clearly articulated the relation between human limitations
and sin: "Sin is occasioned precisely by the fact that man refuses to admit
his 'creatureliness' and to acknowledge himself as merely a member of the
total unity of life. He pretends to be more than he is."[30] Niebuhr further
observes that "the evil arises when the fragment seeks by its own wisdom
to comprehend the whole or attempts by its own power to realize it."[31]

In order to avoid the sin of pride, we must understand and acknowledge our limitations. We must adopt a posture of epistemic humility
grounded in our creation from dust, in God's reminders of our proper
stance before him, and in God's concrete demonstration of that appropriate posture through the incarnation.

Humans as Sinners

The *imago Dei* in all people beckons us to be humbly open to what we may have to learn from "the other." Humility is also the proper response to our finite creaturely existence, which places severe restrictions on what can be known by any one of us individually, or by all humans collectively. We furthermore possess a third reason to be humble, namely that we are fallen persons whose thinking is distorted by our sin. The corrupting influence of sin on our thinking is a theme woven throughout the Bible, featured with special prominence in the Gospel of John.

John notes that people frequently fail to *understand* who Jesus is and fail to *accept* Jesus for who he is. John's prologue proclaims simply that the Word "was in the world, and though the world was made through him, the world did not recognize him. He came to that which was his own, but his own did not receive him" (1:10-11). Herman Ridderbos paraphrases: "The world to which the Logos came was his own creation. The world did not know him, not because he was a stranger but because it was estranged from him, from its origin. The world *should* have known him."[32] C. H. Dodd concurs "that God's people *ought* to 'know' Him is always assumed: it is unnatural that they should not know Him."[33] In the words of Rudolf Schnackenburg, John proclaims that the world "has deliberately and culpably closed its heart to the enlightening and salvific work of the Logos and in doing so has rejected God himself."[34]

John repeatedly narrates people's problems in receiving Jesus as the Son of God, the Messiah sent by His heavenly Father from above. In John 6:36 Jesus tells a crowd simply that, "you have seen me and yet do not believe." Rodney Whitacre paraphrases: "They saw him with their physical eyes, but they did not have the faith that sees the revelation of the Father in what Jesus was doing."[35] George Beasley-Murray comments that "to see and not believe is tantamount to a refusal of faith."[36] As Calvin puts it, Jesus' statement "is pointing to their voluntary blindness."[37]

Why this problem in responding properly to Jesus? John explains that people's perceptual failure to recognize Jesus, their cognitive failure to understand him, and their volitional failure to receive him are rooted in the fact that they love darkness and do evil. John provides a summary statement in 3:19-20. "This is the verdict: Light has come into the world, but men loved darkness instead of light because their deeds were evil. Everyone who does evil hates the light, and will not come into the light for fear that his deeds will be exposed." John proclaims that people's sin (loving darkness and doing evil deeds) is intimately connected with their failure to respond properly to Jesus. As Schnackenburg puts it, "the fault can only be on the side of men [and women]. Their inexplicable 'hatred' (v. 20; cf. 15:24) rises up from the abyss of a heart darkened by sin."[38]

Leon Morris comments astutely that "there is a moral basis behind much unbelief."[39] Personal sin (loving darkness and doing evil) distorts our wills and our thoughts, so that we deny the truth about ourselves and God by engaging in a wide range of cognitive distortions.[40]

On top of that, communal sin further compounds the problem. Jesus points to a sinful communal influence when he asks his hardened audience in John 5:44: "How can you believe if you accept praise from one another, yet make no effort to obtain the praise that comes from the only God?" Thomas Brodie notes that Jesus' audience here rejects him because "zeal for human glory shuts out God's glory."[41] As Brodie observes, "the problems of pride and prestige," often manifested on the corporate, communal level, "are powerful factors, often blinding."[42] The same hindrance of communal sin reappears in John 12 when people fail to confess faith in Jesus because "they loved praise from men more than praise from God" (v. 43).[43]

John 8:42-47 further elaborates on the noetic effects of sin. In verses 43 and 44 Jesus says to his hearers: "Why is my language not clear to you? Because you are unable to hear what I say. You belong to your father, the devil, and you want to carry out your father's desire." Jesus then describes the devil as "the father of lies," as a prelude to telling his hearers that "because I tell the truth, you do not believe me!" (v. 45). In Dodd's words, "it appears that failure to know God is a failure on the ethical plane."[44] Or, as Raymond Brown puts it, "the children of lying hate the truth."[45] These people do not understand what Jesus says and are unable to accept his message because they want to carry out wicked desires that blind them to the truth in Jesus. John's gospel repeatedly highlights how people's sin obscures the clarity with which they understand and accept Jesus and his message.

If we add to John's gospel the rest of the Christian Scriptures, the case becomes even stronger. Merold Westphal has argued that if we are to take the apostle Paul seriously we must see sin as a significant epistemological category.[46] George Zemek's biblical study led him to conclude that, "the noetic effects of the Fall are attested on nearly every page of the Holy Scriptures."[47] Put simply, the Christian Scriptures teach that both our personal sins and our corporate sins exert undesirable influences on our thinking and knowing. The fact that sin blinds or warps our thinking should drive us to greater humility, and to greater dependence on God and others to help us identify the distortions in our thinking. In the words of David Myers, "the belief we can hold with greatest certainty is the humbling conviction that some of our beliefs contain error."[48]

This, then, is our tripartite rationale for cultivating humble learners. Humility is the proper response to the fact that (1) others are made in God's own image, and may have something valuable to teach us, (2) we are limited creatures whose knowledge is tightly circumscribed by our finitude, and (3) we are fallen creatures whose thinking is distorted by our sin, both personal and corporate.

PEDAGOGICAL STRATEGIES FOR CULTIVATING HUMILITY IN STUDENTS

How might one use this framework to cultivate humility in students? In what follows, we each illustrate teaching strategies that are rooted in one of the three aspects of Christian anthropology and that draw upon discipline-specific resources. We demonstrate that our disciplines—international studies, psychology, and theology—offer plentiful resources for cultivating humility in students.

The *Imago Dei* and Cultivating Humble Learners in International Studies (Waalkes)

My international studies courses require that students learn about such others as French diplomats, Palestinian Christians, United Nations bureaucrats, and Jamaican farmers. I assume that many students start with negative images of people different from themselves. Therefore, to learn about these others, students must develop humility. But how can this be accomplished in the classroom? At least three strategies have worked well for me, each of them implicitly grounded in the doctrine of the *imago Dei*.

First, I seek to promote humility by creating an environment conducive to discussion and active learning—a hospitable classroom community that is open to others. I assign case studies of foreign policy decisions, a simulation of the United Nations General Assembly, and debates on global issues to force students to think about how non-Americans view U.S. choices in world politics. In other words, when France opposes the United States, it might be about more than the French hating the United States or being obstinate. When other nations get angry at the United States for its unilateralism, maybe we need to see it from their point of view. They too are God's creatures. Students need to understand why American foreign policy is resented and take a humble look at their own country. Getting students to think critically in this way is the main point of the course, and obviously it requires the cultivation of humility. One way I seek to promote humility in our UN simulation is by requiring that no student be allowed to represent the United States and by requiring that students stay in character in representing another country. Quite simply, they are forced to represent the views of other nations. Some students are struck by the question of how other nations view the United States and express a humble desire to learn more.

Second, I assign novels and narrative nonfiction in each of my upper-level courses, often with positive effects.[49] To translate Martha Nussbaum's "compassion" into Christian terms, humbly reading the stories of others made in the image of God may be an ideal way to practice hospitable community. Here I will touch on two highlights. In my Middle East politics course most students enter with negative images of Arabs in general and Palestinians in particular; they think of terrorists, suicide bombers, or jihadists.[50] Many evangelical students also come with premillennial or Christian Zionist frameworks that suggest that Christians should support the modern state of Israel because it is the fulfillment of biblical prophecy. The central goal of the course is to challenge these views. So, among other things, I assign Elias Chacour's story, told in the book *Blood Brothers* and retold in the book *We Belong to the Land*.[51] A Christian Palestinian, Chacour tells a compelling story about his family being uprooted from their ancestral village by Israelis in 1948, yet Chacour himself remains a pacifist. As part of an assignment on the book, I ask students how they would feel if they were unable to return to their native village, as Chacour was. Those humble enough to look at themselves honestly will admit that they would likely be angry. They can see why some Palestinians would want to lash out in violence. Yet Chacour did not. His example of nonviolent resistance to Israeli injustices humbles students. Several students have said that this book was an important influence in convicting them about their attitudes toward Palestinians and helping them to see Palestinians simply as human beings. Palestinians, too, it seems, are created in the image of God.

In my International Law and Organization course, I also deal with preconceived stereotypes of the subject matter. Thanks in part to the *Left Behind* series, some students now arrive thinking that the United Nations threatens to become a one-world government. If students get nothing else out of this course, they will have these views challenged by a delightful memoir (now sadly out of print) by Brian Urquhart, entitled *A Life in Peace and War*.[52] Urquhart shares his story of working in the United Nations Secretariat from the founding of the organization until the mid-1980s, giving students a firsthand glimpse of what it was actually like to work for the UN. Instead of vague abstractions, they get a poignant account of Urquhart's often frustrating work, an account that makes the United Nations look ineffective and far from a nascent world government. Students relate well to Urquhart's story; even a United Nations bureaucrat starts looking like an intriguing human being. Students who thought they knew what the UN was all about have, perhaps, been humbled. Or at least they have made a connection to the story of another image-bearer.

A final strategy that helps to cultivate humility is the use of film in the classroom.[53] In this highly visual age, it helps students to see images of image-bearers on a screen before them. The film medium sparks identification with characters. In a fictional work or a documentary, students may well inhabit the world of the characters or subjects, seeing the world as they see it. Among many others, one film that has proven powerful in both humbling students and challenging them to see the world through others' eyes is a well-crafted documentary entitled *Life and Debt*.[54] Made by Stephanie Black, this film juxtaposes the Jamaica experienced by tourists with the Jamaica experienced by ordinary residents of the island. Black documents the visible frustration of Jamaican farmers, workers, and business executives who have suffered from the imposition of free trade and International Monetary Fund policies on Jamaica's economy. By letting these others speak, she opens students to an alternative reading of globalization, challenging their complacent assumptions that poverty is simply due to laziness or other deficiencies. Students are humbled to see fellow creatures brought low by circumstances not of their own choosing, fellow creatures in God's image, fellow creatures deserving of their care. Film lets others speak directly to students, helping students to listen humbly.

Human Finitude and Cultivating Humble Learners in Cognitive Psychology (Phelps)

Although I also relate material to the *imago Dei*, in my cognitive psychology course I focus on how limitations of the mind reinforce a biblical view of humans as finite creatures.[55] At the beginning of the semester I present this perspective as an overarching framework for the course. Subsequently, I use the resources of the discipline to remind students that they, like all of us, are finite, limited creatures made from finite elements. Research findings in cognitive psychology are conducive to cultivating epistemic humility in students because they reveal the limitations of the human mind.[56]

One pedagogical strategy I employ is to demonstrate the limits of attention to students, which is easy to convey, since the study of attention is the study of cognitive limitations. We can only process a small amount of the information available to us at any one time. Our pool of mental resources is severely limited. Students can experience attentional limits as they try to do two tasks at the same time, such as repeat a message presented to one ear while a different message is presented to the other ear. Although students can repeat, or shadow, the one message, they are amazed that they process almost none of the meaning of the other, unattended, message.

I also have students experience the limits of visual attention as they perform visual search tasks. For example, I adapt a classic experiment for classroom use by having students search for the letter "T" among a display of many other letters. When the target letter has a unique feature, such at the horizontal line of a "T" among a set of "I"s and "Y"s, it is relatively easy to find; however, when all of the target's features are shared by the other letters, such as when a "T" is searched for among "I"s and "Z"s, it is more difficult to find. The reason, according to one theory, is that combining elementary features into objects requires visual attention to be "shined" on each letter in the display. Since the target in the second task has no unique features, only a unique combination of features, repeated allocations of visual attention to spatial locations are required to find it.[57] I also have students perform the similar, and more engaging, task of solving *Where's Waldo?* puzzles. They must find Waldo, clad in a red-and-white striped shirt and blue pants, among a dazzling collection of objects sharing all of Waldo's features. A key course objective is for students to be humbled by the finitude of human cognition as they study and experience the limits of attention.

A second pedagogical strategy is to reinforce the finitude of human cognition through a study of memory limitations. One kind of memory, working memory, involves the temporary storage and processing of a small amount of information in an active form. For example, we use working memory to hold intermediate steps in mind during mental arithmetic, such as adding 27 and 34. Many students experience the limits of working memory when asked to multiply the numbers instead. Those who can do that in their heads are inevitably humbled when asked to multiply even larger numbers such as 324 by 765. Simple demonstrations such as these can help students understand the nature and limits of working memory.

Another type of memory is long-term memory, which is surprisingly vulnerable to distortion. The most extreme forms of memory distortion are studied under the heading of false-memory research, which focuses on memories for things that never happened. Laboratory studies have produced levels of false memory for words that were not studied during an experiment that approach the level of accurate memory for words that were studied.[58] Students are astonished, perhaps even humbled, when they participate in a classroom demonstration based on this experiment, because they vividly remember words that were not on a list that they studied fifteen minutes earlier.[59] In addition, students appear to be humbled by research which demonstrates the creation of false memories for more life-like events. For example, by suggesting that family members remember the event and by having participants repeatedly try to remember it themselves, about 25 percent of participants come to form a false memory of a complex event that never happened, such as being lost in a mall as a child or spilling a punch bowl at a wedding.[60]

Perhaps the most personal and humbling way to demonstrate the limits of memory to students is to have them apply theories of forgetting to their study habits in college courses. Several conclusions typically emerge from this exercise. First, students forget because they do not engage in deep, elaborate processing that focuses on the meaning of material, its relation to things they already understand, and its relevance to their own lives. They engage in shallow processing instead as they simply read through notes or texts. Second, they mass their encoding attempts rather than distributing them across multiple, brief study sessions. Third, they forget course material due to interference from memories acquired in other, similar subjects. Fourth, they experience retrieval failure due to changes in environmental context or mood state between studying and attempting to recall material, since the contextual cues present when the material was learned are no longer available.

A final strategy I use to cultivate humility is to show that products of the mind, such as scientific theories, are limited, too. One way to do so is to expose students repeatedly to incomplete, transitory theories. For a given topic, we explore the predictions made by specific theories, both confirming and disconfirming experimental results, and an historical progression of theories with each new one attempting to address the weaknesses of the theories that came before it. The goal is to help students see that even our best theories about the mind are limited in scope, unable to account for all of the relevant data, and destined to be revised as were all the theories that came before them.

This point becomes especially clear to students when they work in groups to develop and test a theory of the contents of a sealed black box.[61] Students are typically uncertain about the accuracy of their final theory given the difficulty they experience in testing it. They become even less certain when they are exposed to contradictory theories from the other groups.[62] At its best, the task enables students to see their own limited ability to know, the limits of the scientific method, and the tentative nature of theories. In addition, this activity helps them to share the perspective of cognitive psychologists with respect to theories of cognition: we can evaluate the fit between theory and data, yet we can never be certain about the nature of human thought. We cannot open up the black box of the mind and peek inside.

In my cognitive psychology course, students are confronted with the limitations of attention, memory, and theory construction. I want them to leave the course with the conception that they are finite creatures, not just because their experience is limited to particular times and places during a finite lifespan, but also because their experience of any given time and place is circumscribed by cognitive limitations. It is my hope that studying, experiencing, and reflecting on cognitive limitations will help to cultivate epistemic humility in students.

Human Sin and Cultivating Humble Learners in Theology Courses (Moroney)

Just in case the *imago Dei* in others and finitude in ourselves have not cultivated sufficient humility in us and in our students, perhaps some reflection on sin will help. Theologians, especially those in the Reformed tradition, have historically argued that sin has a specially potent effect in distorting our thinking about God, which is the primary subject matter I teach: theology. John Calvin argued that sinful humans often exhibit marvelous comprehension of "earthly things" or matters relating to this life, but that our efforts to understand "heavenly things" or God are much more likely to be marred by the noetic effects of sin.[63] Abraham Kuyper and Emil Brunner argued similarly that in matters of observation and logic, perhaps most prominent in the natural sciences and mathematics, the noetic effects of sin are minimal in comparison with the study of God and God's requirements for us as God's creatures.[64] In other words, sin is much less likely to distort my thinking about calculus or organic chemistry than it is to distort my thinking about the nature of the afterlife or what God is like. Brunner asserted that "the disturbance of rational knowledge by sin" attains "its maximum in theology."[65] If Calvin, Kuyper, and Brunner are right in their analyses, then it is especially important for us to cultivate humble learners in the theology classroom. But how should this be done?

One technique is simply to show students experientially their need to be humble. This happens when we gently correct students' mistaken proclamations in class and point out their erroneous answers on exams. This also occurs when we craft carefully worded questions for small group discussions that engage students in communal learning with persons from other theological traditions. As they speak with their classmates over the course of several months, most students come to recognize ways in which their own perspectives are limited (that is, in need of enrichment from others) and occasionally just plain mistaken (that is, in need of correction from others). As students come to see their need of enrichment and correction from others, and as they begin to confront their blind spots (some due to finitude and some due to sin), many of them grow in humility.

A second pedagogical aid, also obvious but powerful, is modeling by the instructor. During the first or second week of my systematic theology course I tell students not to assent to a particular doctrine just because their textbook teaches it or I believe it, but only if they are convinced the doctrine is taught by Scripture and supported (or at least not contradicted by) church tradition, reason, and experience. I also tell the students that I am finite and a sinner (which comes as no surprise to them!), and consequently my own theological beliefs are in need of enrichment and correction from others. I tell them that during the course of the semester I will undoubtedly say some things that are incomplete and others that are wrong, and I tell them at those times I want them to raise their hands and question me or correct me. When students helpfully supplement or challenge what I say, if I am able to receive and acknowledge their corrective words, I model for them a higher allegiance to the truth than to my own current beliefs or sinful personal pride. Hopefully this too helps our students grow in humility.

A third approach, even more direct than the first two, is to provide some instruction about the noetic effects of sin and how it should engender humility in us. The Bible teaches that due to sin Christians need to be progressively transformed by the renewing of our minds (Rom 12:2). Part of putting off the old self and putting on the new self is to be made new in the attitude of our minds (Eph 4:23). Even Peter and Barnabas were susceptible to sinful social influences, and had to be shown the error of their ways by Paul (Gal 2:11-14). But can instruction about the noetic effects of sin really help? Is there not an "incoherence of supposing we can detect the noetic effects of sin by means of the very noetic faculties that suffer from those effects"?[66] It is true, of course, that there is no person (Jesus Christ excepted) and no human faculty that is exempt from sin's effects. Still, it is possible to identify, at least partially, the distortions in our thinking caused by sin if we are willing to be self-critical and open to correction from others.

Here I concur with Ted Peters's premise that "even though better understanding may not rid our lives of sin, it will alert us to what is happening and offer insights that can become opportunities."[67] Both for ourselves and for our students, Dewey Hoitenga is right in maintaining that "belief in the noetic effects of sin on their own faculties makes *more* rather than *less* likely that believers will discover their mistakes and be on guard against making them."[68]

A fourth approach, the most direct of all, is to encourage students to be humble about what they learn in their theology courses (humility not just during class but also afterward). During the second week of my course in systematic theology I exhort the students not to be sinfully proud about their knowledge or use it to put others down, but instead to use what they learn to serve others. I discuss with them a lengthy quote from one of their textbooks, that says:

> Those who study systematic theology will learn many things about the teachings of scripture that are perhaps not known or not known well by other Christians in their churches or by relatives who are older in the Lord than they are. They may also find that they understand things about scripture that some of their church officers do not understand, and that even their pastor has perhaps forgotten or never learned well. In all of these situations it would be very easy to adopt an attitude of pride or superiority toward others who have not made such a study. But how ugly it would be if anyone were to use this knowledge of God's Word simply to win arguments or to put down a fellow Christian in conversation, or to make another believer feel insignificant in the Lord's work. . . . Systematic theology rightly studied will not lead to the knowledge that "puffs up" (1 Cor. 8:1) but to humility and love for others.[69]

No subtlety here. Besides showing them experientially their need for humility, modeling humility for them, and instructing them on how sin distorts our thinking, tell them to be humble! While lacking in sophistication, this direct approach is commended by Jesus, who told his followers on four separate occasions that whoever humbles himself will be exalted (Matt 18:4, 23:12; Luke 14:11, 18:14); by Paul, who called on the Ephesians to be completely humble and gentle (Eph 4:2); and by James (Jas 1:10, 1:21, 4:10) and Peter (1 Pet 3:8, 5:6), who repeatedly exhorted their readers to humble themselves before the Lord and in relating to each other. Most humans have a propensity toward sinful pride, and therefore we need to seek humility intentionally.

Fifth, besides learning humility from their classmates, from us, and from Scripture, students can also learn humility from sinful mistakes they encounter in the history of theology. Sinful practices in the medieval church (the Crusades, papal corruption, etc.) humble us in considering how easily we can go astray. The same is true of the Reformation and post-Reformation period. The slaughtering of Anabaptists, the Thirty Years' War, excessive Puritan intolerance, pharisaic Fundamentalist legalism, "Christian German" support of Hitler—the church is replete with humbling illustrations of the blinding effects of sin from our "family history." As students examine the sinful tragedies of our past and their noetic effects, they are often humbled to reflect on how sin may distort their own thinking and that of their generation.

CONCLUSION

This chapter joins a larger discussion of intellectual virtue and moral formation among Christian scholars and educators. We affirm, with many others, that humility is a key to learning. Our contribution to the discussion is to move beyond general calls for humility in professors, and beyond suggestions for cultivating humility outside the classroom or simply by students' "personal choices." We have argued that *students can be humbled by understanding others as made in the image of God and themselves as limited and sinful*. We have also argued that *the very subjects we teach offer plentiful resources for cultivating humility in our students*, as we have demonstrated by describing humility-promoting practices that flow naturally from our three academic disciplines. We hope that our anthropological framework and disciplinary illustrations will inspire others to incorporate the cultivation of humility and other virtues into their teaching practices.

Lastly, we would like to conclude on a balancing note. While this essay focuses on cultivating more humble learners, at times we must also focus on cultivating more hopeful learners.[70] In our classes we aim for a proper balance of epistemic humility (recognizing that our knowledge is limited and contains distortions) and epistemic hope (recognizing that by the Spirit's gracious work in us we do know some truths now and someday we will know fully, even as we are fully known—according to 1 Corinthians 13:12). Our pedagogy must aim to instill humility in the dogmatists who are sure all their beliefs are correct, but also to instill hope in the skeptics and relativists who despair over attaining even a modicum of epistemological certitude. At times we must warn dogmatists against seeing the specks of imperfection in their classmates' eyes but being blinded by the logs in their own. Other times we must encourage skeptics and relativists to take a stand on issues by writing position papers in which they explain their own convictions and the reasons for them. In light of our finitude and fallenness, we should be humble, but we need not be agnostic or silent concerning our convictions. As Steven Stall has said, "knowledge kept to its proper sphere as partial and selective is still knowledge."[71]

Our classroom lectures, discussions, and other activities should aim to inculcate in all students the proper balance of epistemic humility and epistemic hope that is appropriate to our existence as those who are created in God's image, yet finite and fallen. This is part of what it means to live in the period of redemption in which God's kingdom is already present but not yet manifest in its fullness. This aspect of cultivating humility in our students is summed up nicely in the words of Richard Mouw:

We know that only the Creator has a clear and comprehensive knowledge of all things; thus we are humble. But God has also promised eventually to lead us into that mode of perfect knowledge that is proper to us as human creatures; thus we hope.[72]

Notes

INTRODUCTION

1   See the editorial "Intimidation at Columbia," *The New York Times*, April 7, 2005, A22, along with the response of Daniel Pipes in "Conservative Professors Hard to Find," *New York Sun*, April 12, 2005. This recent controversy at Columbia perpetuates a larger, ongoing debate. See Sara Hebel, "Patrolling Professors' Politics," *Chronicle of Higher Education*, February 13, 2004, along with Jeffrey Selingo, "U.S. Public's Confidence in Colleges Remains High," *Chronicle of Higher Education*, May 7, 2004. Despite the latter article's self-congratulatory title, the article itself reports that 51 percent of the respondents to a professionally designed poll "agree" or "strongly agree" that "colleges and universities improperly introduce a liberal bias in what they teach."

2   See Richard Rorty, Julie A. Reuben, and George Marsden, "The Moral Purposes of the University: An Exchange," *The Hedgehog Review* 2 (2000): 106–19; as well as Stanley Fish, "Why We Built the Ivory Tower," *The New York Times*, May 21, 2004, A23.

3   See Derek Bok, *Universities and the Future of America* (Durham, N.C.: Duke University Press, 1990).

4   To cite four examples, see Alexander Astin, "What Higher Education Can Do in the Cause of Citizenship," *Chronicle of Higher Education*, October 6, 1995, B1; Martha Nussbaum, *Cultivating Humanity: A Clas-*

191

sical Defense of Reform in Liberal Education (Cambridge, Mass.: Harvard University Press, 1997); William Galston, "Can Patriotism Be Turned into Civic Engagement?" *Chronicle of Higher Education*, November 16, 2001, B16–17; and Harry R. Lewis, *Excellence Without Soul: How a Great University Forgot Education* (New York: Public Affairs, 2006).

5   Some have accused Bok of providing but a shallow corrective for the ills he diagnosed. For example, John W. Donohue in "Three Cousins of Harvard" says of Bok's work that "President Bok often seems to be gazing upward at a Platonic world where the university exists in ideal form" (*America*, November 17, 1990, 369). Later, Donohue states that "Bok's call for a 'revival of moral education' is an admirable conclusion, but the case made for it is pallid" (370).

6   See Bok, "The Demise and Rebirth of Moral Education," in *Universities and the Future of America*, 55–78 for a useful summary of this important history. For a larger historical account, see Laurence Veysey, *The Emergence of the American University* (Chicago: University of Chicago Press, 1965); D. H. Meyer, *The Instructed Conscience: The Shaping of the American National Ethic* (Philadelphia: University of Pennsylvania Press, 1972); Julie A. Reuben, *The Making of the Modern University: Intellectual Transformation and the Marginalization of Morality* (Chicago: University of Chicago Press, 1996); and Mark Noll, "Introduction: The Christian Colleges and American Intellectual Traditions," in *The Christian College: A History of Protestant Higher Education in America*, ed. William Ringenberg, 2nd ed. (Grand Rapids: Baker Academic, 2006), 17–36.

7   Reuben, *Making of the Modern University*, 1–2.

8   Douglas Sloan, *Faith and Knowledge: Mainline Protestantism and American Higher Education* (Louisville, Ky.: Westminster John Knox, 1994).

9   For a more detailed account of "epistemological crisis," see Alasdair MacIntyre's "Epistemological Crises, Dramatic Narrative, and the Philosophy of Science," in *Why Narrative: Readings in Narrative Theology*, ed. Stanley Hauerwas and L. Gregory Jones (Grand Rapids: Eerdmans, 1989), 138–57.

10   Christopher Jencks and David Riesman, *The Academic Revolution* (New York: Doubleday, 1968).

11   See Mark R. Schwehn, *Exiles from Eden: Religion and the Academic Vocation in America* (New York: Oxford University Press, 1993) and Bruce Wilshire, *The Moral Collapse of the University: Professionalism, Purity, and Alienation* (Albany: State University of Albany Press, 1990).

12   Schwehn, *Exiles from Eden*, 4.

13   For most of the twentieth century, the modern university retained the notion that democratic polity is morally superior to nondemocratic polities. Increasingly, and not surprisingly, however, such commitments are regarded as pragmatic commitments or articles of faith rather than reasoned or principled commitments. See Richard Rorty, "The Priority of Democracy to Philosophy," in his *Objectivity, Relativism, and Truth*, Philosophical Papers 1 (New York: Cambridge University Press, 1991), 175–96.

14   For a good example of such thinking, see Francis Wayland, *The Elements of Moral Science* (Cambridge, Mass.: Belknap Press of Harvard University Press, 1963), the most popular moral philosophy textbook

of the nineteenth century. Wayland, an ordained Baptist minister, was president of Brown University, the first Baptist university in North America.

15   Charles Taylor, *The Ethics of Authenticity* (Cambridge, Mass.: Harvard University Press, 1992).

16   Alasdair MacIntyre, *After Virtue: A Study in Moral Theory*, 2nd ed. (Notre Dame: University of Notre Dame Press, 1984).

17   John Rawls, *Political Liberalism* (New York: Columbia University Press, 1993).

18   Michael Walzer, *Thick and Thin: Moral Argument at Home and Abroad* (Notre Dame: University of Notre Dame Press, 1994).

19   Cf. Nussbaum, *Cultivating Humanity,* and Stephen Macedo, *Liberal Virtues: Citizenship, Virtue, and Community in Liberal Constitutionalism* (Oxford: Clarendon, 1991). Both authors affirm in their own ways that citizenship in liberal societies requires allegiance to the state over more local communities.

20   An excerpt from a well-known British ethicist is instructive: "This book is not about what people ought to do. It is about what they are doing when they talk about what they ought to do. Moral philosophy, as I understand it, must not be confused with moralizing. A moralist is someone who uses moral language in what may be called a first-order way. He, qua moralist, engages in reflection, argument, or discussion about what is morally right or wrong, good or evil. He talks about what people ought to do. . . . By a moral philosopher I mean someone who . . . thinks and speaks about the ways in which moral terms, like 'right' or 'good,' are used by moralists when they are delivering their moral judgments" (W. D. Hudson, *Modern Moral Philosophy* [London: Macmillan, 1970], 2).

21   See Peter Singer, "Philosophers are Back on the Job," *New York Times Sunday Magazine*, July 7, 1974.

22   Bok himself insists that in the appropriate kind of moral education "the principal aim of the course is not to impart 'right answers' " (*Universities and the Future of America*, 73). In contrast, Michael Sandel insists that "republican politics cannot be neutral toward the values and ends its citizens espouse." According to Sandel, republican political theory requires a politics that cultivates in its citizens the kind of character self-government requires. By implication, republican political theory will require a different kind of moral education within which there are right and wrong answers. See Michael Sandel, *Democracy's Discontent: America in Search of a Public Philosophy* (Cambridge, Mass.: Belknap Press of Harvard University Press, 1996), 6.

23   Bok, *Universities and the Future of America*, 77.

24   Bok, *Universities and the Future of America*, 77.

25   Bok, *Universities and the Future of America*, 78.

26   Bok, *Universities and the Future of America*, 77–78.

27   Donohue's criticism has already been noted. For other reviews of *Universities and the Future of America*, see John Rexine, "The Mission of the University," *Modern Age* (Winter 1992): 177–78; and James E. Giles, "The Gripes of the Academe," *Cross Currents* (Spring 1991): 116–17.

28   Bok, *Universities and the Future of America*, 73.

29   Bok's program includes (1) offering courses in applied ethics in the colleges and professional schools, (2) discussing rules of conduct with students and faculty, (3) administering rules of conduct fairly, (4) building strong programs of community service, (5) employing high ethical standards when addressing the moral issues facing the university, and (6) relating to students in ways that are consistent with the institutions' professed ethical standards. See "Toward a Contemporary Program of Moral Education," in *Universities and the Future of America*, 79–102.

30   Bok, *Universities and the Future of America*, 83.

31   Derek Bok, *Beyond the Ivory Tower* (Cambridge, Mass.: Harvard University Press, 1982), 3. This same point was made much earlier in a well-known work by Clark Kerr, *The Uses of the University* (Cambridge, Mass.: Harvard University Press, 1963) and also more recently by Alasdair MacIntyre, "Reconceiving the University as an Institution and the Lecture as a Genre," in his *Three Rival Versions of Moral Enquiry: Encyclopedia, Genealogy, and Tradition* (Notre Dame: University of Notre Dame Press, 1990), 216–36.

32   MacIntyre, *After Virtue*, 6–8.

33   These seem to be offered by Bok as foundational principles for every program of moral education in a democratic society like our own. See Bok, *Universities and the Future of America*, 98, 100.

34   See Warren Bryan Martin, *A College of Character: Renewing the Purpose and Content of College Education* (San Francisco: Jossey-Bass, 1982) for a defense of the centrality of the liberal arts college and an admonition that its purpose is not merely to imitate the research university. He clearly sees as one of its tasks the attempt to help students learn to live ethically fulfilling lives.

35   The characterization of a genuine liberal education by Socratic questioning and skepticism is also advanced by Martha Nussbaum in *Cultivating Humanity*.

36   For an extended defense of this sort of pedagogy, see MacIntyre, *Three Rival Versions*, especially 228–36.

37   See not only *Three Rival Versions* but also MacIntyre's *Whose Justice? Which Rationality?* (Notre Dame: University of Notre Dame Press, 1988), especially 1–11 and 389–403.

38   For the subtitle of this introduction, we are indebted to the fine work of two colleagues of our acquaintance—Daniel Williams and Travis Kroeker—both of whom in different contexts have sought to retrieve neglected traditions and remember vital ends: Daniel H. Williams, *Retrieving the Tradition and Renewing Evangelicalism: A Primer for Suspicious Protestants* (Grand Rapids: Eerdmans, 1999); and P. Travis Kroeker and Bruce K. Ward, *Remembering the End: Dostoevsky as Prophet to Modernity* (Boulder: Westview Press, 2001).

Chapter 1

1   Frederick Rudolph, *Curriculum: A History of the American Undergraduate Course of Study Since 1636* (San Francisco: Jossey-Bass, 1977), 156. In addition to Rudolph, see Reuben's superb history of American education through the 1930s, *Making of the Modern University*.

2	Bruce A. Kimball, *Orators and Philosophers: A History of the Idea of Liberal Education* (New York: Teachers College Press, 1986).
3	T. H. Huxley, "Science and Culture," in *Cultures in Conflict: Perspectives on the Snow-Leavis Controversy*, ed. David K. Cornelius and Edwin St. Vincent (Chicago: Scott, Foresman, 1964), 77. Huxley would not have students receive a purely scientific education, however, for it would "bring about a mental twist as surely as an exclusively literary training" (77).
4	Matthew Arnold, "Literature and Science," in *The Portable Matthew Arnold*, ed. Lionel Trilling (New York: Penguin Books, 1980), 423.
5	MacIntyre, *After Virtue*, 201.
6	Robert Bellah, et al., *Habits of the Heart: Individualism and Commitment in American Life* (Berkeley: University of California Press, 1985).
7	Bok, *Universities and the Future of America*, 97. Chapter 4 is a very helpful discussion of this aspect of moral education in universities.
8	Bok, *Universities and the Future of America*, 98.
9	James Davison Hunter, "Leading Children Beyond Good and Evil," *First Things* 103 (2000): 37. Also see Hunter's important book *The Death of Character: Moral Education in a World Without Good and Evil* (New York: Basic Books, 2000).
10	Stanley Hauerwas, "How Christian Universities Contribute to the Corruption of Youth," in his *Christian Existence Today: Essays on Church, World, and Living In Between* (Durham, N.C.: Labyrinth Press, 1988), 247.
11	Hauerwas, "How Christian Universities Contribute," 248. My emphasis.
12	Hauerwas, "How Christian Universities Contribute," 249.
13	In his essay in this volume Hauerwas quotes from one of MacIntyre's unpublished essays: "What education should be about is the transformation of students' conceptions of their goals. The desires, the needs, the goals that people bring to their education are in general going to be as corrupt as the culture that produced them. So they are going to have to be transformed as persons. . . . Morality thus is in a very important way educative of desire" ("*Pro Ecclesia, Pro Texana*: Schooling the Heart in the Heart of Texas," 208n14).
14	Thomas Kuhn, *The Structure of Scientific Revolutions* (Chicago: University of Chicago Press, 1962), 165.
15	E. M. Adams, "Philosophical Education as Cultural Criticism," *Teaching Philosophy* 3 (1980): 1–2.
16	Bok, *Universities and the Future of America*, 73.
17	Stanley Hauerwas, "*Pro Ecclesia, Pro Texana*," 108.
18	Bok, *Universities and the Future of America*, 77–78.
19	Moreover, a *politically* liberal conception of education does not require that a *comprehensive* moral or philosophical liberalism be given priority over alternatives. For example, in writing about education, John Rawls argues that while children should be taught the civic values and virtues of democratic liberalism, "justice as fairness does not seek to cultivate the distinctive virtues and values of the liberalism of autonomy and individuality, or indeed of any other comprehensive doctrine. For in that case it ceases to be a form of [merely] *political* liberalism." *Political Liberalism*, 200. My emphasis.

20   AAUP, *Declaration of Principles* (1915), reprinted in *Academic Freedom and Tenure: A Handbook of the American Association of University Professors* (Madison: University of Wisconsin Press, 1967), 164.

21   *Declaration of Principles*, 169.

22   AAUP, "Some Observations on Ideology, Competence, and Faculty Selections," *Academe* 72 (1986): 2a.

23   They must be competent scholars; academic freedom does not protect incompetence. And it does not protect gratuitous remarks unrelated to the subject of the course at issue.

24   Schwehn, *Exiles from Eden*, 58. Schwehn himself attributes the phrase to Leon Kass.

25   Schwehn, *Exiles from Eden*, 137.

26   Schwehn, *Exiles From Eden*, 137.

27   Hauerwas, "How Universities Contribute," 247.

28   I am using "reason" here not in its narrow, scientific/instrumental sense, but in a richer philosophical sense. I have benefited most from E. M. Adams's account of the relationship of morality and rationality. See his "Rationality and Morality," *Review of Metaphysics* 46 (1993): 683–97; "Emotional Intelligence and Wisdom," *The Southern Journal of Philosophy* 36 (1998): 1–14; and his major philosophical work, *The Metaphysics of Self and World* (Philadelphia: Temple University Press, 1991).

29   Hauerwas is right if one reads in a certain way his concern that ethics courses teach students that it is finally "up to us" to decide what to value. If this means there is no right and wrong about it, he's right to be concerned. But it is up to us to decide what to value in this sense: we are responsible for thinking critically about our beliefs and values; we have to decide how to live our lives—and we can do this responsibly or irresponsibly.

30   Quoted in Veysey, *Emergence of the American University*, 84.

31   John Stuart Mill, *On Liberty*, in *The Essential Works of John Stuart Mill*, ed. Max Lerner (New York: Bantam Books, 1965), 287.

32   See Nussbaum, *Cultivating Humanity*, chap. 3.

33   Ian McEwan, "Only Love and then Oblivion," *The Guardian*, September 15, 2001, available at http://www.guardian.co.uk/wtccrash/story/0, 1300,552408,00.html (accessed July 15, 2006).

34   Gerald Graff, *Beyond the Culture Wars* (New York: Norton, 1992), 13.

35   See Brand Blanshard, *The Uses of a Liberal Education and Other Talks to Students* (La Salle, Ill.: Open Court Publishing, 1973), 283.

36   Graff, *Beyond the Culture Wars*, 12.

37   See Robert H. Frank, Thomas Gilovich, and Denis Regan, "Does Studying Economics Inhibit Cooperation?" *Journal of Economic Perspectives* 7 (1993): 159–71.

38   Of course, the Scriptures of all religious traditions address justice and the moral dimensions of our social and economic life. What may be less appreciated is the vast religious literature on justice and economics of the last hundred years. What is central to this literature is the claim that to understand the world of economics we must use moral and religious categories. Economic decisions must take into consideration the dignity of people and respect for what is sacred. People are by nature social beings, born into webs of obligation to other people and to God. If we

are by nature sinful, it is also incumbent on us to rise about self-interest. Religious traditions have emphasized cooperation over competition, and are deeply wary of the corrupting influence of wealth, materialism, and our consumer culture. All religious traditions pay special attention to the needs of the poor—the widow, the orphan, the alien. Needless to say, economics textbooks say nothing about religious ways of understanding economics. They never appeal to the dignity of people, the sacredness of nature, or obligations to any larger community (or God). That is, they demoralize and secularize the economic realm.

39   Indeed, according to the national economics standards developed a decade ago for high school economics courses, students should be taught only the "majority paradigm" or "neo-classical model" of economic behavior, for to include "strongly held minority views of economic processes [only] risks confusing and frustrating teachers and students who are then left with the responsibility of sorting the qualifications and alternatives without a sufficient foundation to do so" (National Council on Economic Education, *National Content Standards in Economics* [New York, 1997], viii).

40   Charles Haynes and I have tried to provide such a map at the high school level in our book *Taking Religion Seriously across the Curriculum* (Alexandria, Va.: Association for Supervision of Curriculum Development, 1998). For economics courses, see chap. 5.

41   See *Taking Religion Seriously across the Curriculum*, chap. 7.

42   Cf. Schwehn, *Exiles from Eden*, chap. 3.

43   I have argued this case at length in *Religion and American Education: Rethinking a National Dilemma* (Chapel Hill: University of North Carolina Press, 1995). See especially chap. 5.

44   This is something of a puzzle. As George Marsden has noted, "Keeping within our intellectual horizons a being who is great enough to create us and the universe . . . ought to change our perspectives on quite a number of things. One might expect it to have a bearing on some of the most sharply debated issues in academia today. . . . Why, in a culture in which many academics profess to believe in God, do so few reflect on the academic implications of that belief?" See his *The Outrageous Idea of Christian Scholarship* (New York: Oxford University Press, 1997), 4.

45   John Dixon once put it this way: because "religious studies" makes studies rather than religion its primary focus, students learn that "truth is in the systems of study" rather than in the religion that is studied—though he acknowledges that the "actual effect is far more muddled than that, simply because so much of the material we study is more powerful than the prejudices of the methods we apply to them, and many teachers are exceedingly respectful of the integrity of their subject" ("What Should Religion Departments Teach?" *Theology Today* 46 [1990]: 369–70).

46   Consider an analogy. Political scientists often assume that the truth is to be found in the scientific method they employ rather than in the (normative) ideological, philosophical, and political beliefs and values of the politicians, voters, and writers they study; as a result, they teach students not to think politically so much as to think scientifically about politics. But surely what is most important in studying politics, at least

from the perspective of a liberal education (and of many students), is sorting out whether Democrats or Republicans, capitalists or socialists, have the more reasonable position. For which party should I vote? What is justice? How should I live? Analogously, the primary value of religious studies lies in its ability to enable students to think in an informed and critical way about the moral and spiritual dimensions of life—about our deepest values and ultimate concerns.

47   I have addressed the relationship of theology (or normative study of religion) and religious studies and their respective roles in liberal education in "Liberal Education and Religious Studies," in *Religion, Education, and the American Experience*, ed. Edith Blumhofer (Tuscaloosa: University of Alabama Press, 2002), 9–40; also see my *Religion and American Education*, chap. 10.

48   *Everson v. Board of Education*, 330 U.S. 1 (1947), 18.

49   *Abington Township v. Schempp*, 375 U.S. 203 (1963), 225.

50   Academic freedom is not meant to protect the claims of incompetent scholars. For example, a historian who taught students that the Holocaust did not happen would almost surely be incompetent. A scholar's defense of, or attack on, religion must be professionally competent if it is to be protected. Needless to say, such judgments are often controversial; the principle is not. For a more complete discussion of religion and academic freedom, see my *Religion and American Education*, chap. 9.

51   The Supreme Court began to address questions of academic freedom in the 1950s, largely as a consequence of legislative efforts to exclude communists from the academy. The landmark case was *Keyishian v. Board of Regents* (1966), in which the Court anchored academic freedom in the First Amendment. Writing for the Court, Justice Brennan held that "our nation is deeply committed to safeguarding academic freedom, which is of transcendent value to all of us and not merely to the teachers concerned. That freedom is therefore a special concern of the First Amendment, which does not tolerate laws that cast a pall of orthodoxy over the classroom. . . . The classroom is peculiarly the 'marketplace of ideas.' The Nation's future depends upon leaders trained through wide exposure to that robust exchange of ideas which discovers truth 'out of a multitude of tongues, [rather] than through any kind of authoritative selection' " (385 U.S. 589, 603).

52   While the Supreme Court has never weighed academic freedom against the Establishment Clause, there is one appellate court decision that clearly cuts against the grain of my position—an appallingly bad decision by the 11th Circuit Court in *Bishop v. Aronov*, 926 F2d 1066 (1991). Interestingly, the District Court had gotten it right; see *Bishop v. Aronov*, 732 F. Supp. 1562 (N.D. Ala 1990). I discuss this case at some length in *Religion and American Education*, 269–74.

53   I want to be clear that I have not argued for including religious voices in the argument for religious reasons: they must be included as part of an open and reasoned search for the truth, and because constitutional neutrality requires fairness to religion. I have argued the case for taking religion seriously in both liberal education and moral education at much greater length in *Religion and American Education*. See especially chaps. 6 and 11.

Chapter 2

1   Quotations from the Theaetetus are from the translation by F. M. Corn-
ford in *The Collected Dialogues of Plato*, ed. Edith Hamilton and Hunt-
ington Cairns (New York: Bollingen Foundation, 1961). In the
quotation from 173d–e. I have rearranged one sentence, and in the
quotation from 176b–c I have substituted "just" and its cognates for
"righteous" and its cognates.
2   Cf. David Jeffrey's illuminating treatment of those biblically grounded
reservations about dividing moral and intellectual virtue in chapter 5 of
this book.
3   John 17:3 (KJ21).
4   See p. 49 above.

Chapter 3

1   Neil Postman, *Technopoly* (New York: Vintage Books, 1992), 186.
2   George D. Kuh and Paul D. Umbach, "College and Character: Insights
from the National Survey of Student Engagement," in *Assessing Character Outcomes in College,* ed. Jon C. Dalton, Terrance R. Russell, and Sally
Kline, New Directions in Institutional Research 122 (2004): 51.
Emphasis mine.
3   Bernard Rosen, "Teaching Undergraduate Ethics," in *Ethics Teaching in
Higher Education,* The Hastings Center Series in Ethics, ed. Daniel Callahan and Sissela Bok (New York: Plenum Press, 1980), 173.
4   One should not exaggerate the definition of *theory* so that it means only
what is traditionally known as casuistry, i.e., a highly systematized set
of axioms and principles designed to generate deductively valid conclusions attended by "an extensive knowledge of natural law and equity,
civil law . . . and an exceptional skill in interpreting these various
norms of conduct" (Dagobert D. Runes, ed., *The Dictionary of Philosophy* [Totowa, N.J: Rowman & Allanheld, 1984], s.v. "casuistry"). By a
"theory" I mean only a distinct understanding of the nature and source
of our moral obligations, and principles of application, broadly construed.
5   As John J. Holder Jr. puts it, "reflective dispositions are cultivated so
that the application of thought to ethical problems may become habit-
ual" ("Ethical Thinking and the Liberal Arts Tradition," in *Moral Education and the Liberal Arts*, ed. Michael H. Mitias [New York: Greenwood
Press, 1992], 159). In the same volume, see also James Gouinlock,
"Moral Pluralism, Intellectual Virtue, and Academic Culture," 77–92.
6   Charles Scriven, quoting MacIntyre, insists that advocacy of a point of
view requires that one "enter[s] into controversy with other rival stand-
points" ("Schooling for the Tournament of Narratives" in *Theology Without Foundations: Religious Practice and the Future of Theological Truth*, ed.
Stanley Hauerwas, Nancey Murphy, and Mark Nation [Nashville:
Abingdon, 1994], 286).
7   Reuben, *Making of the Modern University*, 22–23.
8   Meyer, *The Instructed Conscience*, xi.
9   Meyer, *Instructed Conscience*, xii.

10 In the opening pages of *The Elements of Moral Science*, Francis Wayland compares the study of moral laws to the study of the laws of mathematics, physics, and chemistry, and adopts Newtonian categories when he describes the moral law as "an order of sequence established between the moral quality of actions and their results." John Witherspoon expresses the hope that moral "disquisitions" will one day realize the same degree of precision as mathematics and natural philosophy [science] through employing the inductive methods of Newton, noting merely that the evidence for moral theory is of a different kind. See Wayland, *Elements of Moral Science*, 17–20; and John Witherspoon, *Lectures on Moral Philosophy*, ed. Jack Scott (Newark: University of Delaware Press, 1982), 186. See also Meyer, *Instructed Conscience*, 90.

11 Meyer, *Instructed Conscience*, 137.

12 Meyer, *Instructed Conscience*, 4.

13 Douglas Sloan, "Faith and Knowledge: Religion and the Modern University" in *The Future of Religious Colleges*, ed. Paul J. Dovre (Grand Rapids: Eerdmans, 2002), 5.

14 I regard the work of Alvin Plantinga—that Christian belief has sufficient epistemic warrant independent of evidence drawn from other sources of human knowledge—and J. Budziszewski's view that the precepts of the moral law are known without inference from other more basic sources of knowledge, as highly compatible with Sloan's definitions and distinctions. If it is the case that Christian belief and knowledge of the moral law enjoy independent epistemic warrant, this would, I believe, provide the basis for viewing a moral theory based upon standard Christian orthodoxy as epistemically justified and as teleologically eudaimonistic. See Alvin Plantinga, *Warranted Christian Belief* (New York: Oxford University Press, 2000); J. Budziszewski, *Written on the Heart: The Case for Natural Law* (Downers Grove, Ill.: InterVarsity, 1997); and idem, *What We Cannot Not Know: A Guide* (Dallas: Spence Publishing, 2003).

15 Veysey, *Emergence of the American University*, 50–56.

16 Those familiar with the political history of the twentieth century will note the close affinity between the rise of positivism and individualistic political liberalism.

17 George Marsden, "Beyond Progressive Scientific Humanism" in Dovre, *The Future of Religious Colleges*, 37–38. Sloan refers to this movement more broadly as "the Victorian faith in progress." See Sloan, *Faith and Knowledge*, 2.

18 For examples of teleological eudaimonism among the nineteenth-century moral philosophers, see Wayland, *Elements of Moral Science*, 93, 98–99, and Witherspoon, *Lectures in Moral Philosophy*, 86–87, 186. One problem with the moral philosophers' emulation of scientific methodology was the unfortunate tendency to view moral action almost exclusively as obedience to abstract law rather than as fulfillment of or obedience to one's telos or purpose.

19 Meyer, *Instructed Conscience*, 29, 139–41. The moral tradition following Jonathan Edwards held that benevolence must be "disinterested," and not motivated simply by concern for blessedness in the afterlife. See Meyer, 150. In an earlier Christian tradition, good acts are to be moti-

vated by a sincere love for God and the fact that each human being is a bearer of the divine image. See Augustine, *The Enchiridion on Faith, Hope, and Love*, trans. J. F. Shaw (Washington, D.C.: Regnery, 1961), ccxi; and John Calvin, *Institutes of the Christian Religion*, trans. Henry Beveridge (Grand Rapids: Eerdmans, 1997), 3.7.6–7.

20   The clearest scriptural reference is Romans 8:28: "We know that all things work together for good for those who love God who are called according to his purpose." Just before, in vv. 20-22, Paul emphasizes that the ultimate purposes of God are to be achieved in the entire created order as well.

21   Reuben, *Making of the Modern University*, chap. 2.

22   Meyer, *Instructed Conscience*, 128.

23   Even after the passage of more than 100 years, this outlook is essentially unchanged among progressive thinkers: "The aim in reconstructing 'moral reasoning' as 'ethical thinking' has been to show how determinate ethical judgments are possible without appeal to immutable standards of right and wrong" (Holder, "Ethical Thinking and the Liberal Arts Tradition," 156). That moral relativism was widely held to be a direct implication of Darwin's theory in the late nineteenth and early twentieth centuries is amply demonstrated in Richard Weikhart, *From Darwin to Hitler: Evolutionary Ethics, Eugenics, and Racism in Germany* (New York: Palgrave Macmillan: 2004), 21–43.

24   Sloan, *Faith and Knowledge*, 5.

25   John Dewey, "Are the Schools Doing What People Want Them to Do?" *Educational Review* 21 (1901): 468–69; cited in B. Edward McClellan, *Moral Education in America: Schools and the Shaping of Character from Colonial Times to the Present* (New York: Teachers College Press, 1999), 57.

26   McClellan, *Moral Education in America*, 59.

27   A few years ago, a student related to me how on the first night of her university ethics course, the instructor asked students to discuss a situation in which an obese man is caught in a narrow cave entrance while his companions are trapped inside as flood waters threaten to drown them all. Students were asked to debate whether it would be appropriate for his companions to hack the man to pieces with an axe to save the group. See Stanley Hauerwas's treatment of this stock case of modern ethics courses, along with his devastating critique, in chapter 4 below.

28   McClellan, *Moral Education in America*, 58.

29   George S. Counts, *Dare the Schools Build a New Social Order?* (New York: John Day Pamphlets, 1932), no. 11; cited in Nancy R. Pearcey, "Darwin Meets the Berenstain Bears: Evolution as a Total Worldview," in *Uncommon Dissent: Intellectuals Who Find Darwinism Unconvincing*, ed. William A. Dembski (Wilmington, Del.: ISI Books, 2004), 69.

30   McClellan, *Moral Education in America*, 57.

31   See Richard Yanikoski, "Leadership Perspectives on the Role of Character Development," in Dalton, Russell, and Kline, *Assessing Character Outcomes in College*, 7–23. Yanikoski cites the creation of scholarly societies that shifted professors' allegiance to bodies outside the campus; the adoption of the German university model, which deemphasizes a core curriculum; the growth of enrollment; and the growing percentage

of nontraditional, international, and part-time students, which made
scheduling more difficult, and thus served to encourage administrators
to "trim the fat" and focus on the essentials of professional degree
requirements. At many, if not most, state universities, these factors are
arguably far more significant obstacles to a requirement in moral philosophy than the ideological ones described throughout this volume.
One could also include as a factor competitive hiring practices, which
undermines faculty concern for the broader goals of higher education
at their current (temporary) post.

32   McClellan, *Moral Education in America*, 63.

33   The nineteenth-century moral philosophers thus ignored the nonlogical,
largely intuitive nature of much of our moral experience. Not to over-
simplify, but what Aristotle refers to as *phronesis*, or nondeductive moral
discernment; what Russell Kirk calls "the moral imagination," that is, the
distinctly qualitative mode of moral awareness inspired through engagement with literature and the arts; and what John Henry Newman refers
to as the illative sense, an intuitive knowledge that results from "the
combination of many uncatalogued experiences floating in [our] memory, of many reflections, variously produced, felt rather than capable of
statement," are ineliminable features of the moral life. (Newman's notion
of the illative sense is described by Peter Waters, "Cardinal John Henry
Newman and the Development of Doctrine," *AD2000: A Journal of Religious Opinion* 11 [1998]: 10, available at http://www.ad2000.com.
au/articles/1998/aug1998p10_553.html [accessed July 15, 2006]).

34   See McClellan, *Moral Education in America*, 78–93; and also Hunter,
Death of Character, 70f., 127–28. Even as illustrious a virtue champion
as William Bennett believes the acquisition of virtue can be separated
from systematic exposition and practical application to moral controversies. According to Bennett, "values can and should be taught in
schools without fear of accusations of proselytizing" (qtd. in Michael
Cromartie, "Virtue Man," *Christianity Today*, September 13, 1993: 33;
cited in Hunter, 209), and the "formation of character in young people
is educationally a different task, and a prior task to the discussion of the
great, difficult, controversial disputes of the day" (William Bennett,
"Moral Literacy and the Formation of Character," *NASSP Bulletin* 72
[1988]: 35; cited in McClellan, 93). According to Hunter, another significant reason that contemporary pedagogical approaches fear the
accusation of *indoctrination* and avoid controversy is the desire to be as
inclusive as possible. For Hunter, the trouble with inclusiveness is that
moral reasoning is necessarily a "thick" enterprise, that is, it assumes a
particular understanding of the human good that is universal in scope,
even though it is not by any means universally endorsed (210f.).

35   For a more recent articulation of this view, see C. David Lisman, *The
Curricular Integration of Ethics* (Westport, Conn.: Praeger, 1996), 4–6.

36   Robert T. Hall and John U. Davis, *Moral Education in Theory and Practice* (Buffalo, N.Y.: Prometheus Books, 1975), 50.

37   Hall and Davis, *Moral Education in Theory and Practice*, 172.

38   Callahan and Bok, *Ethics Teaching in Higher Education*, 300–301.
Emphasis mine.

39   Bok, *Universities and the Future of America*, 73, 77.

40   Bok, *Universities and the Future of America*, 83.
41   For searing indictments of the failures of moral educational strategies
        based on the pedagogy of mediation, see Hunter, *Death of Character*,
        151–55, and Paul Vitz, *Psychology as Religion*, 2nd ed. (Grand Rapids:
        Eerdmans, 1977), 76–78. In *Assessing Character Outcomes in College*,
        cited above, several of the studies leave a general impression that the
        curricular and extracurricular design of undergraduate education can
        have at least some positive impact on student attitudes. It is not clear,
        however, what sort of educational pedagogy is used in the ethics
        courses, and to what extent they are required. One problem with at
        least some of the studies is that students are asked to assess their own
        attitudes, which strikes me as a rather unreliable measure of genuine
        character formation. Another is that the studies are flawed by a too-
        heavy reliance on progressive ideas as to what constitutes growth in
        character, e.g., commitment to social activism, degree of volunteerism,
        and sensitivity to diversity, as opposed to a more traditional under-
        standing of "character formation," such as commitment to sexual con-
        tinence, marital faithfulness, avoidance of substance abuse, charitable
        giving, and honesty.
42   Weikart, *From Darwin to Hitler*, 153.
43   This list of implications is an adaptation of a similar list in
        Budziszewski, *What We Cannot Not Know*, 162–63.
44   See J. Budziszewski, "Religion and Civic Virtue," in *Virtue*, Nomos 34,
        ed. John W. Chapman and William A. Galston (New York: New York
        University Press, 1992), 62–65; see also John Gray, *Enlightenment's
        Wake: Politics and Culture at the Close of the Modern Age* (New York: Rout-
        ledge, 1995), 18–30, 120–31.
45   According to Hunter, at the center of the moral universe of progressive
        theories of moral education is "the individual—supreme, autonomous,
        rational, evolving, and basically good" (*Death of Character*, 64).
46   Hauerwas, "How Christian Universities Contribute," 242.
47   Hauerwas, "Truth and Honor: The University and the Church in a
        Democratic Age," in *Christian Existence Today*, 227. Hauerwas here fol-
        lows the argument of Peter Berger, "On the Obsolescence of the Con-
        cept of Honor," *Archives of European Sociology* 11 (1970): 339–47;
        reprinted in *Revisions: Changing Perspectives in Moral Philosophy*, ed.
        Alasdair MacIntyre and Stanley Hauerwas (Notre Dame: University of
        Notre Dame Press, 1984), 172–81.
48   Aristotle can be interpreted as rejecting the Socratic method in the
        opening pages of the *Nichomachean Ethics*. That Socrates' methods
        encouraged moral nihilism and sophistry was one of Aristophanes's
        charges against him. See Martha Nussbaum, "Aristophanes and
        Socrates on Learning Practical Wisdom," in *Aristophanes: Essays in Inter-
        pretation*, Yale Classical Studies 26, ed. Jeffrey Henderson (Cambridge:
        Cambridge University Press, 1980), 43–97; cited in Hauerwas, "How
        Christian University Contribute," 251.
49   All of these benefits assume moral realism and the existence of an
        innate or quasi-innate consciousness of the moral law. This conscious-
        ness, I suggest, is reinforced by the profession of a moral theory in a
        context of moral realism. Thus, the requirement in moral philosophy

and a pedagogy of profession are themselves partisan in the good sense, viz., by their very nature they reject moral relativism and the positivistic notion that morality is merely a product of human experience and reflection. Indeed, I believe students are better off without such a requirement if it is taught along the lines of a social science course construed positivistically—in other words, if morality is treated as a "phenomenon" to be viewed with detachment, and not as a reality demanding our appropriation and response.

50 Scriven, "Schooling for the Tournament of Narratives," 283.

51 I address this point more fully below.

52 William C. Starr, "Ethical Theory and the Teaching of Ethics," in *Ethics Across the Curriculum: The Marquette Experience*, ed. Robert B. Ashmore and William C. Starr (Milwaukee: Marquette University Press, 1991), 35.

53 Robert Van Wyk offers a number of objections to what he describes as "value-neutral" moral education, besides that it teaches relativism and permissiveness, viz., that the instructor provides an impoverished role model, and that such education conveys moral shallowness, which in fact undermines autonomy. See Robert N. Van Wyk, "Is Value Education the Achilles' Heel of Liberalism?" in *Values and Education*, Value Inquiry Book Series 76, ed. Thomas Magnell (Atlanta: Rodopi, 1988), 87–89. For another argument that neutrality is conceptually incoherent, see Theodore G. Ammon, "Teachers Should Disclose Their Moral Commitments" in Mitias, *Moral Education in the Liberal Arts*, 163f.

54 See C. David Lisman, "Ethics Education in Schools," in *Encyclopedia of Applied Ethics*, ed. Ruth Chadwick (San Diego: Academic Press, 1998) and idem, *Curricular Integration of Ethics*, 39–42.

55 In my ethics classes, a plurality if not a majority of students will embrace an ethical outlook grounded in theism if this is allowed as an option.

56 Holder, "Ethical Thinking and the Liberal Arts Tradition," 158ff.

57 Ruth Macklin, "Problems in the Teaching of Ethics," in Callahan and Bok, *Ethics Teaching in Higher Education*, 85. If one observes the philosophical literature, the precise meaning of indoctrination was widely debated into the 1980s, but very few articles have been published on the topic since. This may reflect that a scholarly consensus of some kind was reached in the 1980s, so the topic is no longer philosophically interesting. More likely, however, is a growing awareness of an irreducible indeterminacy as to exactly what constitutes indoctrination beyond certain commonsensical rules-of-thumb, which I shall offer below. According to Hunter, the worry over indoctrination is not merely theoretical, but also prudential; i.e., taking moral differences seriously is "hard and dicey work," so moral educators wish to give the appearance of neutrality to their approach less out of principle than of fear (*Death of Character*, 209).

58 One should note that this definition of *credibility* is fairly narrow; it appears to be derived from the new scholarship of the late nineteenth century, and to be based upon consensus, not upon having plausible grounds or warrant.

59   Hall and Davis, *Moral Education in Theory and Practice*, 38.
60   Macklin, "Problems in the Teaching of Ethics," 86.
61   Rosen, "Teaching of Undergraduate Ethics," 187.
62   In effect, the "fair and objective" presentation of both premodern and religiously based theories—say, Aristotle and Aquinas—alongside the modern theories of Kant, Mill, and Rawls, will provide in most instances the needed range of alternatives.
63   Hall and Davis, *Moral Education in Theory and Practice*, 39. Italics in original.
64   See pp. 36–37 above.
65   In point of fact, the common assumption that Socrates professes only ignorance, drawn from Plato, is substantially gainsaid by Xenophon's portrait in his *Memoirs of Socrates* and other writings. In Xenophon's account, among other things, Socrates uses dialetic to persuade his interlocuters emphatically to have respect for one's parents, to offer guidance in the art of choosing friends, to resist sensuality and to gain self-discipline, to work harder at achieving one's goals, and in the case of Glaucon, Plato's brother, even to discourage a person from pursuing his life's ambition. While it is an open question as to whose portrait of Socrates is closer to the truth, Plato's or Xenophon's, it beggars belief to assume that all the instances of substantive teaching by Socrates in Xenophon are wholly fictitious. See Robin Waterfield's discussion of the evidence for and against Xenophon's portrayal in *Xenophon: Conversations of Socrates*, trans. Hugh Tredennick and Robin Waterfield (New York: Penguin, 1990), 16f.
66   In the preface to the second edition of his *Elements of Moral Science*, Wayland outlines a method of question-and-answer recitation to facilitate maximum comprehension of the content of his theory. However, his stated goal is that "[this method] will cultivate the power of pursuing an extended range of argument; of examining and deciding upon a connected chain of reasoning; and will, in no small degree, accustom the student to carry forward in his own mind a train of *original investigation*" (7). Emphasis mine.
67   See Allen C. Guelzo, "Cracks in the Tower: A Closer Look at the Christian College Boom," *Books & Culture* 11 (2005): 28.
68   Gouinlock, "Moral Pluralism, Intellectual Virtue, and Academic Culture," 78, 89–90. In context, Gouinlock appears to have leftists in mind, though the problem surely goes the other way as well.
69   Writes Victor Davis Hanson, "our academic leadership . . . remains obsessed with a racial, ideological, and sexual spoils system called 'diversity'" ("Profiles in Diversity," *Claremont Review of Books* 5 [2005]: 9).
70   See Warren Nord's illuminating comments on the role of religion in the university in chapter 1 above.
71   Unless one wishes to argue that there is a distinct orthodox Protestant tradition, MacIntyre not implausibly describes the major players in the agon as the Enlightenment (Encyclopedia), postmodernism (Genealogy), and Thomistic-Aristotelianism (Tradition). See MacIntyre, *Three Rival Versions*.

Chapter 4

1   The day after I wrote this sentence an editorial by Condoleezza Rice entitled "A 'freedom deficit' haunts the Middle East" appeared in the *Durham Herald-Sun* (August 8, 2003) that explicitly confirmed my set of claims. While noting that America went to war in Iraq because Saddam Hussein's regime posed a threat to the security of the United States and the world, Rice argues that the goal is to "work with those in the Middle East who seek progress toward greater democracy, tolerance, prosperity and freedom." She then quotes one of President Bush's speeches in which he says, "The world has a clear interest in the spread of democratic values, because stable and free nations do not breed ideologies of murder. They encourage the peaceful pursuit of a better life" (A11). It seems never to occur to Rice or Bush that many people might think that the United States represents a society that "breeds ideologies of murder." America, however, is so powerful that we can call our killing "war." It is also interesting to note that even in her justification of the war in terms of the self-interest of the United States, Rice notes that the security of the world is threatened. So America did not go to war strictly from self-interest, but because the security of the world demanded we go to war. One assumes she assumes that what is necessary for American security is also what is necessary for world security because America is the world.

2   See, for example, my essay, "Why Gays (as a Group) Are Morally Superior to Christians (as a Group)," *Dispatches From the Front: Theological Engagements with the Secular* (Durham: Duke University Press, 1994), 153–55. I was obviously having fun in the essay, but I think I am right that one of the difficulties with the arguments about gays in the church is the failure to see how such arguments are shaped by the accommodation of the church to our culture. If Christians really were prohibited from serving in the military as a group, would the "gay issue" look the same as it currently does? If Christians were not trusted by the military, would gays want to be part of Christian communities? Gays have enough problems. Why would they want to make their lives even more difficult by becoming Christian? Moreover, if the church was constituted by a discipline necessary to sustain a despised people, then the discipline of chastity might not appear so outdated. In such a church, to ask gays to live lives of chastity might not appear so oppressive.

3   See, for example, the wonderful reflections of Rowan Williams on September 11, 2001 in his *Writing in the Dust: after September 11, 2001* (Grand Rapids: Eerdmans, 2002). See also *Dissent from the Homeland: Essays after September 11*, ed. Stanley Hauerwas and Frank Lentricchia (Durham, N.C.: Duke University Press, 2003). Selections of Williams's reflections appear in this book on pp. 25–36.

4   See my "September 11, 2001: A Pacifist Response," in Hauerwas and Lentricchia, *Dissent from the Homeland*, 181–95.

5   Dennis O'Brien calls attention to the universities' beginning in monastic schools in order to remind us that, for monks, speaking and reading took place in the context of prayer and were "enveloped in a life of silence." O'Brien quotes Jeremy Driscoll's observation that in our day the monastic reverence toward words expressed in silence is simply

incomprehensible. We think—and it is certainly true of most university cultures—the more words and images, the better; but "monks attempt to practice silence and be careful when they speak. They sing words which they reverence as the very word of God, and they let this word form some few images in their hearts" ("The University: Before, After, and Beyond" [Unpublished paper given as the Phi Beta Lecture at Holy Cross College, March 10, 2003]).

6   Douglas Harink, *Paul among the Postliberals: Pauline Theology beyond Christendom and Modernity* (Grand Rapids: Brazos Press, 2003), 68.

7   Harink, *Paul among the Postliberals*, 68–69.

8   Robert Wilken, *The Spirit of Early Christian Thought* (New Haven: Yale University Press, 2003), 3.

9   For example, Condoleezza Rice observes that a "freedom deficit" haunts the Middle East that results in "a sense of hopelessness" that "provides a fertile ground for ideologies of hatred and persuades people to forsake university educations, careers and families and aspire instead to blow themselves up—taking as many innocent lives with them as possible" ("A 'freedom deficit' haunts the Middle East," A11). Rice simply cannot understand why someone who is receiving a university education could be so irrational as she takes "terrorists" to be. The task of the university is to produce rational lives well formed for the modern nation state. In short, universities ought to produce more people like Condoleezza Rice.

10   William Cavanaugh, *Theopolitical Imagination: Discovering the Liturgy as a Political Act in an Age of Global Consumerism* (London: T&T Clark, 2002), 10.

11   Cavanaugh, *Theopolitical Imagination*, 20–31. Cavanaugh summarizes his argument noting "the rise of a centralized bureaucratic state *preceded* these wars and was based on the fifteenth-century assertion of civil dominance over the Church in France. At issue in these wars was not simply Catholic versus Protestant, transubstantiation versus spiritual presence. The Queen Mother who unleashed the massacre of St. Bartholomew's Day was not a religious zealot but a thoroughgoing *Politique* with a stake in stopping the nobility's challenge to royal pretensions toward absolute power" (29–30).

12   Of course the church never represented "universal values." The church represented people who were put in contact with one another through the bishop. What Christians shared was not common "values" but a common Lord found in the meal of bread and wine.

13   Cavanaugh, *Theopolitical Imagination*, 99. For an analysis quite similar to Cavanaugh's, see John Milbank, "Sovereignty, Empire, Capital, and Terror," in Hauerwas and Lentricchia, *Dissent from the Homeland*, 63–82.

14   In a paper that as far as I know has never been published, MacIntyre observes that "there is a widespread conception among our students that to learn, to grow in knowledge and understanding, is to acquire means to implement desires and goals which the student had already, which the student brings to his or her education from outside it. Sometimes students are asked by their parents or by their advisors at the outset, 'What do you want to do?' And when they have produced some

kind of stumbling answer to this, they are then advised as to what they should learn in order to achieve what it is they want. One's education is to be useful to one in reaching certain goals. Against this, I want to suggest that what education should be about is the transformation of students' conceptions of their goals. The desires, the needs, the goals that people bring to their education are in general going to be as corrupt as the culture that produced them. So they are going to have to be transformed as persons. Aristotle pointed out that what pleases and pains the virtuous person is very different from what pleases and pains the vicious person, and both again are different from what pleases the merely immature person. Morality thus is in a very important way educative of desire. And the desires that people bring to their education are ones which they are going to have to modify, or even abandon, if they are to acquire the intellectual and moral virtues. If we treat the students' desires as given, the students' original goals as given, we are in effect abdicating from the task of educating them into the intellectual and moral virtues" ("Values and Distinctive Characteristics of Teaching and Learning in Church-Related Colleges" [Unpublished Manuscript]). I do know that MacIntyre gave this lecture to those responsible for Methodist colleges and universities. He told me that what he had to say was not well received.

15   Alasdair MacIntyre, "Is Patriotism a Virtue?" in *Theorizing Citizenship*, ed. Ronald Beiner (Albany: State University of New York Press, 1995), 209.

16   Disciplines in the university that continue to claim they are "objective" because they insist on a strict distinction between facts and values are also the disciplines that are most destructive for the moral training students should receive. The very notion of "information" is used to sustain the legitimacy of descriptions that should require further justification. Information, however, legitimates the formation of students without acknowledging that the student is receiving a moral education. Wendell Berry observes, "Education is not properly an industry, and its proper use is not to serve industries, either by job-training or by industry-subsidized research. Its proper use is to enable citizens to live lives that are economically, politically, socially, and culturally responsible. This cannot be done by gathering or 'assessing' what we now call 'information'— which is to say facts without context and therefore without priority. A proper education enables young people to put their lives in order, which means knowing what things are more important than other things; it means putting first things first." See Wendell Berry, "Thoughts in the Presence of Fear," in Hauerwas and Lentricchia, *Dissent from the Homeland*, 41.

17   I am well aware of the ongoing dispute among historians concerning the status of history—that is, whether history is one of the humanities or one of the social sciences. The increasing dominance in the social sciences of rational choice methodologies has seemed to force history increasingly to acknowledge it as a humanity. If I were a historian, I would consider that a very welcome development for history. The legitimating character of the social sciences for a capitalist order is nowhere better revealed than the development of rational choice as the explana-

tory paradigm in the disciplines of economics, political science, sociology, and psychology.

18 For a more extensive analysis of the implications of the compartmentalized character of our lives, see my "How Risky is *The Risk of Education?* Random Reflections from the American Context," *Communio: International Catholic Review* 30 (2003): 79–94. The account I give in this essay about these matters draws heavily on MacIntyre's work.

19 MacIntyre, "Teaching and Learning in Church-Related Colleges," 2.

20 James Burtchaell, C.S.C., *The Dying of the Light: The Disengagement of Colleges and Universities from Their Christian Churches* (Grand Rapids: Eerdmans, 1998), 462.

21 Burtchaell, *Dying of the Light*, 842.

22 Burtchaell, *Dying of the Light*, 844.

23 Quoted in Burtchaell, *Dying of the Light*, 849.

24 This is actually a true story. I have discovered that there exist stories about what I have said in this or that circumstance that are not true. For example, I have been introduced at least three times with a story that is not true. It seems I was in Cambridge walking across the Yard at Harvard trying to find my way to the library. I am alleged to have stopped an undergraduate and asked, "Can you tell me where the library is at?" The student responded, "We do not end sentences with prepositions at Harvard." To which I responded, "Can you tell me where the library is at, asshole?" I realize this is the kind of story that seems so true it should be true, but in fact it did not happen. Of course "did not happen" may be an inadequate way to understand "true."

25 Curtis Freeman informs me that the motto of Wake Forest University is *Pro Humanitas.*

26 I believe the most important book about the difference the church should make for the university is Dennis O'Brien's *The Idea of a Catholic University* (Chicago: University of Chicago Press, 2002). What makes O'Brien's book so significant is his insistence that what matters is truth. He argues that Christian universities should not, indeed cannot, avoid the "signatured nature of truth." He argues that art most determinatively exhibits the character of truth that is signatured just to the extent that art works are "essentially historical insofar as they are connected to and express particular visions and historical placement" (35). He argues this is true for all the knowledges of the university except the sciences. Even though I am not convinced he is right about the sciences, I am sure he is right to insist that the signatured character of truth means no truth is available abstracted from a tradition. In his Holy Cross Lecture he puts the argument he makes in his book succinctly, observing that humans may signature art, but we cannot signature life: "The shock of Christianity is the proclamation that there is one who can signature life itself, one who can appropriate chaos, waste, misery, sin and death. Jesus makes his Cross Holy by taking on all the destruction of mankind and without himself being destroyed. He can say 'I am the way, the truth, and the life.'"

27 Cavanaugh, *Theopolitical Imagination*, 111.

28 John Graves, *Goodbye to a River* (New York: Knopf, 2001), 145. I suppose it is not necessary to have fished Possum Kingdom Lake to

appreciate Graves's book, but it has got to help. I caught the largest Brim I ever caught trolling by those wonderful red rock cliffs.

29   See my "A Tale of Two Stories: On Being a Christian and a Texan," in my book, *Christian Existence Today*, 25–45.

30   For my reflections on truthfulness and lying, see *Performing the Faith: Bonhoeffer and the Practice of Nonviolence* (Grand Rapids: Brazos Press, 2004).

31   Mary Margaret Nussbaum, in an article entitled, "How to Sing Our Days," argues that few developments are more disastrous for our lives than the debasement of our language. She teaches high school English in New York. She describes the minds of her students as "full of ad copy and full of the cruel language of a culture that has falsely married beauty to cash and love to exploitation. . . . Our own language has become windy and vague—full of important-sounding acronyms and prose fit to novel technologies. As a result our language is more capable of deception" (*The New York Catholic Worker* [June–July 2003], 7). Ms. Nussbaum notes that "[o]ne cannot fight an impersonal and mechanized culture with android language or vagueness with vagueness. The great witnesses of peace in the last century—Mahatma Gandhi, Dorothy Day, Nelson Mandela—did not accept the dominant means of speech, action or thought. As prophets, they saw a better way. As readers, they were given language to articulate their vision, knowing as Wendell Berry writes, that 'by their ignorance people enfranchise their exploiters' and that 'the only defense against the worst [language] is a knowledge of the best' " (8). Accordingly, Nussbaum directs us to poetry. The implications of Nussbaum's article for thinking about the way universities should school hearts I think is obvious. Universities have become far too "noisy." I blame the tenure process for some of the noise. Faculty are forced to say something before they can have anything to say. Surely we must find some way to recover the importance of silence. Without silence we will be devoid of the time it takes to see and hear the beautiful.

Chapter 5

1   Nicholas Hans, in his study of educational trends at the peaking of Enlightenment reflection, notes that advances in technology after the mid-eighteenth century encouraged a technical and pragmatic view of education: "At the end of the century, the utilitarian motive becomes all important and the religious and intellectual reasons recede into the background" (*New Trends in Education in the Eighteenth Century* [London: Geoffrey Bles, 1951], 13).

2   Jacques-Paul Migne, *Patrologia Latina* (Paris, 1844–1864), 91:937.

3   Thomas Aquinas, *Summa Theologica*, trans. Fathers of the English Dominican Province (New York: Benziger Brothers, 1948), IIaIIae 9.2.

4   John Bunyan, *The Pilgrim's Progress* (Uhrichville, Ohio: Barbour, 1993), 90–91.

5   René Descartes, "Rules for the Direction of the Mind," in *The Philosophical Writings of Descartes*, vol. 1, trans. John Cottingham, Robert Stoothoff, and Dugald Murdoch (New York: Cambridge University Press, 1985), 9.

6   See Isaac Watts, *The Improvement of the Mind* (Edinburgh: Thomas Nelson, 1844); cf. Col. 1:9, 17–18.
7   Anselm, *Monologion,* in *Monologion and Proslogion: With the Replies of Gaunilo and Anselm,* trans. Thomas Williams (Indianapolis: Hackett, 1995), chap. 47.
8   Augustine, *On Christian Doctrine,* The Library of Liberal Arts 80, trans. D. W. Robertson Jr. (Upper Saddle River, N.J.: Prentice-Hall, 1958), 4.5.
9   Augustine, *Lectures or Tractates on the Gospel According to St. John,* trans. John Gibb and James Innes, *Nicene and Post-Nicene Fathers: f.s.* 7, ed. Philip Schaff (New York: Christian Literature Publishing, 1888), tractate 1.
10 Augustine, *Sermons on Selected Lessons of the New Testament,* trans. R. G. MacMullen, *Nicene and Post-Nicene Fathers: f.s.* 6, ed. Philip Schaff (New York: Christian Literature Publishing, 1888), sermon 67 (Benedictine ed. 117), chap. 3; cf. Col. 1:17.
11 Augustine, *On Christian Doctrine,* 1.11.
12 John Henry Newman, *The Idea of a University,* ed. Martin J. Svaglic (Notre Dame: University of Notre Dame, 1982), xlvii.
13 See Stephen Prickett, "Managerial Ethics and the Corruption of the Future," in *Education! Education! Education! Managerial Ethics and the Law of Unintended Consequences,* ed. Stephen Prickett and Patricia Erskine-Hill (London: Imprint Academic, 2002), 185.
14 Ernest L. Boyer, "The Scholarship of Engagement," in *Selected Speeches: 1979–1995* (Princeton: Carnegie Foundation for the Advancement of Teaching, 1997), 85.
15 Lucius Annaeus Seneca, *Epistolae morales ad Lucilium,* trans. Robin Campbell (Hammondsworth: Penguin Classics, 1969), 88.
16 Augustine, *The City of God against the Pagans,* trans. R. W. Dyson (Cambridge: Cambridge University Press, 1998), 19.14.
17 Charles Habib Malik, *A Christian Critique of the University* (Downers Grove, Ill.: InterVarsity, 1982), 70.
18 Bertrand Russell, *Education and the Good Life* (New York: Boni & Liveright, 1926), 62.
19 Cf. Aristotle, *Nicomachean Ethics,* 1103a15.
20 See Warren Nord's useful discussion of some of these issues in chapter 1 above.
21 Augustine, *On Christian Doctrine,* 4.27–4.29.
22 Thomas Hughes, *Tom Brown's Schooldays* (London: Oxford, 1921), 151–52. David Newsome, in his rich study of Victorian education (*Godliness and Good Learning* [London: Cassell, 1961]), makes this account a signal exemplum of the Victorian Christian ideal (28–29).

Chapter 6

1   Charles Taylor, *The Ethics of Authenticity* (Cambridge, Mass.: Harvard University Press), 1991.
2   For Taylor's treatment of the confusion regarding authenticity, see esp. pp. 25–29. While we in no way disagree with Taylor's depiction of the malaises of modernity, we believe a more precise diagnosis of such widespread and profound malaise is captured more accurately in terms of a vice—an element not found in Taylor's excellent discussion.

3   Thomas Aquinas, *Summa Theologiae*, II–II, 20,4. The text of the *Summa
         Theologiae* (*ST*) used throughout this essay is the Blackfriars edition
         (New York: McGraw-Hill, 1966).
4   Aquinas, *ST*, IIaIIae 20,4.
5   Aquinas, *ST*, IIaIIae 35,1. Aquinas writes, "Damascene teaches that
         spiritual apathy is a kind of oppressive sorrow which so depresses a
         man that he wants to do nothing."
6   Aquinas, *ST*, IIaIIae 20,4.
7   Aquinas, *ST*, IIaIIae 20,4.
8   Walker Percy, *The Moviegoer* (New York: Ballantine Books, 1960).
9   Percy, *The Moviegoer*, 40–41.
10   Paul Elie, *The Life You Save May Be Your Own: An American Pilgrimage*
         (New York: Farrar, Straus & Giroux, 2003), 306. Our interpretation of
         The Moviegoer relies heavily on Elie's account.
11   Percy, *The Moviegoer*, 135–36.
12   Elie, *The Life You Save*, 302.
13   Brian S. Hook and Russell R. Reno, *Heroism and the Christian Life: Reclaim-
         ing Excellence* (Louisville, Ky.: Westminster John Knox, 2000), 212.
14   Hook and Reno, *Heroism and the Christian Life*, 212.
15   Brian J. Mahan, *Forgetting Ourselves on Purpose: Vocation and the Ethics of
         Ambition* (San Francisco: Jossey-Bass, 2002).
16   Mahan, *Forgetting Ourselves on Purpose*, 3.
17   Mahan, *Forgetting Ourselves on Purpose*, 7.
18   Mahan, *Forgetting Ourselves on Purpose*, 4–5.
19   Mahan, *Forgetting Ourselves on Purpose*, 5.
20   Mahan, *Forgetting Ourselves on Purpose*, 6.
21   Aquinas, *ST*, IIaIIae 129,1.
22   Hook and Reno, *Heroism and the Christian Life*, 211.
23   Hook and Reno, *Heroism and the Christian Life*, 212. Although Hook
         and Reno do not use the language of *acedia*, their threefold account for
         the loss of aspirations for excellence helpfully illuminates our argument
         for the widespread phenomenon of *acedia*.
24   Hook and Reno, *Heroism and the Christian Life*, 213–14.
25   Hook and Reno, *Heroism and the Christian Life*, 214.
26   Hook and Reno, *Heroism and the Christian Life*, 215.
27   Hook and Reno, *Heroism and the Christian Life*, 217.
28   Aquinas, *ST*, IIaIIae 35,1.
29   Elie, *The Life You Save*, 291–92.
30   Hook and Reno, *Heroism and the Christian Life*, 207.
31   Mahan, *Forgetting Ourselves on Purpose*, 30.
32   Mahan, *Forgetting Ourselves on Purpose*, 30.
33   Mahan, *Forgetting Ourselves on Purpose*, 14.
34   On this point see Paul J. Wadell, *Friendship and the Moral Life* (Notre
         Dame: University of Notre Dame Press, 1989), 40–42.
35   Mahan, *Forgetting Ourselves on Purpose*, 20.
36   Mahan, *Forgetting Ourselves on Purpose*, 135.
37   Mahan, *Forgetting Ourselves on Purpose*, 151.
38   Servais Pinckaers, O.P., *The Sources of Christian Ethics*, trans. by Sr. Mary
         Thomas Noble, O.P. (Washington, D.C.: The Catholic University of
         America Press, 1995), 142.

39   Josef Pieper, *Faith, Hope, and Love* (San Francisco: Ignatius Press, 1997), 99.
40   Pieper, *Faith, Hope, and Love*, 91.
41   Pieper, *Faith, Hope, and Love*, 98.
42   Pieper, *Faith, Hope, and Love*, 122.
43   Aquinas, *ST*, II–II, 17,8.
44   For a trenchant analysis of the virtue of courage, see Stanley Hauerwas and Charles Pinches, *Christians among the Virtues: Theological Conversations with Ancient and Modern Ethics* (Notre Dame: University of Notre Dame Press, 1997), 149–65.
45   Aquinas, *ST*, IIaIIae 123,3.
46   Aquinas, *ST*, IIaIIae 123,3.
47   Aquinas, *ST*, IIaIIae 137,1.
48   Aquinas, *ST*, IIaIIae 137,1.
49   Aquinas, *ST*, IIaIIae 137,3.
50   Newman, *Idea of a University*, 124. Italics in original.
51   One such helpful book is Michael Novak, *Business as a Calling: Work and the Examined Life* (New York: Free Press, 1996).

Chapter 7

1   From Mill's inaugural address at St. Andrews. The quote is taken from George Marsden, *The Soul of the American University: From Protestant Establishment to Established Nonbelief* (New York: Oxford University Press, 1994), 413.
2   Amy Gutmann, "Undemocratic Education," in *Liberalism and the Moral Life*, ed. Nancy L. Rosenblum (Cambridge, Mass.: Harvard University Press, 1989), 83.
3   This list includes virtues identified by the following authors: William Galston, "Civic Education and the Liberal State," 89–101 and Gutmann, "Undemocratic Education," 71–88, both in Rosenblum, *Liberalism and the Moral Life*. See also Macedo, *Liberal Virtues*.
4   Amy Gutmann, "Introduction," in *Multiculturalism: Examining the Politics of Recognition*, ed. idem (Princeton: Princeton University Press, 1994), 23–24.
5   Gutmann, "Introduction," 23.
6   Gutmann, "Introduction," 24.
7   Aquinas does not place humility alongside the traditional theological (or "infused") virtues of faith, hope, and charity. Yet my purpose in describing humility as a *theological* virtue is simply to highlight the theological context in which Aquinas develops his view.
8   Readers will notice similarities between my project and Mark Schwehn's *Exiles From Eden*. There, Schwehn eloquently defends the claim that the vocation of learning depends on the proper exercise of religious virtues, including humility, faith, and self-denial. While I have benefited from Schwehn's account in many ways, the present paper is more narrowly focused on humility and its relevance to those educative practices prized by the liberal academy.
9   Stanley Fish, *The Trouble with Principle* (Cambridge, Mass.: Harvard University Press, 1999), 249. Also published as "Why We Can't All Just

Get Along," *First Things* 60 (1996): 18 26. Fish is not himself an advocate of liberalism, but attempts to speak on its behalf in this essay.

10   Fish, *Trouble with Principle*, 247.
11   Fish, *Trouble with Principle*, 248.
12   Fish, *Trouble with Principle*, 248.
13   As Richard John Neuhaus argues: "In the Christian view, tolerance is not a compromise of truth but obedience to truth. . . . This tolerance is made necessary by two factors: cognitive humility and love for neighbor." See "Why We Can Get Along," *First Things* 60 (1996): 31. Several others—most notably Michael McConnell and George Marsden—make similar points in their responses to Fish. See "Correspondence," *First Things* 64 (1996).
14   Marsden, *Outrageous Idea of Christian Scholarship*, 45.
15   "Correspondence," *First Things* 64 (1996): 2.
16   This objection has received a considerable amount of attention from others, so I am providing only a truncated version of it here. For a more developed (and enthusiastic) expression of this objection, see Richard Rorty, *Philosophy and Social Hope* (New York: Penguin Books, 1999), 168–74. For a more critical treatment of the assumptions behind the objection, see Stephen Carter, *The Culture of Disbelief: How American Law and Politics Trivialize Religious Devotion* (New York: Basic Books, 1993); Marsden, *Outrageous Idea of Christian Scholarship*, chap. 3; and Nicholas Wolterstorff, "Why We Should Reject What Liberalism Tells Us about Speaking and Acting in Public for Religious Reasons," in *Religion and Contemporary Liberalism*, ed. Paul Weithman (Notre Dame: University of Notre Dame Press, 1997), 162–81. All of these sources were helpful to me in writing this section.
17   Rorty, *Philosophy and Social Hope,* 170.
18   Amy Gutmann and Dennis Thompson, "Moral Conflict and Political Consensus," *Ethics* 101 (1990): 70. Both Gutmann and Thompson (and Rorty for that matter) are concerned with what counts as a legitimate political claim or argument. Yet their writings are relevant to the present subject. After all, many in the liberal academy are suspicious of religious claims because (allegedly) these claims cannot be appraised by means of established rules of evidence and inquiry.
19   Marsden, *Outrageous Idea of Christian Scholarship*, 47.
20   Or, if such expression does have a place, it is within the confines of the extracurricular sphere of the academy. As Marsden notes: "While [religion] is recognized as a legitimate extracurricular activity, so far as the academic dimensions of a university are concerned, it is expected to have no more importance than would membership in a bridge club. Bridge players are not discriminated against in the university; it's just that their pastime is irrelevant to academic life" (*Outrageous Idea of Christian Scholarship*, 20).
21   Marsden, *Outrageous Idea of Christian Scholarship*, 52–53.
22   Michael Baxter, "Not Outrageous Enough," *First Things* 113 (2001): 14.
23   Marsden, *Outrageous Idea of Christian Scholarship*, 48.
24   Wolterstorff, "Why We Should Reject What Liberalism Tells Us," 175.
25   Schwehn, *Exiles from Eden,* 49.
26   Aquinas, *ST* IIaIIae 161.4; Cf. 141.2.

27   Aquinas, *ST* IIaIIae 161.1; Cf. IIaIIae 161.4.
28   Aquinas, *ST* IIaIIae 161.2 obj 1.
29   Aquinas, *ST* IIaIIae 162.1 ad 2 and 162.2.
30   Aquinas, *ST* IIaIIae 162.1 ad 2 and 162.2; Cf. ad 3.
31   Aquinas, *ST* IIaIIae 161.2.
32   Aquinas, *ST* IIaIIae 161.4; Cf. IIaIIae 137.2 ad 1; 157.3 ad 2.
33   Aquinas, *ST* IIaIIae 157.3.
34   Aquinas, *ST* IIaIIae 161.3 ad 3.
35   I say "roughly" along these lines because Daniel Statman does think that humility (a term he uses interchangeably with *modesty*) has an important cognitive dimension. Still, the account he defends is appropriately deemed *behavioral* because he takes humility to be a disposition to act in certain ways. See Daniel Statman, "Modesty, Pride, and Realistic Self-Assessment," *The Philosophical Quarterly* 42 (1992): 420–38.
36   Statman, "Modesty, Pride, and Realistic Self-Assessment," 425; Cf. 433.
37   Statman, "Modesty, Pride, and Realistic Self-Assessment," 433–34.
38   Statman, "Modesty, Pride, and Realistic Self-Assessment," 434.
39   Statman recognizes that this phenomenon is a matter of concern for other philosophers interested in humility (425). Yet he does not appear to take seriously just how severely this phenomenon undermines the account of humility he wishes to defend.
40   Stephen K. Moroney, *The Noetic Effects of Sin: A Historical and Contemporary Exploration of How Sin Affects Our Thinking* (Lanham, Md.: Lexington Books, 2000), 90–97.
41   The wealth of data compiled by Moroney on this subject is helpful. See *Noetic Effects of Sin*, esp. 90–93.
42   I deal more extensively with this problem in "How to Cure Self-Deception: An Augustinian Remedy," *Logos: A Journal of Catholic Thought and Culture* 7 (2004): 60–86.
43   Technically, the virtue to which vainglory is opposed is magnanimity, which concerns the appropriate measure of honor and glory (*ST* IIaIIae 132.2). The vice to which humility is most opposed is pride (IIaIIae 162.1 ad 3). Yet these virtues and vices are intertwined. Whereas magnanimity concerns the moderate pursuit of honor and glory, humility seeks to restrain the inordinate desire for honor and glory. As Aquinas explains: "humility restrains the appetite from aiming at great things against right reason: while magnanimity urges the mind to great things in accord with right reason" (IIaIIae 161.1 ad 3). Understood this way, magnanimity and humility are related insofar as they concern the same subject. Also, the sins associated with vainglory are often attributed to pride as an interior cause. For example, arrogance is a kind of pride that can lead to boasting, whereby one seeks glory from others (IIaIIae 112.1 ad 2). So while vainglory is most opposed to magnanimity, its inordinate nature requires an appetitive restraint so that one no longer seeks glory in others' praise. Humility produces that restraint.
44   Aquinas, *ST,* IIaIIae 132.1.
45   Aquinas, *ST,* IIaIIae 132.1.
46   Aquinas, *ST,* IIaIIae 132.1.
47   Aquinas, *ST,* IIaIIae 153.4.
48   Aquinas, *ST,* IIaIIae 132.5 ad 1.

49   Aquinas, *ST,* IIaIIae 132.5 ad 2.
50   Aquinas, *ST,* IIaIIae 132.5.
51   Aquinas, *ST,* IIaIIae 132.5.
52   Aquinas, *ST,* IIaIIae 132.5.
53   Aquinas, *ST,* IIaIIae 132.5.
54   Paul Weithman, "Toward an Augustinian Liberalism," in *The Augustinian Tradition,* ed. Gareth Matthews (Berkeley: University of California Press, 1999), 313.
55   Aquinas, *ST* IIaIIae 166.2 ad 3.
56   Thomas Hibbs, "Aquinas, Virtue, and Recent Epistemology," *The Review of Metaphysics* 52 (1999): 587.
57   Hibbs, "Aquinas, Virtue, and Recent Epistemology," 587.
58   Aquinas, *ST,* IIaIIae 161.5 ad 2.
59   Aquinas, *ST,* IIaIIae 161.5 ad 4; 161.6.
60   This is Statman's view of most traditional accounts of humility ("Modesty, Pride, and Realistic Self-Assessment," 431–32). I address what I take to be the fundamental weakness of his alternative account above.
61   Aquinas, *ST,* 161.1 ad 5.
62   Aquinas, *ST,* IIaIIae 161.6 ad 2.
63   Aquinas, *ST,* IIaIIae 161.6.
64   Aquinas, *ST,* IIaIIae 23.7 ad 1.
65   Aquinas, *ST,* IaIIae 65.2.
66   Although the sources on which he relies are different than mine, Mark Schwehn also insists that humility can find legitimate expressions outside the Christian tradition. He makes similar claims about justice, charity, and self-denial. In fact, he denies that "there is some sort of absolute and necessary connection between religious belief and [these virtues]." Nevertheless he wishes to argue for both "a historical connection between religious beliefs and these virtues and for an epistemological connection between the exercise of these virtues and the communal quest for knowledge and truth" (*Exiles from Eden,* 53).
67   While Weithman's argument concerns liberal constraints on political advocacy, it appears to have broader application for people living in "maturely pluralistic democratic societies," namely those "with a democratic political culture and democratic institutions and traditions" ("Toward an Augustinian Liberalism," 309). I take it, then, that his argument is relevant to the kinds of ideals we can promote in institutions for which democratic commitments are central. Thus I am adapting his argument somewhat to the context of this paper.
68   Weithman, "Toward an Augustinian Liberalism," 318. Notice here that offering reasons nonreligious people can accept is a normative requirement of liberalism. It is not (as Marsden and Wolterstorff would have it) just a pragmatic strategy for arguing effectively in public contexts.
69   Weithman, "Toward an Augustinian Liberalism," 317.
70   Weithman, "Toward an Augustinian Liberalism," 318.
71   Weithman, "Toward an Augustinian Liberalism," 317. The need for such argumentative restraint seems especially urgent whenever the conflicts in question are political: "To the extent that simply barring certain reasons from political argument makes that argument more civil, consensus building is advanced and intransigence and pertinacity are curbed" (313).

72   Weithman, "Toward an Augustinian Liberalism," 318.
73   Weithman, "Toward an Augustinian Liberalism," 318.
74   This suggestion is made by Wolterstorff, "Why We Should Reject What Liberalism Tells Us," 180.
75   Statman, "Modesty, Pride, and Realistic Self-Assessment," 426. What follows is an abbreviated version of his argument.
76   Statman, "Modesty, Pride, and Realistic Self-Assessment," 426.
77   Statman, "Modesty, Pride, and Realistic Self-Assessment," 426. Statman is quoting Norvin Richards, "Is Humility a Virtue?" *American Philosophical Quarterly* 25 (1988): 256.
78   Statman, "Modesty, Pride, and Realistic Self-Assessment," 427.
79   Statman, "Modesty, Pride, and Realistic Self-Assessment," 427.
80   Statman, "Modesty, Pride, and Realistic Self-Assessment," 427.
81   Statman, "Modesty, Pride, and Realistic Self-Assessment," 427.
82   Statman, "Modesty, Pride, and Realistic Self-Assessment," 429.
83   Statman, "Modesty, Pride, and Realistic Self-Assessment," 430. A quibble: I think it is misleading to describe traditional religious perspectives as promoting a pessimistic view of human life and value. While it is true that, compared to God's greatness, "even the worthiest man, such as Abraham, is really only 'dust and ashes,'" this does not imply that human beings have little worth in the moral sense. On the contrary, we have a significant degree of worth just in virtue of being made in the likeness of a God who loves and is concerned about us. Of course, this issue is one that goes far beyond the parameters of this paper.
84   Augustine, *Confessions*, trans. F. J. Sheed (Indianapolis: Hackett, 1993), 1.1.
85   Statman, "Modesty, Pride, and Realistic Self-Assessment," 431.
86   Statman, "Modesty, Pride, and Realistic Self-Assessment," 431.
87   Statman, "Modesty, Pride, and Realistic Self-Assessment," 432.

Chapter 8

1   MacIntyre, *After Virtue*, 191.
2   For an extended treatment of humility as an intellectual virtue, see Robert C. Roberts and W. Jay Wood, "Humility and Epistemic Goods," in *Intellectual Virtue: Perspectives from Ethics and Epistemology*, ed. Michael DePaul and Linda Zagzebski (Oxford: Clarendon, 2003), 257–79.
3   Mark Schwehn, "A Christian University: Defining the Difference," *First Things* 93 (1999): 28.
4   Parker J. Palmer, *To Know as We are Known: A Spirituality of Education* (New York: Harper & Row, 1983), 108.
5   Elton Trueblood, *The Idea of a College* (New York: Harper & Brothers, 1959), 60.
6   Schwehn, *Exiles from Eden*, 48–49. Italics in original.
7   James Sire, *Habits of the Mind: Intellectual Life as a Christian Calling* (Downers Grove, Ill.: InterVarsity, 2000), 124.
8   Richard J. Foster, *Celebration of Discipline: The Path to Spiritual Growth*, rev. ed. (San Francisco: Harper & Row, 1988), 66.
9   Palmer, *To Know as We are Known*, 114–16; Douglas V. Henry, "Intellectual Integrity in the Christian Scholar's Life," *Christian Scholar's Review*

33 (2003): 55–74, also focuses on cultivating virtue in scholars more than students.

10   W. Jay Wood, *Epistemology: Becoming Intellectually Virtuous* (Downers Grove, Ill.: InterVarsity, 1998), 51–52. Although Wood emphasizes heightened individual awareness of deficiencies and resolve to change as central to the cultivation of intellectual virtue, he also acknowledges the value of being confronted with human finitude and sin (75; 97–98).

11   Schwehn, "A Christian University," 28.

12   Nussbaum, *Cultivating Humanity*, 9–11. For a lucid critique of Nussbaum's view of critical thinking, see Michael Beaty and Anne-Marie Bowery, "Cultivating Christian Citizenship: Martha Nussbaum's Socrates, Augustine's *Confessions*, and the Modern University," *Christian Scholar's Review* 33 (2003): 23–54.

13   Nussbaum, *Cultivating Humanity*, 91, 92.

14   Nussbaum, *Cultivating Humanity*, 92–99.

15   At times Nussbaum appears to view religious commitment as an obstacle to liberal learning, but we see religious commitment as a compelling reason for understanding others. See Nussbaum, *Cultivating Humanity*, 292 and Beaty and Bowery, "Cultivating Christian Citizenship," 40–43.

16   Genesis 5:1 repeats this language. Unless otherwise noted, all Scripture references are from the New International Version (NIV).

17   Herman Bavinck, *Gereformeerde Dogmatiek*, 3rd ed., vol. 2 (Kampen: Kok, 1918), 621. Citation and translation from Anthony A. Hoekema, *Created in God's Image* (Grand Rapids: Eerdmans, 1986), 99.

18   Richard Mouw, *When the Kings Come Marching In: Isaiah and the New Jerusalem* (Grand Rapids: Eerdmans, 1983), 47.

19   Nicholas Wolterstorff, *Until Justice and Peace Embrace* (Grand Rapids: Eerdmans, 1983), 78.

20   Thomas Merton, *New Seeds of Contemplation* (New York: New Directions, 1961), 60.

21   C. S. Lewis, "The Weight of Glory," in *The Weight of Glory and Other Addresses* (New York: Touchstone, 1996), 39–40.

22   On a related note, see Elizabeth Newman, "Hospitality and Christian Higher Education," *Christian Scholar's Review* 33 (2003): 75–93.

23   Larry Crabb, *Connecting: Healing for Ourselves and Our Relationships* (Nashville: Word, 1997), 53. Pope John Paul II's teaching on sexuality as an icon of the Trinity also reflects a deep understanding of communities of persons reflecting God's communal image. See George Weigel, *Witness to Hope: The Biography of John Paul II* (New York: HarperCollins, 1999), 335–43.

24   Paul Ferguson, "Adam," in *Evangelical Dictionary of Biblical Theology*, ed. Walter A. Elwell (Grand Rapids: Baker Books, 1996), 10.

25   Richard J. Foster, *Prayer: Finding the Heart's True Home* (San Francisco: HarperSanFrancisco, 1992), 61.

26   Foster, *Prayer*, 61.

27   Robert H. Culpepper, "The Humanity of Jesus the Christ: An Overview," *Faith and Mission* 5 (1988): 14–27; W. Norman Pittenger, *Christ and Christian Faith: Some Presuppositions and Implications of the Incarnation* (New York: Round Table Press, 1941), 19–25.

28   Reinhold Niebuhr, *The Nature and Destiny of Man: A Christian Interpretation* (New York: Charles Scribner's Sons, 1941), 167.

29   C. Stephen Evans, *Preserving the Person: A Look at the Human Sciences* (Grand Rapids: Baker Books, 1977), 143.

30   Niebuhr, *Nature and Destiny of Man*, 16.

31   Niebuhr, *Nature and Destiny of Man*, 168.

32   Herman N. Ridderbos, *The Gospel According to John: A Theological Commentary*, trans. John Vriend (Grand Rapids: Eerdmans, 1997), 44. Italics in original.

33   C. H. Dodd, *The Interpretation of the Fourth Gospel* (Cambridge: Cambridge University Press, 1953), 157. Italics in original.

34   Rudolf Schnackenburg, *The Gospel According to St. John* (New York: Herder & Herder, 1968), 257–58. Raymond Brown summarizes aptly that "for John the basic sin is the failure to know and believe in Jesus" (*The Gospel According to John, I–XII* [New York: Doubleday, 1966], 10).

35   Rodney A. Whitacre, *John* (Downers Grove, Ill.: InterVarsity, 1999), 161.

36   George Beasley-Murray, *John* (Waco, Tex.: Word Books, 1987), 92.

37   T. H. L. Parker, trans., *Calvin's Commentaries: The Gospel According to St. John 1–10* (Grand Rapids: Eerdmans, 1959), 160.

38   Schnackenburg, *The Gospel According to John*, 405.

39   Leon Morris, *The Gospel According to John* (Grand Rapids: Eerdmans, 1971), 234.

40   Moroney, *Noetic Effects of Sin*.

41   Thomas L. Brodie, *The Gospel According to John* (New York: Oxford University Press, 1993), 243.

42   Brodie, *The Gospel According to John*, 255.

43   In the past century we might think of the way in which communal sin distorted the thinking of those associated with the Ku Klux Klan or Hitler's Nazi regime. Within American culture today, perhaps materialism and consumerism blind us to truths we would otherwise see.

44   Dodd, *Interpretation of the Fourth Gospel*, 159.

45   Brown, *The Gospel According to John*, 365.

46   Merold Westphal, "Taking St. Paul Seriously: Sin as an Epistemological Category," in *Christian Philosophy*, University of Notre Dame Studies in the Philosophy of Religion 6, ed. Thomas P. Flint (Notre Dame: University of Notre Dame Press, 1990), 200–226.

47   George J. Zemek, "Aiming the Mind: A Key to Godly Living," *Grace Theological Journal* 5 (1984): 205.

48   David Myers, *The Inflated Self* (New York: The Seabury Press, 1980), 117.

49   In addition to the courses mentioned in the text, I list here the other upper-level courses I teach along with the novels or memoirs I use in them. *International Political Economy:* David Liss, *The Coffee Trader* (New York: Random House, 2003); *Comparative Politics:* Chinua Achebe, *Anthills of the Savannah* (New York: Anchor Books, 1987); *U.S. Foreign Policy:* Philip Caputo, *A Rumor of War* (New York: Henry Holt, 1977), or Tim O'Brien, *If I Die in a Combat Zone* (New York: Broadway Books, 1975).

50   The late Edward Said would call these Orientalist stereotypes, and many American college students, reflecting the culture as a whole, seem to hold them. See Edward W. Said, *Orientalism* (New York: Pantheon, 1978).

51   Elias Chacour with David Hazard, *Blood Brothers*, 2nd ed. (Grand Rapids: Chosen Books, 2003); Elias Chacour with Mary Jensen, *We Belong to the Land* (New York: HarperCollins, 1990).

52   Brian Urquhart, *A Life in Peace and War* (New York: W. W. Norton, 1987).

53   See Scott Waalkes, "Using Film Clips as Cases to Teach the Rise and 'Decline' of the State," *International Studies Perspectives* 4 (2003): 156–74.

54   *Life and Debt*, DVD, directed by Stephanie Black (New York: New Yorker Films, 2001).

55   See Matthew P. Phelps, "*Imago Dei* and Limited Creature: High and Low Views of Human Beings in Christianity and Cognitive Psychology," *Christian Scholar's Review* 33 (2004): 345–66, where I explore in more detail how the study of human memory reinforces a biblical view of human beings as limited creatures made in God's image. I also argue that cognitive limitations are good aspects of the creation rather than instances of natural or moral evil.

56   The cognitive phenomena mentioned in this section can be found in a good cognitive psychology textbook, such as Mark H. Ashcraft, *Cognition*, 3rd ed. (Upper Saddle River, N.J.: Prentice-Hall, 2002).

57   This task is analogous to searching for your car in a crowded parking lot when you do not remember precisely where you parked it.

58   Henry L. Roediger and Kathleen B. McDermott, "Creating False Memories: Remembering Words Not Presented in Lists," *Journal of Experimental Psychology: Learning, Memory, and Cognition* 21 (1995): 803–14.

59   One such list contains words such as tired, bed, pillow, etc., but does not contain the word sleep, which is related to all of the words on the list. Nevertheless, most students recall sleep when asked to remember the list.

60   Amy Tsai, Elizabeth Loftus, and Danielle Polage, "Current Directions in False-Memory Research," in *False-Memory Creation in Children and Adults: Theory, Research, and Implications*, ed. David F. Bjorklund (Mahwah, N.J.: Lawrence Erlbaum Associates, 2000), 31–44.

61   I adapted this activity from one suggested in Carolyn Hildebrandt and Jennifer Oliver, "The Mind as a Black Box: A Simulation of Theory Building in Psychology," *Teaching of Psychology* 27 (2000): 195–97.

62   Several factors contribute to the differences between the groups' theories, such as formulating different initial assumptions, using different methods to experiment on the box, and arriving at different interpretations of the same evidence.

63   John Calvin, *Institutes of the Christian Religion*, 2 vols., ed. John T. McNeill, trans. Ford L. Battles (Philadelphia: Westminster, 1960), II.2. 15–25.

64   Abraham Kuyper, *Principles of Sacred Theology* (Grand Rapids: Eerdmans, 1954), 104, 110, 157, 159, 600. Emil Brunner, *The Christian*

Doctrine of Creation and Redemption Dogmatics, vol. 2 (Philadelphia: Westminster, 1952), 26–27.

65   Emil Brunner, *Revelation and Reason* (Philadelphia: Westminster, 1946), 383.

66   Dewey J. Hoitenga Jr., "A Futile Search for Sin?" *Perspectives* 8 (March 1993): 8.

67   Ted Peters, *Sin: Radical Evil in Soul and Society* (Grand Rapids: Eerdmans, 1994), 5.

68   Hoitenga, "A Futile Search," 9. Italics in the original.

69   Wayne Grudem, *Systematic Theology: An Introduction to Biblical Doctrine* (Grand Rapids: Zondervan, 1994), 33.

70   For an alternative view of humility interacting with the virtue of magnanimity in preparing one for the theological virtue of hope, see Josef Pieper, "On Hope," in *Faith, Hope, Love*, trans. Mary Frances McCarthy (San Francisco: Ignatius Press, 1997), 100–103, 122. Also, we acknowledge the valuable perspective on the need for Christian hope within the context of higher education offered above by Paul Wadell and Darin Davis.

71   Steven W. Stall, "Sociology of Knowledge, Relativism, and Theology," in *Religion and the Sociology of Knowledge*, ed. B. Hargrove (New York: The Edwin Mellen Press, 1984), 67.

72   Richard J. Mouw, "Humility, Hope, and the Divine Slowness," *The Christian Century* 107 (1990): 367. The authors are listed in alphabetical order; each author made an equal contribution. We would like to thank the Malone College Writers Group, the faculty development forum at Malone, David Smith, and the editors of this volume for feedback on earlier versions of our essay.

List of Contributors

MICHAEL D. BEATY is professor of philosophy at Baylor University, where he has served since 1987. Currently chair of the department, he has previously held posts at Baylor as vice provost for faculty development and director of the Institute for Faith and Learning. A specialist in moral and social philosophy, the philosophy of religion, and Christianity and higher education, he is the author of numerous articles and is the editor or coeditor of four books: *Christian Theism and the Problems of Philosophy*; *Christian Theism and Moral Philosophy*; *Cultivating Citizens: Soulcraft and Citizenship in Contemporary America*; and *Christianity and the Soul of the University: Faith as a Foundation for Intellectual Community*.

DARIN H. DAVIS is associate director of the Baylor Institute for Faith and Learning, an appointment taken following four years as assistant professor of philosophy at St. Norbert College in De Pere, Wisconsin. A native of Amarillo, Texas, he holds a B.A. in philosophy and English from the University of Texas, an M.A. in philosophy from Baylor University, and a Ph.D. in philosophy from Saint Louis University. His research interests are focused on contemporary moral philosophy, moral psychology, and business ethics. His work has appeared in the *American Catholic Philosophical Quarterly* and (with William Rehg) in the *Southern Journal of Philosophy*.

SHAWN D. FLOYD is currently associate professor of philosophy at Malone College in Canton, Ohio. He received his B.A. and M.A. in philosophy from Baylor University and his Ph.D. in philosophy from Saint Louis University. His research interests include virtue ethics, Thomas Aquinas, and philosophy of religion, and he has published articles in journals such as *The Modern Schoolman*; *History of Philosophy Quarterly*; *Logos: A Journal of Catholic Thought and Culture*; and *The Heythrop Journal*.

STANLEY HAUERWAS is Gilbert T. Rowe Professor of Theological Ethics at Duke Divinity School and the author of numerous books including *Resident Aliens*; *A Community of Character*; *The Peaceable Kingdom*; *A Better Hope*; *With the Grain of the Universe*, his 2000–2002 Gifford Lectures; and *Cross-Shattered Christ: Meditations on the Last Seven Words*. Described by *Time* magazine as "America's Best Theologian" and "contemporary theology's foremost intellectual provocateur," Hauerwas is a keen cultural critic whose considerable opus has significantly shaped conversation about postliberalism, narrative theology, and virtue ethics.

DOUGLAS V. HENRY serves as director of the Institute for Faith and Learning and associate professor of philosophy in the Honors College at Baylor University. In addition to work in ancient philosophy, ethics, and the philosophy of religion, his research interests include the history, philosophy, and theology of Christian higher education. Coeditor of *Faithful Learning and the Christian Scholarly Vocation* and of *Christianity and the Soul of the University: Faith as a Foundation for Intellectual Community*, he is currently working on *For Freedom, for Love: Liberal Education and the Baptist Vision*.

DAVID LYLE JEFFREY is Distinguished Professor of Literature and Humanities at Baylor University. An expert in medieval English literature, Jeffrey is also a gifted speaker and prolific writer whose recent book, *Houses of the Interpreter: Reading Scripture, Reading Culture*, joins his *Dictionary of Biblical Tradition in English Literature*; *People of the Book*; *English Spirituality in the Age of Wyclif*; and *Rethinking the Future of the University*, an examination of the relationships and contributions of historic Christian thought to the intellectual life of university disciplines.

NICHOLAS K. MERIWETHER is associate professor of philosophy at Shawnee State University in Portsmouth, Ohio, where he teaches a junior level ethics requirement. He has published articles on Jurgen Habermas's discourse ethics and moral sanctions in *Telos* and *The Journal of Moral Education*. His primary area of research is the nexus of ethics, civil society, religion, and political theory.

STEPHEN K. MORONEY is professor of theology at Malone College, where he has been recognized with the college-wide distinguished faculty award for teaching. He has degrees from Wheaton College, Gordon-Conwell Theological Seminary, and bachelor's and doctoral degrees from Duke University. He is the author of *The Noetic Effects of Sin: A Historical and Contemporary Exploration of How Sin Affects Our Thinking*, and he is working on a subsequent book addressing the subject of judgment, both human and divine.

WARREN A. NORD works in the areas of philosophy of the humanities, philosophy of religion, philosophy of education (especially moral education), and the relationship of religion and education. For twenty-five years he served at the University of North Carolina-Chapel Hill as director of the Program in the Humanities and Human Values, where he continues to serve as lecturer in philosophy. He is the author of many articles and book chapters, primarily on religion and education, as well as two books: *Religion and American Education: Rethinking a National Dilemma*, and with Charles C. Haynes, *Taking Religion Seriously across the Curriculum*. He is currently working on a book tentatively entitled *God and Education*.

MATTHEW P. PHELPS is associate professor and chair of psychology at Malone College. He completed his M.S. and Ph.D. in (cognitive) psychology at The Pennsylvania State University. He has coauthored several articles on human episodic memory. His current scholarship centers on relations between cognitive limitations and Christian anthropology. Matt lives in Canton, Ohio with his wife, June (a clinical psychologist), and their daughters, Rayna and Ana. Their family's primary community is First Mennonite Church.

ROBERT C. ROBERTS is Distinguished Professor of Ethics at Baylor University. His papers have appeared in such journals as the *Philosophical Review*; *American Philosophical Quarterly*; *Philosophical Studies*; *Journal of Religious Ethics*; *Scottish Journal of Theology*; *Journal of Religion*; *Philosophy and Phenomenological Research*; and *Inquiry*. His books include *Rudolf Bultmann's Theology: A Critical Interpretation*; *Spirituality and Human Emotion*; *The Strengths of a Christian*; *Faith, Reason, and History: Rethinking Kierkegaard's Philosophical Fragments*; *Taking the Word to Heart: Self and*

Other in an Age of Therapies; Limning the Psyche; and *Emotions: An Essay in Aid of Moral Psychology.*

PAUL J. WADELL is professor of religious studies at St. Norbert College in De Pere, Wisconsin. He is the author of six books, including *The Moral of the Story: Learning From Literature about Human and Divine Love; Becoming Friends: Worship, Justice, and the Practice of Christian Friendship; The Primacy of Love: An Introduction to the Ethics of Thomas Aquinas;* and *Friendship and the Moral Life.* His primary areas of interest include virtue ethics, the role of friendship in the Christian life, the relationship between worship and Christian ethics, and how the church as a community of discipleship is called to witness Christ in the world.

SCOTT T. WAALKES is associate professor of international politics at Malone College, where he has taught since 1998. During the 2004–2005 academic year, he was on sabbatical as a Fulbright Scholar in the Middle Eastern nation of Bahrain. Scott's B.A. is in political science from Calvin College, and his M.A. and Ph.D. are in foreign affairs from the University of Virginia. The author of several articles and book reviews in international studies, he is currently writing a book on Christian responses to globalization.

Index